6/03

The New Autonomous House

The New Autonomous House

Design and Planning for Sustainability

Brenda and Robert Vale

Thames & Hudson

© 2000 Brenda and Robert Vale
Preface © 2000 John Perlin

First published in hardcover in the United States of America in 2000 by
Thames & Hudson Inc., 500 Fifth Avenue, New York, New York 10110

thamesandhudsonusa.com

First paperback edition 2002

Library of Congress Catalog Card Number 99-66918
ISBN 0-500-28287-0

Printed in Hong Kong by H&Y Printing Ltd

Contents

Preface

John Perlin

Brenda and Robert Vale show us the step by step approach they took towards designing and planning to build an autonomous house that would serve as an ideal of sustainability. By meticulously describing the arduous procedure they went through in coming to a decision as to what should comprise each aspect of the house, the reader learns that, though in the abstract concepts such as autonomy and sustainability appear simple to define, the terms become fraught with complexity when applied to a concrete project. Trying to find the best solution at each juncture required many factors to be weighed in the balance: these factors and this process are ably described by the Vales.

In sun-scarce England a wind generator rather than photovoltaics (the use of solar cells to convert sunlight into electricity) would appear to be the better choice, but real-world constraints forced the authors to decide on photovoltaics instead because, in their words: 'Although more expensive than a wind turbine in terms of expected electricity per pound of capital cost, the photovoltaics have the twin advantages of having no moving parts (so no need of regular maintenance) and being far less intrusive – important in a town-centre site.'

The dogmatist would have forced the Vales to rely only on the sun once they had made this choice. But what happens at night or on a rainy day? Should the occupants do without the various amenities electricity makes possible during these periods? Since the Vales wished to build a house that would function like a normal 20th-century home, they found themselves having to choose between a battery pack (to store the energy produced by the solar cells for times when they cannot work) or hooking up to the national electricity grid for backup. The more self-righteous would have taken immediately to batteries – does not an autonomous house mean having no connection to the outside world for its power? For the Vales, who wanted a house that treads as lightly as possible on the environment, the choice once again is not that simple. Batteries contain lead, they note, a highly toxic material, especially threatening to people and the environment during their production and disposal. Therefore, using the electricity grid as the storage unit actually turns out as the better option when attempting to eliminate reliance on non-renewable resources and minimize pollution, as the power generated by photovoltaics would offset at least a portion of the electricity derived from the burning of fossil fuels or the use of nuclear fission. In fact, the Vales conclude, 'if the environmental impacts of the manufacture of the batteries are taken into account, the grid-linked system [combined with photovoltaics] is likely to appear even more favourable (since the grid already exists, it has already made its impact) ...'. This kind of holistic thinking, exemplified by the Vales' choice of power linkage, pervades every other issue they confront as they build from windows to thermal mass. By always considering 'the reasons for building the house rather than the house as abstract concept', *The New Autonomous House* becomes a universal guidebook on designing and planning for sustainability, even if it focuses on a particular project in a specific locale with its own special criteria.

1 | *Definitions and Introduction to the Problems*

DEFINITIONS

Before addressing the theoretical and practical aspects of the autonomous house, it is necessary to clarify what is meant here by the expression 'autonomous house'. The term has been used to describe a number of projects, the first of which was undertaken in the 1970s at the Technical Research Division (later to become the Martin Centre) at the University of Cambridge School of Architecture. The original autonomous-house concept was proposed by Alexander Pike, lecturer at the University of Cambridge School of Architecture, as part of the lead-up to the United Nations Conference on the Environment in Stockholm in 1972;[1] work began on the project in 1971. In a paper for the Science Research Council (SRC, a UK-government research-funding body), the project is described by Pike as follows: 'The main object of this research is to devise a servicing system for houses which reduces dependence on limited localized consumables.'[2] The paper goes on to point out that part of the rationale behind the autonomous house was to allow '... outlying and marginal lands to be utilized, leading towards a more rational policy for land use and the availability of cheaper land for housing. This could provide an alternative planning strategy to help relieve the spatial pressure now being experienced in most of our cities and towns.'[3] The report by Pike and his colleagues, published by the SRC/Department of the Environment (DOE) in 1974, was the culmination of three years' work. In its conclusion Pike wrote: 'Aware of the problems of a low research budget for a large objective, the Cambridge team decided to devote the primary research investment to the establishment of a sound theoretical base before starting the experimental work which might otherwise carry the high risk of waste of resources. Sufficient theoretical work has now been completed to enable the project to proceed to the experimental stage.'[4]

Because of the length of time between the start of the research and the publication of the SRC/DOE report, other members of the Technical Research

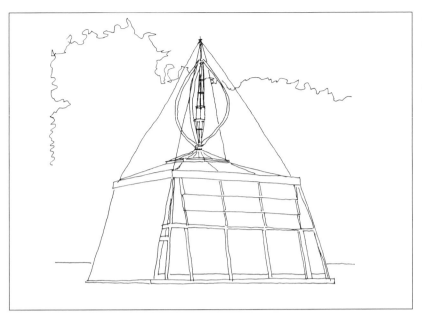

Fig. 1
The Alexander Pike autonomous house (after Architectural Design 44 [November 1974], p. 681)

Division also penned definitions of the autonomous house as part of their own research activities. Perhaps the most poetic of these, and the most different from Pike's definition, is in a paper by Lapthorne that seeks to make apparent the links between industrialized building and autonomous servicing:

> *Once again the house must express the transition from hand to horizon; be shaped by climate and living patterns; create rich visual variety; create shade and coolness in summer, warmth and shelter in winter; store its water; consume its wastes; draw energy from the environment; enrich the soil; support its inhabitants; maintain itself; and be in tune with the natural rhythms. In short the autonomy of any other animal group ... The mark of the autonomously serviced house will be the mark of the individual.*[5]

Another definition is given by Vale and Vale: 'The autonomous house on its site is defined as a house operating independently of any inputs except those of its immediate environment. The house is not linked to the mains services of gas, water, electricity or drainage, but instead uses the income-energy sources of sun, wind and rain to service itself and process its own wastes.'[6] By the time the SRC/DOE report was being compiled, the term autonomous house had become common parlance, so much so that Alexander Pike was moved to conclude: 'During the three years that have elapsed since this investigation was commenced some confusion appears to have arisen in the use of the term *autonomous house*, which is now used, incorrectly, to describe a range of projects which seek, to some degree, to exploit the use of ambient energy and recycling methods for providing services supplementary to the conventional systems. A unique feature of the Cambridge project is its aim to provide complete self-sufficiency with a fully integrated servicing system, an essential factor in the development of an alternative, less constrained strategy for planning.'[7] Pike's emphasis on the planning implications of the autonomous house, both here and in the definition given earlier, is interesting, yet seems odd in view of the energy and carbon dioxide implications of the likely increase in private transport that settlement of areas 'beyond the grid' would engender.

By 1976 the Cambridge autonomous house had become the 'autarkic house',[8] perhaps to distance it from those projects which did 'seek, to some degree, to exploit the use of ambient energy and recycling methods for providing services supplementary to the conventional systems'. The *Shorter Oxford Dictionary*[9] defines autonomous *inter alia* as 'self-governing', and autonomy as 'freedom (of the will)', while autarchy (or autarky) is 'self-sufficiency'; autarchy is also defined as 'absolute sovereignty, despotism'. The revised name for the Cambridge house is therefore the more accurate, but the term autonomous house is used here for two reasons. The first is that the political overtones of the term are quite appropriate, in that the house described in this work is seen as more than merely self-sufficient; this will become apparent later. The second reason is that the term autonomous house has become, as Pike realized, common parlance. The Solar Energy Society of Canada Inc. (SESCI, the Canadian branch of the International Solar Energy Society [ISES]) runs the annual SESCI Autonomous House Competition for houses that have minimal energy and other resource demands (but not zero demands).[10] In Hungary an 'autonomous energy school' was intended to use photovoltaics, solar collectors and wind generators to meet its electricity and hot-water demands, with a bio-briquet-fired boiler for back-up heating; it will also collect water from a bored well and create biogas from sewage.[11] These projects may bear out Pike's concern that the term autonomous house was being misused as far as his definition was concerned, but some later references still demonstrate an understanding of the difference between 'autonomous' and 'low-impact'. For example, in their guide to the solar houses of Australia, Parnell and Cole define autonomous housing as 'housing with completely independent energy, service and waste disposal systems',[12] although this definition fails to clarify the rôle of renewable resources. In their description of the autonomous Butt House at Ararat near Melbourne, built in 1981 and using passive solar heating, rainwater collection, a wind generator and wood-burning slow-combustion stoves, they describe a 'seldom used' 2-kW diesel generator as being part of the autonomous systems, something Pike would never have accepted.[13]

INTRODUCTION TO THE PROBLEMS

The perception of the problems in the 1970s

Before beginning to discuss such strategies as might be appropriate for the design of an autonomous house, it is necessary to set out some of the reasons why the concept of autonomy itself is worth pursuing. The United Nations conference in Stockholm in 1972 and the publicity leading up to it brought into widespread public consciousness the twin problems of pollution and resource depletion. The United Nations Brundtland Report[14] demonstrated that the problems aired at Stockholm had not declined in significance by the end of the 1980s, and issues such as ozone depletion and global warming that were perceived in the 1970s as being concerns of the distant future, were now the preoccupations of the present. Yet the environmental problems were clearly understood in the 1970s and earlier. The following is taken from a 1973 textbook on climatology: 'It is estimated that the concentration [of carbon dioxide in the atmosphere] may rise to 375 ppm. Given this, the Manabe and Wetherald study previously cited suggests that this will result in a warming of the surface layer by 0.5°C'.[15] The Manabe and Wetherald study mentioned is considerably earlier, dating from 1967.[16] Another example of 1970s understanding of global warming is seen in a paper by Professor Brown, the Professor of Microbiology at the University of New South Wales in Australia, reprinted in *Soil and Health* (the official journal of the Soil Association of New Zealand), which had a special issue on conservation and the environment in the run-up to the 1972 Stockholm conference. Brown wrote: 'One thing seems to be obvious and that is that there should be no continuous increase in atmospheric carbon dioxide. Atmospheric carbon dioxide in the northern hemisphere is increasing measurably. How are we going to fulfil a criterion of no increase in atmospheric CO_2?'[17] The article is not the only one in that issue of the journal that points out the dangers of increasing levels of carbon dioxide in the atmosphere. Another concern current in the 1990s, that of ozone depletion in the stratosphere, was first expressed on 28 June 1974 in a paper in *Nature* written by two US scientists, who were subsequently guests at a dinner given to mark the twentieth anniversary of their discovery. A description of the 1994 anniversary event in the *ASHRAE Journal* pointed out that it had taken 13 years from the initial publication of the paper to the agreement of the Montreal Protocol to limit and eventually abandon the use of chlorofluorocarbons.[18]

The principle of sustainable development in the 1990s

The principal rallying cry from the United Nations' 1992 'Earth Summit' conference in Rio de Janeiro, held 20 years on from the Stockholm conference, was for 'sustainable development', defined as 'development that meets the needs of the present without compromising the ability of those in the future to meet their own needs'.[19] This principle was enshrined in Agenda 21, the primary document of the conference, which has been summarized as follows: 'Agenda 21 is the major outcome of the United Nations Conference on Environment and Development (UNCED) which was held in Rio de Janeiro in June 1992. It provides a common framework of action for all countries to achieve sustainable development ... The compartmentalized ways of dealing with environmental and developmental issues which have been used in the past have caused many of the social, economic and environmental problems facing humanity.'[20] A more detailed description of the nature of Agenda 21, with its emphasis on the interdependent nature of human interaction with the Earth, is given in Appendix 1.

The New Zealand Ministry for the Environment produced a guide to Agenda 21 in an attempt to render this bulky document more intelligible to a wider audience. The guide lists the various aspects of the document under the headings: 'a sustainable economic environment'; 'an equitable social environment'; and 'a liveable built environment'.[21] The last of these three sections includes the following subheadings:

human settlements	*sustainable land use planning and management*
	integrated provision of environmental infrastructure
	provision of adequate shelter for all
	improving human settlements
sustainable energy and transport	*energy development, efficiency and consumption*
	transport
waste management	*minimising wastes*
	waste reuse and recycling
	waste disposal and treatment[22]

These subheadings together constitute all aspects of the sustainable development goal that are of relevance to the design of buildings. 'Environmental infrastructure' must include all aspects of the servicing of dwellings, such as water-supply systems, and 'waste disposal and treatment' must relate to methods of managing sewage from buildings. It is clear from these subheadings that architects and building designers have a significant rôle to play in the fulfilment of Agenda 21's aims, and through this to the achievement of sustainable development.

Non-renewable fuels and global warming

For architects and civil engineers, two groups of people who deal with the design of artifacts that tend to have a long life, one of the logical implications of the concept of sustainable development is that buildings should be designed so as to eliminate the need for non-renewable fuels; the subheading 'sustainable energy and transport' above highlights this. This need to eliminate the use of non-renewable fuels follows for two reasons. The first is that non-renewable fuels (coal, oil, gas and uranium) are, by definition, not sustainable: once they have been dug up and used, they are gone and not available for the use of future generations. Estimates of the availability of non-renewable fuels vary. The British Wind Energy Association describes the situation for the United Kingdom as follows: 'There is much debate as to how long our supplies of oil, gas and coal will last, but nobody denies that one day they will run out. The Government has estimated that remaining reserves in the United Kingdom at current rates of use will last 13 years for oil and 25 years for gas.'[23] How long the reserves of fossil fuels will actually last depends on cost, ease of extraction, rate of increase or decrease of demand, discovery of new deposits and similar factors that interact to produce a constantly varying result. What cannot be avoided in calculations is the fact that once any of these fuels has been converted into heat, it is gone for ever.

The second reason for the unsustainability of fossil fuels as an energy supply is that their use has considerable environmental impact. The burning of coal, oil and gas to provide energy results in the release of carbon dioxide into the atmosphere. This carbon dioxide is leading to an alteration in the global climate, which has been described as follows: 'There is no single issue in contemporary human affairs that is of greater importance.'[24] The Intergovernmental Panel on Climate Change (IPCC) set up by the United Nations General Assembly in 1988, has stated that carbon dioxide accounts for 55% of the total global warming effect of all the so-called 'greenhouse gases' (carbon dioxide, CFCs and related gases, methane and nitrous oxide).[25] Writing in 1990, Leggett states:

> Fossil fuels – coal, oil and gas – are made of carbon derived from once living organisms. Coal is made primarily of compacted plant remains. Oil is derived chiefly from the thermal maturation (chemical change resulting from burial) of organic matter, principally ancient phytoplankton in marine sediments. Gas is derived primarily from the thermal maturation of organic matter, principally plant remains, in a variety of sediments. All this carbon – in the absence of extraction and burning by humans – is effectively cut off from the natural carbon cycle. But humans are burning fossil fuels at a rate which currently adds 5.7 (± 0.5) Gigatonnes (Gt) of carbon to the atmosphere each year. To this

must be added approximately 2 Gt of carbon derived from burning and clearing forests. Taking into consideration the 2 Gt or so sequestered in the oceans and the 2 Gt or so of carbon retained in the terrestrial biota, there is a net increase of about 3 Gt of carbon in the atmosphere each year.[26]

Leggett gives values for carbon in the atmosphere as shown in Table 1.1.[27]

Table 1.1: Quantities of carbon in the climate system in Gt

CO_2 in the atmosphere today	750
CO_2 in the pre-industrial atmosphere	575
present annual release from fossil-fuel burning	> 5
present annual release from deforestation	approx. 2
amount of carbon in phytomass (all plants)	560
carbon in recoverable coal and oil	4,000
carbon in potentially recoverable fossil fuels	5,000–10,000

World fossil-fuel demand has grown by 5% every year since the end of World War II,[28] and the concomitant rise in the amount of carbon in the atmosphere can be seen from Table 1.1, which shows an increase of 175 Gt in atmospheric carbon on pre-industrialization levels as a result of the burning of fossil fuels to date. This increase of 30% in the atmosphere's carbon content pales into insignificance when compared with the amount of carbon represented by the fossil-fuel reserves. Leggett says:

> *... the burning of all 4,000 Gt of known coal and oil reserves would increase the CO_2 content of the atmosphere by almost 2,000 Gt of carbon, more than trebling that of today's atmosphere. By exactly how much this would elevate the surface temperatures on Earth it is impossible to say, because of uncertainties in climate response ... temperatures during the age of the dinosaurs (in the Cretaceous period, 140 to 66 million years ago) were up to 10°–15° [C] higher than today. Geochemists have calculated that these involved an atmospheric CO_2 content four to eight times higher than that observed today.[29]*

Given that the figure for 'carbon in potentially recoverable fossil fuels' is quoted as being between 5,000 and 10,000 Gt, which is 7–13 times the current carbon content of the atmosphere, it seems likely that the combustion of all known as well as potentially recoverable fossil fuels really could alter the climate of the entire planet to that of the Cretaceous period.

The sad fact demonstrated by these figures is that the message has not changed in the 20 years between the 1972 United Nations Conference on the Environment in Stockholm and the 1992 United Nations Conference on Environment and Development in Rio de Janeiro. In the 1970s there was concern about the depletion of non-renewable resources, which is discussed in Rattray Taylor[30] and Friends of the Earth.[31] This concern was also very much the guiding idea behind *Limits to Growth* by Meadows et al.[32] The three works cited are typical examples of books that were widely available to the public in the early 1970s, not academic reports of limited circulation. All three books also cover the effects of carbon dioxide emissions in the atmosphere. For example, Rattray Taylor states: 'The one thing that is beyond doubt is that the carbon dioxide levels are rising, and doing so at an increasingly rapid rate. Plotted on graph paper, the curve suggests that the average temperature of the earth would rise at least 5°C by 1990.'[33] The three books deviate in only one major fashion from current thinking, and that is in the field of 'thermal pollution' – the effect of adding energy to the atmosphere as a result of the heat produced from burning fossil fuels and uranium. Rattray Taylor, who was the editor of the BBC Television science series *Horizon*, says: 'I don't doubt that the world could continue for thousands of years at least before becoming bankrupt of energy. Long before it did so we should upset the earth's heat balance.'[34] Meadows et al. quote Holdren: 'Thermal pollution may have serious climatic effects worldwide, when it reaches some appreciable fraction of the energy normally absorbed by the earth from the sun.'[35]

There are some scientists who think that global warming is not a reality. The Business Roundtable of New Zealand, a pressure group representing the interests of business in New Zealand, arranged a lecture early in 1995 by an American meteorological scientist, Professor Richard Lindzen, who says that the effect of water vapour in the atmosphere will cancel any global warming effects.[36] The New Zealand Minister for Science and Research, Simon Upton, commented to the Business Roundtable that he was '... frankly surprised that you have chosen to sponsor a public tour by a scientist who has to date failed to convince his peers in normal scholarly exchanges'.[37] A report in *The Times* of 18 October 1995 states:

> ... the United Nations Intergovernmental Panel on Climate Change have concluded that global warming is under way and is now fact rather than speculation ... The report by the Intergovernmental Panel on Climate Change, to be officially unveiled in Rome in December, has concluded for the first time

that global rises in temperature can be partly blamed on industrial activity, which increases emissions of gases such as carbon dioxide that trap the sun's heat.[38]

THE FUTURE FOR BUILDINGS

In some ways, whether global warming exists or not is irrelevant to the designer. The quotation from Rattray Taylor above shows some of the uncertainties in the global warming argument: the temperature rise of 5°C by 1990 that he predicted has not come to pass – perhaps he was intending to shock his readers into action. The original pressure for the design of the autonomous house at Cambridge was resource depletion, but the long-term availability of non-renewable fuels will have an impact on buildings quite apart from that of climate change. The primary energy input to the United Kingdom in 1990 was supplied as shown in Table 1.2 below.

Table 1.2: Primary energy inputs to the United Kingdom, 1990[39]

fuel	energy supplied in Exajoules (EJ)	% of total
oil	3.2	35
coal	2.9	32
natural gas	2.2	24
primary electricity	0.8	9
total	9.1 EJ	

The recent trend in electricity production from coal to gas means that by 1995 at least two thirds of the United Kingdom's primary energy was supplied by oil and gas, fuels which are estimated to be available for no more than 25 years.[40] Because of the long life of buildings, typically 60–100 years, those built today will still exist when the fuels they were designed to use will probably no longer be available. It is appropriate that architects should be looking towards making buildings that do not use fossil fuels, as part of a rational approach to long-term sustainable design. If this is not done, there will be a large stock of buildings that are not at the end of their useful life, but will be unserviceable because they need fuels that are no longer obtainable or too expensive for general use.

The autonomous house described in this work aims to demonstrate that the servicing needs of a small building can be met without the use of fossil fuels, and with minimal impact on the environment. If such a goal can be achieved in a house that has 24-hour occupancy with a relatively low occupant density, then it may be possible to achieve the same goal in commercial buildings that are occupied for shorter periods of the day, and mostly during daylight hours, by large numbers of people.

2 | *The Philosophical and Technical Background*

THE ENVIRONMENTAL MOVEMENT

Any design proposal for an autonomous house will include specifications for the technologies necessary to build and service it. Before embarking on such a design, it is important to consider the type of technology that might be appropriate for such a dwelling. For example, should it make use of the most advanced technology that modern society can offer, and be of mass-produced, prefabricated construction with automated controls, or should it employ simple technologies that could be constructed and managed by the occupants? In the 1960s various aspects of modern technology were increasingly criticized in certain quarters. The criticisms fell into three main categories: pollution of the environment; depletion of finite natural resources; and social and political arguments.

Pollution of the environment
The pollution problem was first brought to widespread public attention by Rachel Carson's *Silent Spring* – the title refers to the death of songbirds as a result of pesticide poisoning, and the resultant dearth of birdsong. Published in 1962, the book demonstrated the effects of the build-up of pesticides. These chemicals, now so widely distributed that they are found virtually everywhere in the environment, are described by Carson as a product of chemical warfare research during World War II:[1] when some of the chemical agents under test during the war were found to be poisonous to insects they were developed for pest control. Carson explains that what set these new insecticides apart from the largely organically derived products used in the past was their potential as carcinogens and their ability, in very small doses, to cause damage to animals or human beings.[2] In the final chapter of the book she suggests, as an alternative, the use of sterilized male insects, artificial sex attractants, bacteria that attack only the pest

concerned, and also that introduction of predators should be encouraged.[3] All of these control methods have the advantage of being harmless to other species. She concludes that:

> The 'control of nature' is a phrase conceived in arrogance, born of the Neanderthal age of biology and philosophy, when it was supposed that nature exists for the convenience of man. The concepts and practices of applied entomology for the most part date from that Stone Age of science. It is our alarming misfortune that so primitive a science has armed itself with the most modern and terrible weapons, and that in turning them against the insects it has also turned them against the earth.[4]

Writing a decade later, Barry Commoner looked at causes of pollution other than pesticides, including fallout from nuclear weapons tests, smog caused by car exhausts, and nitrates found in drinking water as a result of the heavy use of nitrogen fertilizers. He found that the increase in pollution since 1945 could not be attributed to rising population or increasing affluence, since the rise in pollution levels was some 5–50 times greater than the rise in population or in affluence indicators such as the production of basic commodities like steel, textiles and food.[5] What he found in a sector-by-sector analysis of US production was that there had been considerable growth in certain sectors – for example, the production of 'non-returnable soda bottles' had increased by 53,000% in the period 1946–71, synthetic fibres by 5,980%, and mercury for chlorine production (to make detergents) by 3,930%.[6] During the same period, production of other more 'sustainable' technologies, such as returnable bottles, cotton and wool fibres, and soap production had declined. Commoner concluded that pollution was the result of the substitution of existing technologies and products with new ones, combined with a lack of foresight and concern on the part of those who were making the substitution without looking beyond the immediate purpose of the new technologies and products at the side-effects.

Depletion of finite natural resources

Commoner refers briefly to another factor that influenced the critics of modern technology, the fact that 'Unlike the constituents of the ecosphere, mineral resources are *nonrenewable*.'[7] The best known expression of this problem is contemporary with Commoner's work and can be found in the Club of Rome's computer study *Limits to Growth* published in 1972. This extrapolated the exponential demand rates for various resources and concluded that '... the great majority of the currently important non-renewable resources will be extremely costly one hundred years from now ... as long as the demand for resources continues to grow exponentially.'[8] A similar point is raised in the 'Blueprint for Survival' published the same year by *The Ecologist* magazine as a plan for '... a society which is sustainable and which will give the fullest possible satisfaction to its members. Such a society by definition would depend not on expansion but on stability.'[9] The 'Blueprint' states that 'Indefinite growth of whatever type cannot be sustained by finite resources,'[10] and concludes that 'Synthetics and substitutes are likely to be of little help, since they must be made from materials which are themselves in short supply.'[11]

Social and political arguments

The concerns about pollution and resource depletion described above are rooted in measurable factors: levels of contaminants in the air or water, or consumption of a resource compared with its known reserves. However, many critics of the 1960s and 1970s also expressed dissatisfaction with the ideas and technology of society at that time. Several of these critics wrote of technology becoming the overriding power in society. For example, Jacques Ellul said:

> *Technique* [i.e., technology] *requires predictability and, no less, exactness of prediction. It is necessary, then, that technique prevail over the human being. For technique, this is a matter of life and death. Technique must reduce man to a technical animal, the king of the slaves of technique. Human caprice crumbles before this necessity; there can be no human autonomy in the face of technical autonomy. The individual must be fashioned by techniques ... in order to wipe out the blots his personal determination introduces into the perfect design of the organization.*[12]

Roszak criticized 'technocracy', which he defined as a society:

> *... in which those who govern justify themselves by appealing to technical experts who, in turn, justify themselves by appeal to scientific forms of knowledge. And beyond the authority of science there is no appeal ... [This technocracy] easily eludes all traditional political categories ... Its assumptions about reality and its values become as unobtrusively pervasive as the air we breathe.*[13]

The creation of such a society appears to have produced not an educated and scientifically literate population, but its exact opposite: 'Under the technocracy we become the most scientific of societies; yet, like Kafka's K., men throughout the 'developed world' become more and more the bewildered dependents of inaccessible castles wherein inscrutable technicians conjure with their fate.'[14]

Bookchin referred to changes in the popular attitudes towards technology that had occurred in the previous few decades. The optimism of the 1920s and 1930s, when industrialization seemed the key to social progress, had been replaced by a schizoid attitude to technology 'divided into a gnawing fear of nuclear extinction on the one hand, and a yearning for material abundance, leisure and security on the other.'[15] Increasingly this dual attitude was leading to a 'blanket rejection of technology',[16] which Bookchin regarded as dangerous. He states: 'There is a very real danger that we will lose our perspective toward technology, that we will neglect its liberatory tendencies.'[17]

ALTERNATIVE TECHNOLOGY

These ideas and others led to the emergence of the counter-culture or 'alternative' movement: not an organization, but a loosely defined and changing set of attitudes to life. Dickson says of this movement: 'Whatever one feels about the political significance of the counter-culture movement, one of the more important practical ideas to have emerged from it is ... the need to develop an alternative technology.'[18] He stresses the fact that alternative technology (A.T.) does not have a firm definition, and concludes that it is ' ... a set of approaches to the alternative design and use of machinery and tools, rather than ... a particular set of machines'.[19]

The lack of cohesion of the A.T. movement makes a more detailed definition, and one that is acceptable to all shades of opinion, difficult to achieve. Writing in *Architectural Design* in 1974, Peter Harper admitted this:

> *What is alternative technology? You tell me; I've been trying to track it down for years:*
> *– A means of throwing the Apocalypse off the scent?*
> *– Pandora's toolbox for graduate odd-job men?*
> *– The canonical technics of sun, wind and shit?*
> *– DIY writ large?*
> *– Bucky Fuller writ small?*[20]

Godfrey Boyle and Peter Harper were still having problems with the definition in 1976. They chose the term 'radical technology' for their view of the new technology, and said: 'we are perpetually tracking the elusive beast which we now call "Radical Technology" in order to cage it once and for all. In spite of all our efforts it remains at large.'[21]

The most detailed set of definitions of the new technology was produced by Robin Clarke in his proposal for a 'soft-technology' (yet another name for alternative-technology) research community. These definitions are in the form of pairs of short phrases, each pair of which contrasts some aspect of a 'soft-technology' community with its 'hard' equivalent.[22] The full list is given in Appendix 2. Of the 36 separate items in Clarke's list, 29 can be assumed to relate to the technological aspects of the society being described, rather than to the social or agricultural ones (assuming that agriculture is not regarded as a technology, which is itself debatable). It can be seen that the proponents of technological alternatives do not even have a common name for their endeavours: Boyle and Harper write of 'radical technology'; Robin Clarke calls it 'soft technology'; and Dickson lists, in addition, 'low-impact technology', 'intermediate technology', 'peoples' technology' and 'liberatory technology', as other names for the same thing.[23] However, 'alternative technology' and its abbreviation A.T. were in common use throughout the 1970s, when the movement was at its height.

As a definition of A.T., Robin Clarke's 36 characteristics are still the best available, but they are rather unwieldy for general use. Dickson summarizes the common elements that can be found in the various overlapping proposals for technological alternatives as follows: 'The minimum use of non-renewable resources, minimum environmental interference, regional or sub-regional self-sufficiency, and the elimination of alienation and exploitation of individuals.'[24] This list of attributes defines the ecological, social and political elements that make up alternative technology in a reasonably succinct fashion and may be used as a standard against which technological proposals may be judged.

UTOPIAS – TECHNOLOGY AND SOCIETY

Although the idea of alternative technology appears to be a recent phenomenon, a symptom of dissatisfaction with modern technological progress, it is possible to trace many of the concepts of alternative technology to earlier times. Robin Clarke refers to the 'Utopian characteristics of soft technology' in his list of comparisons, and Utopian writing provides a useful place to observe past attitudes to technology and its rôle in society. Thomas More's *Utopia* (1516)[25] lent its name to the genre of writing that gave '... a literary form to the dreams of a Golden Age and of ideal societies which had doubtless been haunting man since the beginning of the conscious discussion of social problems'.[26] This definition, with the authors' additional observation that the ideal society should exist in this life rather than in a heaven reached after death, will be used to determine whether or not a given work should be included in the survey of Utopian writing that follows. This proviso is intended to ensure that a given Utopia could be considered as being, in the mind of its author, a possible model for an achievable society. Utopian fiction should not be confused with writing which describes an imaginary society in order to highlight the shortcomings of an existing one. Examples of the latter type include Butler's *Erewhon* (1872),[27] Orwell's *Nineteen Eighty-Four* (1949),[28] and Huxley's *Brave New World* (1932),[29] and these will not be discussed here since, although the societies described in them are imaginary, they are intentionally designed not to be ideal societies.

Speaking in New York in 1904, the poet W.B. Yeats said: 'Wherever men have tried to imagine a perfect life, they have imagined a place where men plough and sow and reap, not a place where there are great wheels turning and great chimneys vomiting smoke.'[30] By Yeats' definition, all Utopias ought to paint a picture of simple rural pleasures and honest labour on the land. However, even a superficial survey of the Utopian fiction written prior to 1904 reveals that for every Utopia offering the simple life, there is another that gives pride of place to science and technology. Utopias can also be classed according to their political framework: there are two extremes, authoritarian and libertarian Utopias. In the former, the individual, although often enjoying material comfort, is subordinate to the state or some other authority, and must conform to a code of rules laid down by that authority. In the libertarian Utopias, the happiness of the individual is derived from free expression of personality without submission to externally applied moral or legal codes. As well as attempting to demonstrate that the idea of alternative technology has a long history, the following survey of Utopian fiction examines the types of technology that have been deemed appropriate by the authors of Utopian fiction for different kinds of society.

The first work that can properly be said to describe a Utopia is Plato's *The Republic* (written in *ca* 400 BC), which describes Plato's ideal, authoritarian society, ruled by Guardians. To prevent change, the Guardians control all artistic activities to keep out subversive new ideas. There is no mention of technology as such in *The Republic*, which is largely a description of the selection and training of the Guardians. There is, however, a suggestion of the technological specialization of the modern assembly line in the following passage:

Well, we forbade our shoemaker to try his hand at farming or building and told him to stick to his last, in order that our shoemaking should be well done. Similarly with other trades, we assigned each man to the one for which he was naturally suited, and which he was to practise throughout his life to the exclusion of all others, and so become good at his job and never miss the right moment for action.[31]

The opposite view to Plato's authoritarian version of the ideal society was expressed by Zeno of Kittion (*fl. ca* 320 BC), the first thinker in the Stoic school of philosophy. Zeno believed that people could govern their actions without the need for external compulsion. Berneri says:

> In Zeno's ideal commonwealth, there were to be no States or political institutions, but complete freedom and equality for all human beings, while marriage, temples, law-courts, schools and money, were to be abolished. Zeno did not, however, confuse freedom with license or irresponsibility. He believed that human social instinct has its roots in communal life and finds its highest expression in the sense of justice, and that man combines a need for personal freedom with a sense of responsibility for his own actions.[32]

Just as Zeno offered a libertarian view of society to set against Plato's repressive ideal, the playwright Aristophanes provided a satirical contrast to Plato's rigid technological specialization. In *The Birds* (written in 414 BC)[33] Aristophanes ridicules the whole idea of technological progress, and shows how it destroys a carefree and happy society. In the play the birds are persuaded by an Athenian politician to give up their quiet life and become a super-power to challenge the gods and men. They build and arm a huge city, and achieve a powerful position. By the end of the play they have become the servants of the technology they have created and must spend all their time keeping up their defences. It is interesting to find the idea that 'progress' is not necessarily beneficial being expressed so long before the problems of pollution and resource depletion became apparent, with the advent of the industrial revolution.

After the speculations of the Greeks of antiquity there was a lull in the production of Utopian fiction until Thomas More's *Utopia* (1516). More's ideal world is technically advanced for its time and there is no poverty, but its society is rigidly controlled, militarily expansionist, and dependent on slave labour. It inspired a series of Utopias described a century later and typified by Andrea's *Christianopolis* (1619).[34] Other descriptions of Utopias from this period include Burton's introduction to *The Anatomy of Melancholy* (1621),[35] Campanella's *City of the Sun* (written in 1602 and published in 1623),[36] and Gott's *Nova Solyma* (1648).[37] Like More, these writers describe in detail the construction of their buildings and cities. Mumford[38] admired Andrea for his use of zoning regulations to separate industrial and residential areas.[39] Christianopolis also boasts building inspectors and street lights,[40] piped water and a modern sewage system: ' ... flowing water frees the houses of their daily accumulations.'[41] Its houses are fireproof,[42] double-glazed, centrally heated and passively cooled: 'The buildings have double windows, one of glass and one of wood, inserted in the wall in such a way that each may be opened or closed as is desired ... They drive out cold with furnace heat, and counteract heat with shade.'[43]

The workers who live in Christianopolis are all highly educated and use their knowledge of science to improve their work processes and products continually. This technological effort is backed up by a central research institute. The life of the inhabitants of Christianopolis is a curious mix of the liberal and the repressive. In many ways, Christianopolis provides a far more satisfactory existence for its inhabitants than the other Utopias, the descriptions of which were penned at about the same time: working conditions are comfortable, education is universal, and there is no private property or money. There is an ample stock of well built comfortable houses, and food and wine are provided for all the population from the public stores. Housework is shared by husbands and wives and, unlike earlier Utopias, children are not bred according to eugenic requirements. On the other hand, recreational sex is frowned upon, attendance at prayers three times a day is compulsory, books are censored and women 'have no voice'[44] in the church and council. Crimes are treated differently according to their type: '... they punish most severely those misdeeds which are directed straight against God, less severely those which injure men, and lightest of all those which harm only property.'[45] It seems that Andrea would like to have trusted people to manage their own affairs and lead a good life, but his religion told him that they were sinners and must be prevented from sinning further:

> In the same way we may say of penalties, there is no use of these in a place that contains the very sanctuary of God and a chosen state, in which Christian liberty can bear not even commands, much less threats, but is borne voluntarily toward Christ ... It is the art of arts to guard against permitting sin to become easy for anyone.[46]

However, *Christianopolis* shows that Andrea believed in technological progress through the use of science in the workplace, as well as in the laboratory, and that this technology could provide comfortable living and working conditions for all members of his Utopian community.

The first Utopia to give full emphasis to the possibilities offered by science and technology is Bacon's *New Atlantis* (1672).[47] The book contains only a brief description of the society on which it is based, and is largely an account of the scientific research institute that Bacon would like to have created. Osborne expounds the idea behind Bacon's writing, that the old learning based on Aristotle needed to be replaced by a new learning based on scientific observation as follows: 'Bacon believed that the salvation of mankind was to be sought in the extension of our practical knowledge. That age did not pursue the ideal of knowledge for its own sake, but advocated experimental research because of the immense benefits which they hoped to achieve from it.'[48]

Salomon's House, the research centre described in Bacon's book, is an Aladdin's cave of technological gadgets and scientific wonders. There are laboratories for every subject from plant breeding to mathematics, as well as devices such as submarines and flying machines,[49] and much attention is given to the production of synthetic materials, both metals and foodstuffs. Little is said of Bensalem, the country where Salomon's House is located, but the few hints that are given show that it is a static and thoroughly regulated society. There is a king, but the real power must rest with the scientists and technologists, who decide which of their inventions and discoveries to reveal to the state and which to keep secret.

In the latter half of the 18th century, the genre of Utopian fiction was largely replaced in England by books such as Harrington's *Oceana* (1656)[50] and Winstanley's *Law of Freedom* (1652).[51] These works lack the fictional framework of the earlier Utopias and are more in the nature of political manifestos. As such, they fall outside the scope of this particular discussion. It was not until the 19th century that technology again became a central concern to writers of Utopian fiction. This is not surprising, since the effects of the industrial revolution were at this time causing far-reaching changes in society. Technology began to play a central rôle in Utopias at the same time as it began to play a central part in the real world. Although early Utopias showed a knowledge of the benefits of technology, they tended to view human progress as freedom from want in a society that embodied mental, physical and moral improvement. Luxuries were regarded as tending to undermine morals, so ideal societies were often austere and egalitarian. However, in the 19th century, mass production held out the promise of wealth for all, and the concept of progress tended to be viewed in material rather than spiritual terms.

These 19th-century Utopias and their abundance are typified by Bellamy's *Looking Backward* (1888), which sold about 180,000 copies.[52] In Bellamy's ideal society of the year 2000, the state is the sole employer and everyone is conscripted into the 'industrial army' from the age of 21 to 45.[53] After three years of compulsory service on unpleasant work of the state's choice, a person can select a particular trade, provided that there is a vacancy. After retirement at 45, people are free to do as they like. Only those over the age of 45 can vote for the president, and the other leaders are chosen from the managerial élite which is made up of those who rise through the ranks of the industrial army. So that every worker can be regularly graded, and promoted or reduced in rank as appropriate, an elaborate piece-work scheme is operated in all sectors of employment. People who refuse to work are 'cut off from all human society'.[54] Each member of

Bellamy's society is given an equal share of its wealth by means of a credit card. With this card people can buy goods from large showrooms whence the items are dispatched to their homes through pneumatic tubes. The cards can also be used to buy services, such as concerts, relayed into the home by telephone, or to subscribe to newspapers or magazines which are controlled by the subscribers.

Bellamy appears to have been unable to believe that work could ever be pleasant. One of his characters says of it: 'It is a necessary duty to be discharged before we can fully devote ourselves to the higher exercise of our faculties, the intellectual enjoyment and pursuits which alone mean life.'[55] The residents of Boston in the year 2000 look forward to their retirement at 45: 'As the time when we shall first enter upon the full enjoyment of our birthright.'[56] Perhaps because he could not imagine that work might be enjoyable, Bellamy believed in the application of technology to improve life, particularly in the field of labour-saving devices: 'Now that we all have to do in turn whatever work is done for society, every individual in the nation has the same interest, and a personal one, in devices for lightening the burden.'[57] The central character of the book, a resident of 19th-century Boston, who wakes from a hypnotic trance to find himself in the future, is so impressed by the technology of this new society that he says: 'It appears to me ... that if we could have devised an arrangement for providing everybody with music in their homes, perfect in quality, unlimited in quantity, suited to every mood, and beginning and ceasing at will, we should have considered the limit of human felicity already attained, and ceased to strive for further improvements.'[58]

Bellamy's was not the only vision of the machine-dominated future that was popular in the 19th century. In France, Cabet's *Voyage en Icarie* (1845)[59] enjoyed great popularity and inspired the building of a number of Utopian communities in America.[60] Cabet takes the regulation of his society to ludicrous extremes; committees of experts decide all matters of life down to what one should eat, when one should eat, what one should wear, and when one should talk during work. Mumford says of these 19th-century visions: 'These Utopias become vast reticulations of steel and red tape, until we feel that we are caught in the Nightmare of the Age of machinery ...'[61]

William Morris was so dismayed by *Looking Backward* that he wrote his own Utopian novel, *News from Nowhere*, as a reply to it. Reviewing Bellamy's book in *The Commonweal*, Morris wrote: 'A machine life is the best which Bellamy can imagine for us on all sides; it is not to be wondered at when his only idea of making labour tolerable is to decrease the amount of it by means of fresh and ever fresh developments of machinery.'[62] He described Bellamy's future world as a 'cockney paradise', and railed against its burgeoning consumerism.[63] Morris, as well as being a socialist, was an artist and designer, not a technologist, and in the buildings, clothes and manufactured articles of his Utopia, there is none of the uniformity of earlier writers. If people want to wear beautiful clothes, there is nothing to stop them, as this description of a dustman demonstrates: 'We only call him Boffin as a joke, partly because he is a dustman and partly because he will dress so showily and get as much gold on him as a baron of the Middle Ages. And why should he not if he likes?'[64] (Boffin, the 'golden dustman' was a character in Dickens' novel *Our Mutual Friend* who made a fortune out of waste recycling.) Berneri's introduction to her discussion of *News from Nowhere* sums up the differences between Morris' approach and that of Bellamy and Cabet:

> *Here we can work without having a foreman at our elbow, we can sleep without having to set the alarm clock, eat what we like and not what the experts have decided to be best suited to our constitution; we can love without having to consider tyrannical laws or a no less tyrannical public opinion; here we can dress as we like, read what we like and, above all, think what we like. Here we can live because we have not been catalogued and directed, but left to arrange our lives as we think fit.*[65]

Not all Morris' critics are so complimentary; Hough says of *News from Nowhere*: '... it becomes plain that Morris is talking a good deal of nonsense.'[66]

The changes in the society in Britain described by Morris are brought about by popular revolution, followed by a long civil war. He did not believe, as did Bellamy, that capitalism would give up its hold without a struggle. Morris also differed from Bellamy in his attitude to work: he thought that work which was not compulsory, which was carried out in pleasant conditions and which allowed full scope for personal creativity, would not be a burden to the worker. In Morris' Utopia, people go off for a couple of weeks of haymaking or road mending as a pleasant change from their usual tasks. The attitude to work, and to the use of machinery, is described in this passage:

> *The wares which we make are made because they are needed: men make for their neighbours' use as if they were working for themselves, not for a vague market of which they know nothing, and over which they have no control: as there is no buying and selling, it would be mere insanity to make goods on the chance of their being wanted: for there is no longer anyone who can be compelled to buy them. So that whatever is made is good, and thoroughly fit for its purpose. Nothing can be made except for genuine use; therefore, no inferior goods are made. Moreover, as aforesaid, we have now found out what we want, so we make no more than we want; and as we are not driven to make a vast quantity of useless things, we have time and resources enough to consider*

our pleasure in making them. All work which would be irksome to do by hand is done by immensely improved machinery; and in all work which it is a pleasure to do by hand machinery is done without. There is no difficulty in finding work which suits the special turn of mind of everybody so that no man is sacrificed to the wants of another. From time to time, when we have found out that some piece of work was too disagreeable or troublesome, we have given it up and done without the thing produced by it. Now surely you can see that under these circumstances all the work that we do is an exercise of the mind and body more or less pleasant to be done: so that instead of avoiding work, everybody seeks it: and since people have got defter in doing this work generation after generation, it has become so easy to do, that it seems as if there were less done though probably more is produced.[67]

This quotation sums up, perhaps, the most important difference between Morris and the other 19th-century writers of Utopian fiction: Morris believed that creative work was an important element of human life and that it could be more than a necessary duty.

News from Nowhere could be seen as the first description of an alternative-technology Utopia. While Andrea's *Christianopolis* shows a society where technology is used to serve the inhabitants and allow them more control over their work, Morris is the first writer to reject much of the advanced technology of his time, because of its tendency to alienate those who operate it. The passage from *News from Nowhere* quoted above satisfies many of Robin Clarke's 'characteristics' of alternative technology discussed earlier – Morris' ideal society is making deliberate technological choices. It does not shrink from employing machinery to eliminate the drudgery of work, but the use of machinery has not been allowed to take the skills out of labour. The society also has a decentralized energy supply grid, supplying power wherever needed, as an alternative to the 19th-century technology of steam engines, layshafts and belts, which was tending to centralize production: 'Why should people collect together to use power, when they can have it at the places where they live, or by any two or three of them; or anyone, for the matter of that?'[68] Victorian steam power has been replaced by 'force vehicles'[69] on land and water which move without any visible means of propulsion, and the kilns for pottery- and glass-making operate without smoke. One of the characters says of the attitude of this society to technology: 'This is not an age of inventions. The last epoch did all that for us, and we are now content to use such of its inventions as we find handy, and leaving those alone which we don't want.'[70]

The 19th-century boom in the popularity of Utopian fiction was partly supplanted in the 20th century by the anti-Utopias of, for example, Zamyatin's

We (1924),[71] Huxley's *Brave New World* (1932)[72] and Orwell's *Nineteen Eighty-Four* (1949).[73] However, Wells produced two Utopias in the traditional vein: the first, *A Modern Utopia* in 1905, and the very different *Men like Gods* in 1923. In the first Wells says: 'Were we to have our untrammelled desire I suppose we should follow Morris to his Nowhere, we should change the nature of man and the nature of things together ... warm our hands to a splendid anarchy.'[74] He goes on to describe an efficient and rigidly controlled world society. In the later book, Wells changes his mind and describes an advanced anarchistic society existing in a parallel universe. He says that the people in it are little different from the people of a Bronze Age community, but they are not distorted by the social pressures typical of the early 20th century as they grow up: 'Innately better to begin with, the minds of these children of light had grown up uninjured by any such tremendous frictions, concealments, ambiguities and ignorances as cripple the growing mind of an Earthling.'[75]

The second half of the 20th century saw an increase in the output of Utopian fiction, particularly from the United States of America. Not surprisingly, several of these more recent novels incorporate the idea of alternative technology, but they display differing types of social structures. For example, while Ethel Mannin's *Bread and Roses* (1944),[76] an English Utopia, describes an anarcho-syndicalist society of natural liberty and mutual aid, Skinner in *Walden Two*[77] depicts a community in the United States controlled by behavioural psychology, where the residents have voluntarily submitted to a code which is designed to modify and control their behaviour so as to make them happy: 'Our members are practically always doing what they want to do ... but we see to it that they will want to do precisely the things which are best for themselves and the community. Their behaviour is determined, yet they're free.'[78] Although they rest on different foundations, both Mannin's and Skinner's societies offer a high standard of living allied to a low consumption of goods, facilitated by avoiding waste and using communal facilities.

Huxley's *Island* (1962)[79] describes another society in the tradition of Morris and Mannin, which has made careful choices in its use of technology, summed up by the comment: 'Electricity minus heavy industry plus birth control equals democracy and plenty.'[80] The Island of Pala described in the novel combines Western science with Eastern mysticism, to produce a society that enables individuals to develop their potential without interfering with the rights of others: 'There's plenty of scope for small-scale initiative and democratic leaders, but no place for any kind of dictator at the head of a centralized government.'[81] At the end of the book, the enlightened Pala is invaded by a neighbouring dictatorship, implying perhaps that Huxley thought a society like the one he described could not exist, or would not be permitted to exist, in the real world.

Mannin, Skinner and Huxley set their Utopias in the present, but Callenbach's *Ecotopia* (1975)[82] is placed in 1999, 24 years after it was published, and depicts the steady-state society formed by the secession of Washington, Oregon and Northern California from the rest of the United States of America in order to create an ecological society (hence the title). The book is reminiscent of *New Atlantis* in its enthusiastic description of the devices and processes that have been introduced to conform to the 'stable state life systems which are our fundamental ecological and political goal'.[83] Ecotopia offers its citizens a relaxed communal style of life but they also have ritual war games, in which the men (the women do not take part), armed with spears, try to kill members of an opposing team. It is a society which demands conformity to its extrovert, communal outdoors-loving style of life, and contains elements of authoritarian, as well as libertarian, Utopias of the past. Libertarian was defined at the beginning of this survey of Utopias as 'free expression of personality without submission to externally applied moral or legal codes'. Ecotopia seems to allow its citizens free expression while expecting them to conform to its codes. Callenbach does not say what happens to dissenters, but his ideal society is backed up by armed forces, police, prisons, and a counter-intelligence service.

Two other relatively recent Utopias from the United States are Le Guin's *The Dispossessed* (1975),[84] and Piercy's *Woman on the Edge of Time* (1976).[85] Both are distant from the present; Le Guin's is set on another planet and Piercy's is far in the future in Massachusetts. *The Dispossessed* is interesting because it looks at the disadvantages of the libertarian society described so enthusiastically by others; Le Guin shows how public opinion in such a society may become as powerful a force for preventing change as the moral and legal restraints of a more authoritarian society. Technically speaking, the book is not a Utopia, because it describes the society established by a group of anarchists on the barren, inhospitable moon of a fertile planet whose political system they have rejected. Rather than a generalized ideal society, *The Dispossessed* describes an attempt to create a specific ideal society in a particular given situation. The emphasis of the society is the avoidance of waste – 'excess is excrement'[86] – and the technology used is simple and geared to the best possible use of natural resources, such as solar and wind power.

In *Woman on the Edge of Time*, the experiences of a poor Mexican-American woman in a mental hospital are contrasted with the society of the future. When Connie, the woman from the 20th century, first visits the future, she is disappointed to find that the people live in villages with small buildings, vegetable gardens and goats, rather than in a more futuristic environment. They use solar collectors and windmills for energy supply and each region aims at self-sufficiency in proteins. Gradually, a more advanced technology becomes apparent, with computers, automated factories and holographic films, but all these systems are manufactured in the villages and are used to increase decentralization. There are no big cities any more because they have been found not to work. The principal difference between Piercy's Utopia and other similar visions is in the child rearing; children are conceived and grown to birth in a building called the brooder, and are then allocated to three male and female 'mothers' who (with the aid of suitable drugs) breast feed and care for them. This system was found to be the only way to remove the distinctions between men and women whilst giving individual attention to the children. Politically, organization is by lengthy meetings of 'reps', chosen by lot, at village, township and regional level, who discuss and argue until a consensus is reached. If one side in an agreement loses, they are feasted and given presents by the winners:

> Political decisions – like whether to raise power production, go a different route. We talk locally and then choose a rep to speak our point on area hook-up. Then we all sit in holi simulcast [ie. holographic simultaneous television broadcast] and the rep from each group speaks their village point. Then we go back into local meeting to fuse our final word. Then the reps argue once more before everybody. Then we vote.[87]

In a similar vein to the last two Utopias, but set in Britain, is Brenda Vale's *Albion* (1982). This describes life in Britain in the middle of the 21st century, and is probably the first fully alternative-technology Utopia, containing detailed descriptions of the devices and techniques that are used to provide the necessities of daily life. The society depicted is one in which care of resources has become part of daily life:

> He had pegged out all the clothes. He pulled the line up and tied it to a hook on the wall of the house. He looked into the large underground cistern below the pulley. It was not very full. Perhaps he had been too free with the rainwater he had used for rinsing. Nevertheless, he pumped water up from the cistern into the tank in the scullery roof. There was nothing else to do ... He emptied the water from the bucket under the mangle into the water butt in the garden, then, looking down at the seedlings he refilled the bucket and watered them instead.[88]

In Albion fossil fuels are no longer available; coal is reserved for the manufacture of chemicals. Enthusiasts make petrol to enable them to drive treasured 1980s cars at occasional rallies:

I make it from the bits of waste wood. There's no problem with the technology, you must have come across it surely, but it's a question of only using the surplus wood that the community doesn't want. That's why I can't travel very far. It's meant a bit of adjustment to the engine, but even I can see that you can't use the coal for making proper synthetic petrol.[89]

Like *The Dispossessed*, *Albion* does not describe a society that is ideal (as More's original was intended to be) but one that has been created out of the collapse of the present. An account of the changes is given in a history book read by one of the characters:

Eventually he stood up, went into the front and looked along the shelves of Michael's desk for the copy of Albion Revolution *he had seen there ... the little book made the changes seem sharp and clear, untroubled and obvious. It traced the changing patterns that a society without abundant energy and transport had to make to survive. With little investment in the nuclear programme, at the end of the oil boom the government found itself forced to import oil again but had no money and no loans to do so. There was no alternative energy programme and, although there was coal, no cheap way had been developed of making it into a fuel for the transport system. Without the transport system the economy had to change. However, before any major economic planning the people had started to implement the alternative for themselves. They had moved out from the towns and cities and squatted on marginal and derelict land to grow food ... John turned to the back of the book and began to read:- "Far more insidious, from the point of view of the state, was the orderly revolution that continued, noticed but unmolested, for many, many years. It was a revolution so decentralized and individualistic that there was nothing for the state to react against. The revolution ignored the state and turned to its own gardens and solar collectors, windmills and looms, bicycles and cooperatives, and the state could do nothing. There were no heroes and heroines to persecute, no ruling élite and no mastering committee. There was nothing to seize and confiscate, for the revolutionary propaganda was only spread by demonstration and example. The state that belonged to the Albion revolution was no more than a state of mind. When land-squatting began in the time of hardship then those who appeared as leaders were arrested, but even then it was difficult to distinguish who was leading from who was being led. When it became obvious that without transport even the police and government were going to starve in the city then the revolution was given the respectability of an alternative solution."*[90]

TECHNOLOGIES AND SOCIETIES

An authoritarian society was defined earlier as one which demands the submission of the individual to some higher authority and its legal and moral codes. A libertarian society was seen as one which was based on individual liberty. It is possible to divide Utopias into two general categories according to which type of society they portray, and also to divide them technologically into conventional or alternative-technology societies. These distinctions are less easily made in the case of the earlier Utopias, because their technology and form of society are too far removed from the present to allow a judgment to be made. The following table shows some more recent Utopias, ranked according to date of publication.

Table 2.1: Social and technological aspects of some 19th- and 20th-century Utopias

author, date	more or less authoritarian	more or less libertarian	conventional technology	alternative technology
Cabet, 1842	x		x	
Bellamy, 1888	x		x	
Morris, 1891		x		x
Wells, 1905	x		x	
Wells, 1923		x	x	
Mannin, 1944		x		x
Skinner, 1948	x			x
Huxley, 1962		x		x
Le Guin, 1974		x		x
Callenbach, 1975		x		x
Piercy, 1976		x		x
Vale, 1982		x		x

The table shows that the majority of writers on Utopia have considered that more or less libertarian societies need an alternative to conventional 'advanced' technology. This table cannot examine in detail either the degree of libertarianism in a given Utopia, nor the extent to which its technology matches Clarke's 36 characteristics, but it does reveal the trends of thought in Utopian writing in the past 130 years. It can be argued that the two works (Skinner, and Wells' second Utopia) which do not fit the pattern are, to some extent, outside the mainstream of Utopias; Skinner's behaviourist community is only a village or small town rather than a whole region or country, so it need not concern itself with the technological problems of a larger unit; and the parallel universe that Wells depicts in *Men like Gods* is so far removed from the present that its technology cannot easily be compared. It could be argued that the technology mentioned in the book fulfils the criteria for A.T., but Wells does not give enough detail to allow this to be done confidently.

Perhaps the most important aspect of Utopian thought highlighted by the brief study above is that most writers have considered that the technology of their time cannot meet the needs of a society which places the needs of the individual above the demands of the state. The implication, therefore, is that advanced technology is not appropriate to a freer society, and that it represents a barrier to freedom. The survey demonstrates, in addition, that the idea of alternative technology is not merely a recent phenomenon, but one that has been current for many years. Even if one disregards Aristophanes' mocking of the concept of progress in *The Birds*, alternative technology can be seen as an idea running parallel to the development of conventional technology, and as representing the technology suited for many differing views of what constitutes an ideal society, one that values individual freedom. This conclusion has an impact on the design of an autonomous house, as it implies that the alternative-technology approach to a house might be the more appropriate route to follow, as the one tending to encourage individual freedom. This would presuppose a design that was simple and could be controlled and repaired by the users, as well as one that minimized environmental impact and energy use.

APPROPRIATE TARGETS

In addition to being faced with a fundamental strategic choice between two technological approaches, advanced and alternative technology – or hard and soft, high-tech and low-tech, etc. – the designer of an autonomous house also has a wide range of finer tactical decisions within that strategy. It was shown above that 29 out of the 36 criteria listed by Clarke defining the 'hard-technology' society could be attributed to technology *per se*. Individual constituents of the technology used to build an autonomous house might turn out to share certain characteristics with advanced technology, such as 'high pollution rate', 'capital intensive', 'operating modes too complicated for general comprehension', even if the aim of the building's design was the laudable goal of eliminating the use of mains services and non-renewable fuels.

In contrast to Clarke's list of criteria, it is interesting to look at a much more recent list that applies specifically to the built environment. This list was produced by Graeme Robertson of the University of Auckland, and was developed originally for the 1992 Earth Summit, the United Nations Conference on Environment and Development in Rio de Janeiro.[91] There are many parallels in tone as well as substance with Clarke's list, and the majority of Robertson's criteria could similarly be applied to the technology of a house, such as 'elimination of the concept of waste', 'low renewable-energy approaches', and 'respect for the notion of "craft"'; the full list is given in Appendix 3.

The adoption of an advanced-technology strategy at the outset of the design process for an autonomous house might lead the designer to attempt to create a home that meets the levels of servicing currently provided in a 'standard house'. For example, in a description of the Cambridge Autonomous House, Alexander Pike said: '... the proposals illustrated represent a personal approach, attempting to provide facilities as closely comparable as possible to those expected by the average family, thereby hoping to make the benefits available to the widest section of the population.'[92] This is an approach that is fraught with difficulties; not only must the 'standard house' be defined, along with its servicing provision, but the autonomous house must attempt to provide, from the resources it collects from its immediate environment, the same degree of apparently limitless servicing that the conventional house can offer thanks to its connection to a much larger resource pool. A definition of the standard house might be achieved using published data for average temperatures in rooms, or *per capita* water consumption, for example. These data would furnish a limit for practical purposes to apparently limitless servicing. However, the autonomous house cannot provide servicing without limits, a theoretical possibility in the conventional house. The occupants of a conventional house may have a general tendency to heat the house to an average temperature of 20°C, but they could, if they wanted to, heat it to 30°C, provided that they could pay the fuel bill resulting from their decision and the heating system was capable of supplying the heat. The occupants of an autonomous house could not do this, because they would not have the resources to do so. Even if the design of an autonomous house is based on a set of standard performance data for a conventional house, the autonomous house would fall short, at a conceptual level, of the standards of servicing that are conventionally accepted, and never reach the state of 'advanced' technology.

However, no such problems confront the designer whose autonomous house design is based on alternative-technology criteria. An alternative-technology approach to design implies an idea of sufficiency of resource provision, rather than excess – a position elaborated by Le Guin in *The Dispossessed* where 'excess is excrement' in her idealistic community.[93] The conventional method of servicing houses works on the premise that the occupants may have as much of a service (and therefore of a resource) as they can afford. If they want to heat the house to a constant temperature of 30°C, they can do so. Similarly, in a conventional house an occupant may choose to use large amounts of water by having many baths or using a lawn sprinkler. The only control of these activities is the price the user pays for the resource consumed. The mechanism of control by price takes no account of the effect on the global environment of one consumer's choice of service provision. The person who heats a house to 30°C is adding carbon dioxide to the atmosphere (54 kg of CO_2 per Gigajoule [GJ] for gas, and 190 kg of CO_2 per GJ for electricity)[94] at a greater rate than the person who chooses a temperature of 20°C. They are also increasing their rate of consumption of non-renewable resources in the form of fossil fuels. Similarly, the result of high water consumption is that water becomes unavailable to other users, requiring the construction of new supplies, or the diversion of water from agriculture to supply consumers: 'In the western United States, for instance, the future water demands of rapidly growing Las Vegas will almost certainly be satisfied by diverting water from irrigation. Similarly in China, most cities suffer from severe water shortages, and many of them will meet their future needs by taking water away from irrigation.'[95] It could be argued that the market mechanism will control these transactions, but there is often no direct link between the use of a resource and its effects. The water company may have to build a new reservoir to meet the water demands of its consumers, and it can then pass the cost of the reservoir on to its customers. Here the market mechanism appears to operate in a relatively straightforward way, but there are a number of problems. One is that the users who consume little water have to help pay towards making provision for the users who consume a lot of water; the effect is that the cost of water goes up, even for those who have not caused the increased demand. Another problem is that the construction of the new reservoir will cause problems that have an impact outside the concerns of the individual water customers, as it may involve the flooding of an existing valley, the destruction of existing houses and the inundation of landscape and wildlife habitat. In the case of the overheated house, the effect of global warming resulting from increased carbon dioxide emission due to increased fossil fuel consumption may cause a rise in sea level, requiring increased expenditure on coastal defences to reduce the possible effects of flooding. This cost is not easily passed on to the consumer by the power company under presently existing market arrangements, even when the cost of flood protection measures is incurred in the same country that causes the increase in carbon dioxide emissions. Many of the environmental effects of energy use are trans-boundary effects, in that the cause and effect are geographically separated: the burning of coal containing sulphur in one country may result in the acidification of lakes in another. Even in a situation where it is clearly agreed that the effect is attributable to a particular cause, such as in the case of the Chernobyl nuclear power station accident, there is no market mechanism that adds the cost of radioactive sheep in Wales onto the bills of electricity consumers in the Ukraine.

Alternative servicing

An autonomous house will not be able to provide the same level of service provision as a conventional house. If a house is providing services from the resources that fall on it, it can never achieve that level of apparent limitlessness that is offered by conventional servicing. An electrical system based on batteries, for example, will run out of stored power if all the lights are left on. A rainwater storage tank will be emptied if everyone wants a bath at once. At first sight, the autonomous house looks less attractive than the conventional system, in which the limits are imposed by circumstances out of sight of the occupant of the house; when someone turns up their heating, they tend not to be thinking of a possible rise in sea-level caused by the carbon dioxide emissions connected with this action. Even if that person is aware of the emissions, he or she is likely to feel, with some justification, that the effect of an individual's action can have little impact on the global climate. Conventional servicing of houses encourages the user to pass the buck and to assume that the global problems are caused by, and can be solved by, someone else.

In the autonomous house, the user cannot pass the buck. Responsibility for conserving a given resource, be it water, electricity or space heat, will lie with the occupants. If they leave the taps running they will run out of water until it rains again. This makes such a house sound a very unattractive proposition, but the autonomous-house concept has one major practical advantage over the conventionally serviced house – apart from reduced environmental impact – and that is that the services are provided at no cost to the user.

In the 1950s, British newspapers talked of electricity too cheap to meter as a result of the nuclear fusion experiments being carried out with the zero-energy thermonuclear array (ZETA) device at Harwell. Electricity was to be supplied unmetered, like water, for a fixed payment per household, and the consumer would use as much as required. The reality 40 years later in the United Kingdom is that water is now metered like electricity and has become an expensive commodity. A press report in February 1994 showed that 95 low-income households surveyed in Merseyside were paying an average of £4.70 per week for their metered water supplies,[96] giving an annual bill of nearly £250.

Whereas in the conventional house access to services is limited by the ability to pay – in the Merseyside case cited above, 42% of the households surveyed said that they were washing less often because of the cost of water – in the autonomous house access to services is limited by the amount that the house can collect. This seems to have some very real advantages. The users are put into direct touch with the resources, rather than being separated from them by a market mechanism. As a result of this, users are given direct control of those resources, and also control and direct awareness of the environmental impact created by the use of the resources. In a conventional house it is very difficult to see the connection between the use of a service, which is good from the user's standpoint, and the environmental impact, such as global warming, or water shortage, which is bad from the viewpoint, often not of the service user, but of someone far away. In the autonomous house, resource depletion begins at home: it is possible for the occupants to misuse their resources without damaging anyone but themselves. Their over-use of electricity will not harm the global environment, but it will leave them in the dark if they allow their batteries to go flat. This relationship between user and resources, and the effect that this use of resources has on the Earth as a whole, constitute an important step in putting people into control of their circumstances. People may learn to value a resource if they appreciate the effect of scarcity of that resource.

The concept of satisfaction

A number of thinkers on environmental questions have put forward this concept of 'enough' rather than 'more' over the years: 'It is not life which occasions our shortages – not even the 'good' life; but is the constantly *better* life as measured by increasing use of resources ... which brings us to the limit of resources.'[97] This statement was made at the conclusion of the International Symposium on 'Man's Rôle in Changing the Face of the Earth' held at Princeton, New Jersey, in June 1956. The participants invited to the symposium, including Lewis Mumford and Teilhard de Chardin, were of international standing, and the event was organized by the Wenner-Gren Foundation for Anthropological Research and the National Science Foundation. Its deliberations were published in two volumes by the University of Chicago Press, and subsequently reprinted several times. One of the participants, the Professor of Economics at the University of Michigan, was moved to write a poem setting out the two strands of thought that were apparent at the symposium. His words are still relevant today:

A conservationist's lament

The world is finite, resources are scarce,
Things are bad and will be worse.
Coal is burned and gas exploded,
Forests cut and soils eroded.
Wells are dry and air's polluted,
Dust is blowing, trees uprooted.
Oil is going, ores depleted,
Drains receive what is excreted.
Land is sinking, seas are rising,
Man is far too enterprising.
Fire will rage with Man to fan it,
Soon we'll have a plundered planet.
People breed like fertile rabbits,
People have disgusting habits.
Moral:
The evolutionary plan
Went astray by evolving Man.

The technologist's reply

Man's potential is quite terrific,
You can't go back to the Neolithic.
The cream is there for us to skim it,
Knowledge is power, and the sky's the limit.
Every mouth has hands to feed it,
Food is found when people need it.
All we need is found in granite
Once we have the men to plan it.
Yeast and algae give us meat,
Soil is almost obsolete.
Men can grow to pastures greener
Till all the earth is Pasadena.
Moral:
Man's a nuisance, Man's a crackpot,
But only Man can hit the jackpot.[98]

The poem makes explicit both the environmental situation to which the concept of the autonomous house is an appropriate response, and the use of technological imagination to allow that concept to be realized. However, it is clear that the technologist who replies to the conservationist's lament is not an alternative technologist.

The idea that 'enough is as good as a feast' was expressed by Rattray Taylor, whose work *The Doomsday Book* was an important contribution to the publicizing of the environmental debate in the United Kingdom:

> One of the best-established principles in economics is the one which says that the more you have of anything, the less satisfaction you get from having some more; otherwise known as the principle of marginal returns. One car may make a great difference to your life. The fourth car just gives you the choice whether you will go there in the sedan or the convertible. One crust of bread may save a man from starvation; a thousand crusts would simply be a litter problem ... industrial civilizations have reached the point where a majority of the population is consuming goods which yield only marginal satisfactions.[99]

A similar position is reflected in the journal *Architectural Design*, which published a special issue on 'Design for Survival' in July 1972 reflecting the concerns expressed at the United Nations Stockholm Conference. In an introduction to the special edition, Colin Moorcroft says: 'It is a patent fraud for the rich nations to pretend that the poor nations will ever be able to consume equal amounts of resources. They are prevented from doing this by more than economic controls: they are prevented by the fact that there isn't anything like enough to go around ...'[100] He goes on to criticize advanced technology, seeing it as part of the problem that keeps the world's poor in a state of poverty, rather than as part of the solution to their condition: 'The new technology is more than an unsuccessful alternative to previous technologies: it actively blocks any other ways out.'[101]

CONCLUSION: THE ALTERNATIVE-TECHNOLOGY APPROACH

The conclusion that may be drawn from writings on the environment from the 1970s and earlier (when the effect of human impact on the environment first came to prominence), from the study of Utopian literature, and from more recent work on the area of sustainability, is that the alternative-technology approach to the design of an autonomous house is the appropriate one. An autonomous house has to depend on the resources that can be collected on its site, and the technology that it uses to harvest these resources needs to be simple, robust and controllable by the occupants. Only in this way will the inhabitants of the house gain that sense of control which will allow them to use their share of the Earth's resources sensibly. The alternative-technology approach appears to be intellectually justifiable and will form the basis of the house design that is described in the rest of this book. However, under this overall design umbrella of alternative technology, there are many areas where the choice of technological approach is not clear cut, and subsequent chapters will attempt to consider the possibilities and to steer a route through the choices that might be made.

3 | *The Autonomous House as Built*

INTRODUCTION

In addition to meeting various criteria for self-sufficiency, an autonomous house has to constitute a home. This chapter considers the design of the authors' autonomous house, largely from an architectural standpoint, and attempts to explain both the decisions that were made during the design process and the effect that these decisions had on the overall form of the finished building. In many ways it is artificial to separate the design from the technical aspects, and there will be seen to be considerable overlaps; these too will be highlighted as the discussion progresses. However, there is some value in isolating aspects of the design, as it helps clarify some of the thinking that was involved. At the same time, it is important to give a sense of the relative degree of importance assumed by different factors at different stages of the design process. The original intention was not that the house should be fully autonomous, but that it should be a home, the occupation of which should create no carbon dioxide emissions; that it should require no space heating; and that it should use solar energy for water heating and electricity production. As will be seen, autonomy in water supply and sewage were added later in the design.

The descriptions of the design process and its outcome that follow are given before the discussion of the technical options that were considered and the account of the technical decisions that were reached during the process. This is in order to provide the reader with a mental picture of the house as the technical options are discussed. The present book was written after the construction and occupation of the autonomous house, so it would be disingenuous to attempt to make the design process fit into a neat historical progression. The design process for most buildings is less a progression than a series of iterations, often carried out in parallel and at a wide range of scales. It is seldom neatly ordered.

WHY A HOUSE?

Before investigating the design of the autonomous house it is worth asking why the authors elected to design a house. Might not a large commercial building have been a more appropriate demonstration of a new technology, or perhaps a public building such as a school or a library? A house seems such a small thing by comparison. The question may appear reasonable, but in the United Kingdom, the domestic sector of the economy is a large energy consumer. Its consumption of fossil fuels (direct as well as indirect, through the use of electricity) accounts for more than a quarter of the United Kingdom's total carbon dioxide emissions. The total emissions for the United Kingdom as given by the Department of the Environment are shown below.

Table 3.1: Carbon dioxide emissions in the United Kingdom, 1990[1]

industry and agriculture	35%
households	26%
road transport	21%
commercial and public sector	15%
other transport	3%

Note: 'just over half' of road transport carbon dioxide emissions are from private car use.

On a basis of delivered energy (or rather, 'energy consumption by final user'), the domestic sector is nearly the largest energy consumer in the United Kingdom.

Table 3.2: Energy consumption by final user in the United Kingdom, 1991[2]

transport	31%
domestic	30%
industry	25%
commerce, public administration, agriculture, etc.	14%

The position of the domestic sector can be compared with energy use by the whole of the building sector, using a different breakdown of the basic statistics.

Pout[3] gives the following breakdown of delivered energy and carbon dioxide emissions under different headings to those used by the DOE.

Table 3.3: Delivered-energy consumption and carbon dioxide emissions for the United Kingdom, 1992

delivered-energy consumption	buildings	48%
	transport	32%
	industrial process	11%
	agriculture	9%
carbon dioxide emissions	buildings	46%
	transport	32%
	industrial process	20%
	agriculture	2%

Note: data have been interpreted from graphs in Pout.

The data from the Department of the Environment can be combined with those from Pout to show the split between the domestic sector and other buildings, as shown in Table 3.4.

Table 3.4: Domestic sector in relation to the buildings sector as a whole

delivered-energy consumption	domestic	30%
	other buildings	18%
carbon dioxide emissions	domestic	26%
	other buildings	20%

Note: it is assumed that the fact that the Department of Environment data relate to the years 1990 and 1991, while Pout's data relate to the year 1992, is of little significance.

The domestic sector can be seen to be not only a large consumer of energy and producer of carbon dioxide when compared with the nation as a whole, it is also the larger part of the whole buildings sector. On this basis alone it seems that the technology applied in a house to eliminate fossil-fuel use could, when applied widely, make a major impact on total national energy consumption. Technology successful at a domestic level and potentially applicable across the buildings spectrum would be of greater significance than technology successful only at a commercial or industrial level.

It is not only in the United Kingdom that the domestic sector is important as a focus for the reduction of consumption of energy and impact on the environment. Henderson states:

> *The housing sector ... accounts for about 20% of all final energy demand in the OECD countries ... This proportion is higher in the West European countries, averaging 28%, due largely to the lower use in other sectors rather than higher use in housing. In former Soviet Bloc countries, the proportion used in housing tends to be lower, averaging 16%, due in part to the emphasis given to heavy industry in those economies and also to the relatively small size of apartments.*
>
> *In developing countries ... biofuels such as wood and straw often meet a considerable proportion of housing energy demand, but do not appear in economic statistics. Including such use of biofuels, housing accounts for over 40% of their energy demand.*[4]

Even in a country where the energy consumption of the domestic sector is relatively small compared to that of the United Kingdom, there are still good reasons for suggesting that an autonomous house is a good way to move towards a more sustainable society. In New Zealand for example, the national energy use can be broken down as follows.

Table 3.5: Total amount of energy used in different New Zealand sectors[5]

	energy (PJ)	% of total
industry	154.5	42
transport	129.8	36
buildings	79.3	22

of which

domestic buildings	47.3	13
commercial buildings	32.0	9

It can be seen that the New Zealand domestic sector, although relatively small in terms of national consumption, is still the larger of the two sectors that make up the built environment, an area of the economy over which architects may be able to exercise some influence. The report from the Centre for Advanced Engineering in Christchurch, New Zealand, from which the data above are taken, reaches the following conclusion about the domestic sector: '… energy efficiency in the domestic homes is important because of the unique structure of the domestic sector. It is the only sector that serves as a base to everyone and a workplace to some.'[6]

This is the key to the significance of the domestic sector: its universality. Everyone has to live somewhere, and the home has an immediate impact on personal circumstances and values in a way that the office or workplace probably do not. If sustainability is to become acceptable (at worst) or desirable (at best), it could be argued that it is only through the home that values can be changed.

THE SITE

The location in Southwell
The site for the autonomous house was bought in 1991 at a cost of £69,000. It is situated near the centre of Southwell, Nottinghamshire, at the top end of Nottingham Road. 'Southwell is a well built clean town, such a one as a quiet distressed family ought to retire to: coals, provisions, and religion to be had good and cheap.'[7] This comment, made by the diarist John Byng in June 1789, could have been made about Southwell in 1989. It is still the sort of town he describes, and this was one of the reasons for choosing it as a site for the house. The population in the early 1990s was about 6,665,[8] and the town, perhaps by virtue of its relative isolation (it lies in the centre of a triangle bounded by the main roads from Nottingham to Newark, from Nottingham to Doncaster, and from Newark to Mansfield) has a range of facilities that seems unusually complete for a town of its size: apart from the Norman Minster, these include a magistrates' court, a library, a racecourse, a police station, a market and a varied collection of local shops and industry. From the point of view of sustainable development, the choice of such a town for the site of the house meant that all the necessary requirements for daily life could be obtained within walking distance of the site, reducing the need for car journeys. A further consideration was the presence, again within easy walking distance of the site, of the local school. As the designers/owners of the house were both employed at the University of Nottingham, there was a need for a site within easy travel distance of Nottingham, which lies about 24 km (15 miles) to the south. At the time of the purchase of the site, the housing market was in recession; during the property boom of the 1980s, the site, centrally located on a prominent corner, would

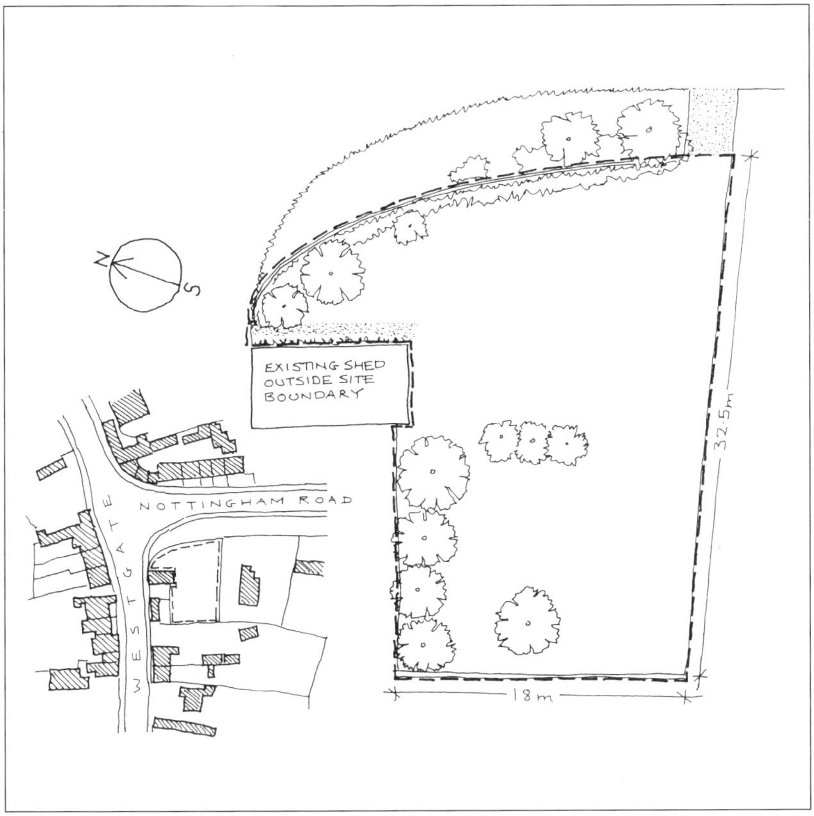

Fig. 2
The site in
Southwell

probably have been bought by a speculative builder. These are the sorts of considerations that guide the selection of any site for a family home.

The site is located at the point where Nottingham Road (the road from Nottingham) enters Southwell at a T-junction with Westgate, one of Southwell's old streets, which is lined, both sides of the junction, with buildings that are at least one hundred years old. Although it has some older buildings such as the Baptist Church, Nottingham Road is largely occupied by houses built in the 20th century, some of which post-date World War II. These houses are on the west side of the road, with older buildings, such as the church and some houses, all on the east. The site itself was part of the garden of a 1950s bungalow, and forms, at its northern end, the corner between Nottingham Road and Westgate. With the exception of the very corner, the site's northern boundary is separated from Westgate by a derelict shop and its neighbouring buildings. The boundary to Nottingham Road is thickly planted with yew, various species of *Prunus*, brambles and other plants, forming a relatively dense visual screen to the road. Between the planting and the road is a mild-steel picket fence. The boundary between the site and the adjoining bungalow was a line marked with two metal posts. The area of the site is approximately 575 m², or one seventh of an acre.

Contextual influences

The existing houses on Westgate in Southwell follow a pattern of being built right up to the inside edge of the footpath, with gardens behind that are not visible from the road. The newer houses on Nottingham Road are more conventional by contemporary standards and stand in the centre of their respective plots, with front gardens and driveways. The only houses on Nottingham Road that follow the Westgate pattern of being built up to the inside edge of the footpath are those of a curved 19th-century brick terrace with a slate roof, built right on the eastern corner of the junction and following round onto Nottingham Road. These existing housing patterns were a strong determinant of the way in which the design of the autonomous house developed.

Other strong influences affected the design. The first was that the site was in an area of the town that was to be designated a conservation area. It lies about 300 m from the Norman St Mary's Minster, which contains the 13th-century chapter house, of whose carved-leaf capitals Pevsner says: '... the leaves of Southwell assume a new significance as one of the purest symbols surviving in Britain of Western thought, our thought, in its loftiest mood.'[9] It was important that any design for a house to be constructed on the site should be able to respond to this historical context for a number of reasons. The first, and most pragmatic, was that a design that was visually in keeping with the area would be more likely to receive planning consent without difficulty, and this would speed up the process of building the house. The second reason was that it was felt to be very important that the house should not be shocking or offensive to the local community. This aspect is controlled in theory by the planning procedure, but a deliberate effort was made to design a house that would look a natural part of its setting. If a radical proposal is made to change the way that houses are serviced, it is perhaps too much to demand that people should also have to change their expectation of what a house should look like. The innate conservatism of the non-architecturally trained public can be seen particularly in homes. The houses offered by speculative builders, which, it must be assumed, satisfy to some extent their customers' expectations, are usually very traditional or conservative in design. This is an aspect of design with which architects will need to come to terms if their ideas are to be taken up in the wider housing market. The point of designing the autonomous house as it is was partly to demonstrate that it was feasible, but also to make the concept itself appear desirable. Had the house been very unconventional in appearance, it might have elicited a response that the idea was interesting, but that the technology was clearly not for the ordinary householder, or even for the ordinary builder.

This approach of designing for the existing housing market rather than for the architects' own preferences, has been applied deliberately in the Canadian government's Advanced Houses Program:

> *Canada's Advanced House Demonstration Project is an example of a national program, involving 10 different projects across the country. Project sponsors include national, provincial and municipal governments, builders, corporations, and power utilities ... Public and private sponsors are interested in transferring residential innovations into mainstream markets. Demonstration projects promote awareness of new technology to consumers, with a view towards creating a demand for the product. Greater consumer demand is necessary to achieve the potential energy savings related to a particular product by reducing per unit costs and pay back periods through economies of scale.*[10]

Throughout the project, it was realized that design alone without the potential for, or the probability of, transfer to the marketplace, would be meaningless. The sustainable house must be recognized as a marketable product by house builders and as an affordable and desirable home by consumers.[11]

A further reason for the decision to respond to the context was founded on architectural arguments, somewhat ironic in light of the conservatism of the house-buying public. One of the most famous slogans of the environmental movement has been 'think globally, act locally'.[12] This means that individual small-scale actions must be based on an awareness of large-scale influences and effects. In architectural terms, it suggests that a design should not represent an international style but should respond to its immediate environment. When one visits Southwell, or any other relatively unaltered English town, there is a great sense of visual continuity in the buildings, which has to do with scale, materials and proportions. These are largely the result of the limited palette of materials from the locality that were available to the builders of the past. The changes that occurred when, for example, the railway allowed Welsh slate to be imported, are clearly visible (– regular steam railway services to Southwell began in 1860; by 1910 there were 26 passenger train departures every weekday).[13] In the late 20th century, materials were coming from all over the world, leading to an international visual homogeneity that is at odds with the particular local character, or *genius loci*, of a place.

THE HOUSE

Embodied-energy considerations

The idea of a *genius loci* is not, in the era of concern for sustainability, merely a whimsical or even Luddite concept. Proponents of the status quo could argue that if the world has materials to offer, it is up to the architect to choose whatever will fit the budget and the designer's visual preferences. However, consideration of the embodied-energy content of materials suggests that the transport of materials over long distances will result in increased energy use and pollution compared to materials obtained locally wherever possible. This is particularly important in the case of heavy materials such as bricks, and potentially less relevant the lighter materials are. Part of the design strategy for the autonomous house was that the heaviest components should be obtained from the closest source, regardless of the financial cost, as this would have the lowest environmental cost. This was particularly important because part of the technical design of the house required the use of high-mass construction, and the transport of this mass could have resulted in considerable embodied energy in these materials. Baird[14] gives a figure of 4.5 MJ/tonne/km for road transport in the United States of America and New Zealand, compared to 0.6 MJ/tonne/km for rail transport. Assuming a brick density of 1,750 kg/m³ (data averaged from Willoughby)[15] and a brick of dimensions 100 × 215 × 65 mm (i.e., a volume of 0.0013975 m³), one brick will weigh 2.45 kg. As a comparison with this theoretical calculation, one of the bricks used for the external skin of the autonomous house, the Yorkshire Brick Company's 'Dales Blend', weighs 2.48 kg. The weights of the theoretical brick and the bricks used give a figure of 403–8 bricks per tonne. The transport of one brick in a lorry over a distance of 1 km therefore takes 0.011 MJ. Given that the embodied-energy content of bricks made in tunnel kilns averages 9.9 GJ per thousand,[16] the embodied-energy content of a single brick is 9.9 MJ. Although these figures relate specifically to the manufacture of bricks in Australia, they are used here as they are a detailed analysis of brick manufacture on a plant-by-plant basis. These figures for transport energy and embodied energy show that 'average' bricks have to travel a distance of 900 km (558 miles) by road before their transport energy demand equals their manufacturing-energy demand. However, even a distance of 300 km (186 miles) would increase the embodied energy by a third. The manufacture of bricks in Australia results in embodied-energy figures in the range 6–50 GJ per thousand,[17] so as the process of making the bricks increases in efficiency, the effect of transport becomes more significant. The most efficiently made bricks (6.0 MJ/brick) would have their embodied energy increased by 50% if transported 300 km. If the lorry bringing the bricks to the building site travels back empty to the brickworks, the effective transport energy of the brick should be related to the total travel distance, so the distance from brickworks to site need be no more than 150 km (93 miles) to make a significant impact on embodied energy.

The use of high-mass materials, produced as locally as possible, makes a significant impact on the form of the building, particularly if the intention is to incorporate as much mass as possible, as will be explained in Chapter 4. Discussion with the Planning Officer of Newark and Sherwood District Council, the Local Authority, showed that a brick exterior would be regarded by the Council as a necessity, given the location of the house. This was acceptable as a design constraint, as the site of the house was a transitional zone between the 18th- and 19th-century houses of Westgate, all made of red brick, and the later houses on Nottingham Road, also made of brick, but with greater variety of colour. It seemed reasonable to ally the house visually with the Westgate housing, so as to act as a transition on the western corner of the Westgate/Nottingham Road junction, just as the curved 19th-century terrace does on the eastern corner. The new house would then reflect the opposite side of the junction, and would create the sense of a gateway as the Nottingham Road enters the town. This implied the use of red brick to match the existing red/orange brick of the 18th- and 19th-century houses.

Siting the house

Having determined the basic appearance of the proposed house – red-brick loadbearing masonry – it remained to determine where the house should be placed on the site, and what form it should take. The site had been a garden and had never had any buildings on it. Apart from the dense planting along the Nottingham Road edge of the site, there were a number of fruit trees, one of which was reputed to be one of the first Bramley apple trees. (The Bramley was first produced in Southwell by accident, and the first Bramley cooking apples appeared in 1837; the original tree still exists.)[18] The site was bought with outline planning consent, obtained by the vendors (of whose garden the site had been part) for a detached bungalow, which was shown on the planning consent drawing as placed conventionally in the centre of the plot, with a front and rear garden and a strip of land down each side. This response implied a building that allied itself firmly in a visual sense with the recent Nottingham Road houses rather than with the older buildings. It would also have resulted in a building that overlooked, and was overlooked by, the next-door bungalow, occupied by the vendors of the site. This siting proposal would have produced a number of small pieces of garden round the new bungalow, all rather narrow and small in area, and considerably shaded by the proposed building. Finally, the construction of the bungalow as shown would have required the removal of the ancient apple trees. Further discussion with the Planning Officer suggested that the Council would look favourably on the design of a two-storey house in lieu of a bungalow, as the argument about forming a 'visual gateway' at the top of Nottingham Road was accepted as a good strategy for the site. Such a gateway would require a building with more bulk than a bungalow, so as to provide definition to the corner and a sense of enclosure of the space at the junction. Through the Planning Officer, the Council made two suggestions concerning the development of the site. The first was the retention of the planting along the Nottingham Road edge; this was fully in accordance with one of the aims of the house design, which was to minimize the impact on the natural environment. The second suggestion, which was made fairly emphatically by the Highways Department, was that the entrance to the site, which had a gate near the junction, should be made as far from the Nottingham Road/Westgate corner as possible, to minimize the dangers entailed in vehicles turning out of the site into the traffic at the junction. This put the access point to the site at the southeast corner, by the boundary with the neighbouring bungalow. The Highways Department also required, as part of any planning consent, that it should be possible to turn a car within the curtilage of the dwelling, so that vehicles would not have to back out onto the main road.

One constraint included as part of the design strategy to minimize the environmental impact of the house was that the area devoted to driveways, car-parking, etc. should be as small as possible. The Council provided a drawing to show the dimensions of a turning area that would meet the requirements of the Highways Department, and when this was laid over the site plan with the site entrance in the position specified by the same department, it demarcated a zone of space adjacent to the site's southern boundary where a house could not be constructed. The desire to make the parking/turning area as small as possible meant that the turning space was to be kept close to the Nottingham Road edge, so that the driveway's intrusion into the site could be minimized. On the northern edge of the site there was a brick shed, not part of the site, which was used as a garage by its owner. Construction had to be kept 'three feet' (sic) from this as a condition of the sale of the site. These various measurements and other requirements, such as preserving the apple trees, began to create a space into which the proposed house would have to fit.

Perhaps the strongest technological influence on the siting of the house was seen to be the need to have the house facing south in order to maximize solar gain through the glazing: several studies have suggested that this is a key factor in the design of a low-energy house. For example, in an early study of solar houses in the United Kingdom, Oppenheim gives a list of rules-of-thumb for low-energy design, which refers to the need for southern orientation and an extended east-west axis to maximize solar gain;[19] the *European Passive Solar Handbook* makes similar recommendations.[20] However, a house with a long east-west aligned axis would have presented its narrow end, rather than a long facade, to the street. The street in this case is Nottingham Road, as the site does not have a boundary with Westgate in any meaningful sense. If the house had occupied this position, the presence of the apple trees on the north side would have meant that the house would have had little garden between it and the neighbouring bungalow, as the trees would have forced it towards the southern boundary of the site. Even if this constraint had been removed by felling the apple trees, the space to the south of the house would have been small, and the building would have seemed to loom over the existing bungalow next door. The problem of the narrowness of the remaining garden would have been exacerbated by the fact that it was intended to have a conservatory on the house to provide, if not solar heating, at least a tempered external space to extend the times of year when one could sit somewhere that felt like outside. The conservatory was also to form a useful space for the production of fruit, vegetables and flowers by extending the growing season. The presence of the conservatory would have made the shorter dimension of the house greater, reducing the available garden by the width of the conservatory and increasing the house's apparent proximity to the adjoining bungalow.

Some sketches were made of a design which followed these classic passive solar design principles, with a parking area on the Nottingham Road side, but it was obvious that the remaining garden space would be constricted, and would also be open to the traffic noise from Nottingham Road. By occupying the full width of their sites, the existing houses on Westgate are able to screen their garden areas from the street, providing a very tranquil private outdoor space behind a relatively hard urban frontage. A parking area to the Nottingham Road side of the site would have lacked the physical bulk necessary to screen the garden; the provision of screening would have entailed the construction of a garage at the very least. This would have been an additional cost that had not been included in the calculations at the outset on account of the general strategy's intention to make minimal provision for the car. A house that faced north and south would also have suffered from the same problem as the bungalow on the outline planning consent, that of having no substantial garden area, with the plot broken up into small strips of ground around the house.

At this point in the consideration of the design strategy, it was decided to abandon the classic passive solar approach. Study of the theoretical research carried out around 1980 for the passive solar Pennyland housing estate in Milton Keynes had suggested that, given the British climate, passive solar energy was unlikely to make a major contribution to fulfilling the energy demand of the proposed house, in comparison with the savings in demand that could be achieved by effective insulation. The calculations made for the Pennyland project showed that a change from the thermal insulation requirements of the then current Building Regulations to an insulation level that was labelled 'very highly insulated' would result in a reduction of space-heating energy demand from 13,000 kWh/year to 6,000 kWh/year. The passive solar measure of concentrating the glazing on the south side of the house would reduce the figure further to about 5,000 kWh/year.[21] The monitoring of the completed houses gave the following conclusion:

> The direct gain passive solar design used at Pennyland seems to have been highly popular with the residents, but unlikely to lead to any large energy savings, mainly due to the high level of window obstruction (net curtains, etc.). The need for the direct gain design to allow sunshine unimpeded access to the interior of the house seems to be in conflict with the needs of the occupants for privacy ... There is still plenty of scope for research in other facets of passive solar design, such as the use of conservatories and the development of selective surfaces in multiply glazed windows.[22]

In the end, the marginal passive solar savings achieved by any one of the Pennyland houses compared to some neighbouring conventional houses were estimated at about 300 kWh/year.[23] This is not a significant contribution to annual space-heating energy demand.

Abandoning the passive solar design constraint allowed greater freedom in the positioning of the envelope within which the house would sit. Contemplating a design strategy that would put the house as near as possible to the Nottingham Road edge of the site, while leaving space for the required turning circle, led to the creation of a block of space about 15 m long, with its long axis aligned roughly north-south; this was the space into which the house would have to fit. Sited in this way, the house provided as much of a screen to the road as possible, with the minimum space for the car adjacent to the southern boundary. By siting the house close to the Nottingham Road side of the site, two advantages could be perceived. The first was that the adjoining bungalow would not be overshadowed, either practically or figuratively, by the new house. The second was that the new house would have a single garden area about 18 metres square, rather than a series of thin strips. At the 'front' or Nottingham Road side, there would be no garden, but the driveway and turning space would allow the preservation of all the planting along the boundary line. Both the existing bungalow and the new house would look into the garden of the house, providing an amenity for both.

Design influences on the house

Once the space that the house could occupy had been ascertained, it was time to consider the plan of the house itself. It was decided early in the design process that the house should be simple, partly as a design principle, and partly to make it cheap to build, so that the additional costs of thick insulation could be offset by low construction costs. The intention was to design a building that would be in some way timeless, rather than one based on current fashions in architecture. The same deliberate attempt to produce a timeless and simple architecture can be seen in the buildings of the Shakers in North America for example (– Sprigg and Larkin describe Shaker architecture as 'relentlessly unadorned').[24] A similar approach is visible in some of the buildings of the Arts and Crafts movement, such as the cottages designed by Ernest Gimson in Leicestershire, Stonywell in particular.[25] This approach is not merely a product of the 19th century or earlier, as is made clear by the publication by Christopher Alexander of *The Timeless Way of Building*[26] (the introductory volume in his Center for Environmental Structure series, which includes *A Pattern Language*).[27] This timelessness would also provide a way in which the new house could be tied in to the context of Southwell by seeming to be part of it rather than a modern intervention into it. The architectural concerns of the late 20th century could be regarded as irrelevant to the autonomous house in a number of ways. The house design was a response to global problems (particularly the problems of global warming through carbon dioxide emissions and of resource depletion), and such a house needed to be driven more by long-term issues of performance and impact than by rapidly changing cultural theories. The building also had to attempt to satisfy the expectations of that portion of the populace with little or no interest in or knowledge of architecture, as to what might constitute a 'house' in order that it might appear acceptable, or even (hopefully) desirable. Finally, if it was to minimize the environmental impact of the use of energy and materials needed to construct it, the house needed to have a very long life and low maintenance. Pullen's studies of the embodied energy of a range of brick-clad Australian houses showed that, when the periodic replacement of components was taken into account, the embodied energy of a house during an 80-year life was roughly 17 times its annual operational energy.[28] The Minster in Southwell is an example of a building that has been in continuous use for a thousand years as a place of worship, the function for which it was originally designed.

The idea of modernity, in which a building responds to a theory that is current at the time of its construction, fits poorly with the idea of a building that might be designed to last for 500 years or longer. Many buildings which were seen at the time of their construction to represent the most up-to-date thinking in formal terms, are now seen as at best misguided and at worst a liability to those

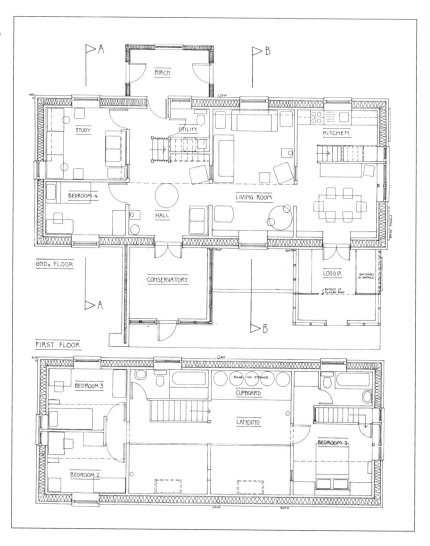

who still have to use them. Alison and Peter Smithson's Hunstanton School in Norfolk is a good example of this problem; Martin Pawley described its environmental performance in a re-visit to the school for the *Architects' Journal*:

> *While a famous architectural critic shows slides of it in the air-conditioned lecture theatres of the University of California, children faint and whole classes are evacuated from heat exhaustion in England. While 100 graduate students type the words 'New Brutalism' into their dissertations, condensation drowns photocopiers and freezing children dare not trust their feet to the tile-bubbling, resistance-heated floors.*[29]

One intention in designing the autonomous house was to make a building that posterity would not consider a liability.

Bay sizing and planning

A way of planning the house that would combine simplicity, reference to the *genius loci*, timelessness and buildability was needed. The result was a house planned as a series of repeated bays of identical structure, reflecting the plan of Southwell Minster. The concomitant of such a construction was that it would need only repeats of identical elements rather than a number of different components for different spans. This, it was hoped, would make it easy to build, which would help to reduce the tender prices that might be received from builders. The considerations of the area of the site where the house would have to be located had resulted in a 'footprint' about 15 m long by 6 m wide. If the external walls were 450 mm thick, this being the depth of a brick and block masonry cavity wall built with the longest wall ties available (giving a 250-mm cavity filled with insulation), the available internal bay dimension would be in the region of 5×3.5 m. A series of sketches was made to look at this bay dimension from the point of view of its adaptability for a number of uses within the house. It had to be possible to divide the bay into two bedrooms or two bathrooms, and to use it as a living room, kitchen/dining area or studio. These projected rooms also had to be able to accommodate existing pieces of furniture. By this stage of the design process the plan of the house, four equal bays on two floors, was beginning to take shape.

On the ground floor one bay would serve as an entrance and utility room, with a stair to the first floor. The bay at the northern end of the house would contain a fourth bedroom and a study, while the kitchen would be at the south end, with the living room between it and the hall. A separate stair to the main bedroom on the first floor would divide the kitchen from the dining area. The bay that formed the hall would have an entry porch to act as an airlock on the road side. It would also have a conservatory on the garden side. Outside the kitchen would be a loggia, with a glazed roof. Between these two indoor/outdoor spaces was to be a buried 4,000-l rainwater tank that would also serve as a reflective pool outside the living-room window. On the first floor were two bedrooms at the north end, a bathroom on the landing, a further landing with a large cupboard containing tanks for the storage of solar heated water, and a main bedroom at the southern end, with en-suite bathroom.

At this point, further considerations relating to the section needed to be taken into account: two factors obtained that would have led the design of the house in opposite directions. The first was the desire to maximize the use of space and resources by making the entire volume of the house habitable; this would be the

Fig. 4
The section of the house (drawing by Brenda Vale)

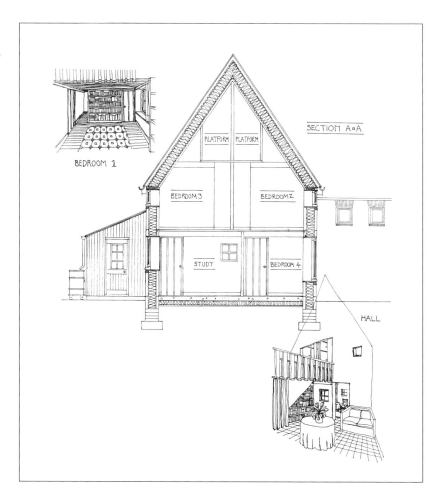

most efficient use of resources in the creation of habitable space. It would also mean, since the thermal insulation would be in the perimeter of the building, that there would be no unheated roof voids or underfloor areas that might lead to problems with freezing of services or penetrations of air/vapour barriers. This factor would lead to an increase in the pitch of the roof in order to create more habitable space under it, and hence an increase in the height of the house. The opposite consideration was an awareness that the site had been bought with outline planning consent for a bungalow. Although in conversation the Planning Officer had indicated that a house would be acceptable, it was felt that a three-storey house might be too much of a jump in scale from a bungalow. There was also the adjoining bungalow to consider, which would have looked and felt very dominated by a tall house. It was therefore decided to form the first-floor rooms within the roofspace in order to keep the eaves height to a minimum.

The point at which the vertical wall of the first-floor rooms became the roof was fixed at 1.50 m, shoulder height – the shoulder height of a 50th percentile adult British male is 1.43 m[30] – which would allow a person to stand up adjacent to the wall. The roof pitch was then manipulated in order to permit the insertion of a third level of floor above the first floor, providing additional attic storage space that was still within the thermal envelope of the house. The roof pitch that resulted from this process was 55°, which is comparable to the roof slope of a number of houses in the immediate vicinity of the site. The use of a 55° roof allowed a headroom of 2.50 m under the ridge in the attic spaces. The overall height of the house was just under 9.00 m to the ridge, with an external eaves height of 4.30 m. A conventional, but superinsulated, two-storey house with flat ceilings might have an eaves height of 5.30 m and a ridge height of just under 8.00 m (based on the Cresswell Road ultra-low-energy houses in Sheffield, designed by Brenda and Robert Vale).

By March 1992, the basic plan of four equal bays and the basic section of two storeys with attic at second-floor level, had been determined. The house design was now submitted for planning approval. The planning drawing showed a pergola in the garden (the 'energy walk', used to support photovoltaic panels), and a total of 8,000 l of rainwater storage, in the tank mentioned above, and in two further tanks at the north end of the building, with the aim of using the water to flush the toilets (using a type with lower water demand, such as the Swedish Ifö Aqua with 3-l flush).[31] On the south wall of the house were to be three banks of evacuated-tube solar water heaters at low level, to allow the heated water to thermosyphon to the five 200-l storage tanks on the first floor.

Redesign for autonomy

Up to this point the design process had proceeded on the basis that the house should produce no carbon dioxide emissions in use; this had resulted in high levels of insulation to eliminate the need for space heating, and the use of solar energy for hot water and electricity supply. The application for planning consent was also made on this basis. Following an invitation to present a paper in Vienna, at the Wiener Symposium für Solar-Architektur[32] (where the authors had the opportunity to see advanced-house designs from the whole of Austria), it was decided, on return to the United Kingdom, that the zero carbon dioxide strategy was not bold enough, and that a fully autonomous strategy would be more interesting. This required a re-think of the house in order to find the space for the autonomous systems, particularly for the storage of water and the treatment of sewage and grey water. The basic four-bay plan was retained, but the extra space required was created by designing the foundations as a cellar. This was estimated to be a relatively low-cost option, since the depth of the topsoil on the site,

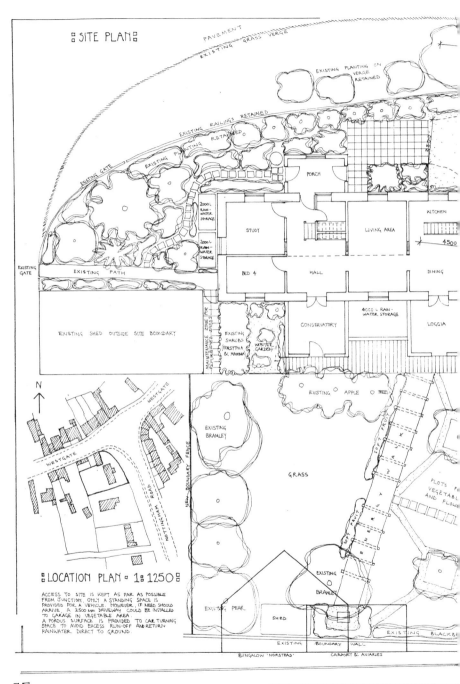

⊹ SITE PLAN ⊹

PAVEMENT

EXISTING GRASS VERGE

EXISTING PLANTING ON VERGE RETAINED

EXISTING RAILINGS RETAINED

EXISTING PLANTING RETAINED

EXISTING GATE

EXISTING PLANTING RETAINED

PORCH

2000 L RAIN-WATER STORAGE

KITCHEN

STUDY

LIVING AREA

4500

2000 L RAIN-WATER STORAGE

EXISTING GATE

EXISTING PATH

BED 4

HALL

DINING

MAINTENANCE ZONE FOR REPAIRS/REPLACEMENT

EXISTING SHRUBS FORSYTHIA & MAHONIA

WINTER GARDEN

CONSERVATORY

4000 L RAIN-WATER STORAGE

LOGGIA

EXISTING SHED OUTSIDE SITE BOUNDARY

N

WESTGATE

WESTGATE

EXISTING APPLE TREES

EXISTING BRAMLEY

GRASS

NEW BOUNDARY FENCE

NOTTINGHAM ROAD

PLOTS FOR VEGETABLES AND FLOWERS

SOFT FRUIT

SOFT FRUIT

⊹ LOCATION PLAN ⊹ 1⊹1250 ⊹

ACCESS TO SITE IS KEPT AS FAR AS POSSIBLE FROM JUNCTION. ONLY A STANDING SPACE IS PROVIDED FOR A VEHICLE. HOWEVER, IF NEED SHOULD ARRIVE, A 2500 MM DRIVEWAY COULD BE INSTALLED TO GARAGE IN VEGETABLE AREA
A POROUS SURFACE IS PROVIDED TO CAR TURNING SPACE TO AVOID EXCESS RUN-OFF AND RETURN RAINWATER DIRECT TO GROUND.

EXISTING BRAMLEY

EXISTING PEAR

SHED

EXISTING BOUNDARY WALL

EXISTING BLACKBERRY

BUNGALOW 'NORSTEAD'

CARPORT & AVIARIES

⊹⊹ HOUSE AT JUNCTION OF NOTTINGHAM RD⊹ & WESTGATE ⊹ SOUTHWELL ⊹

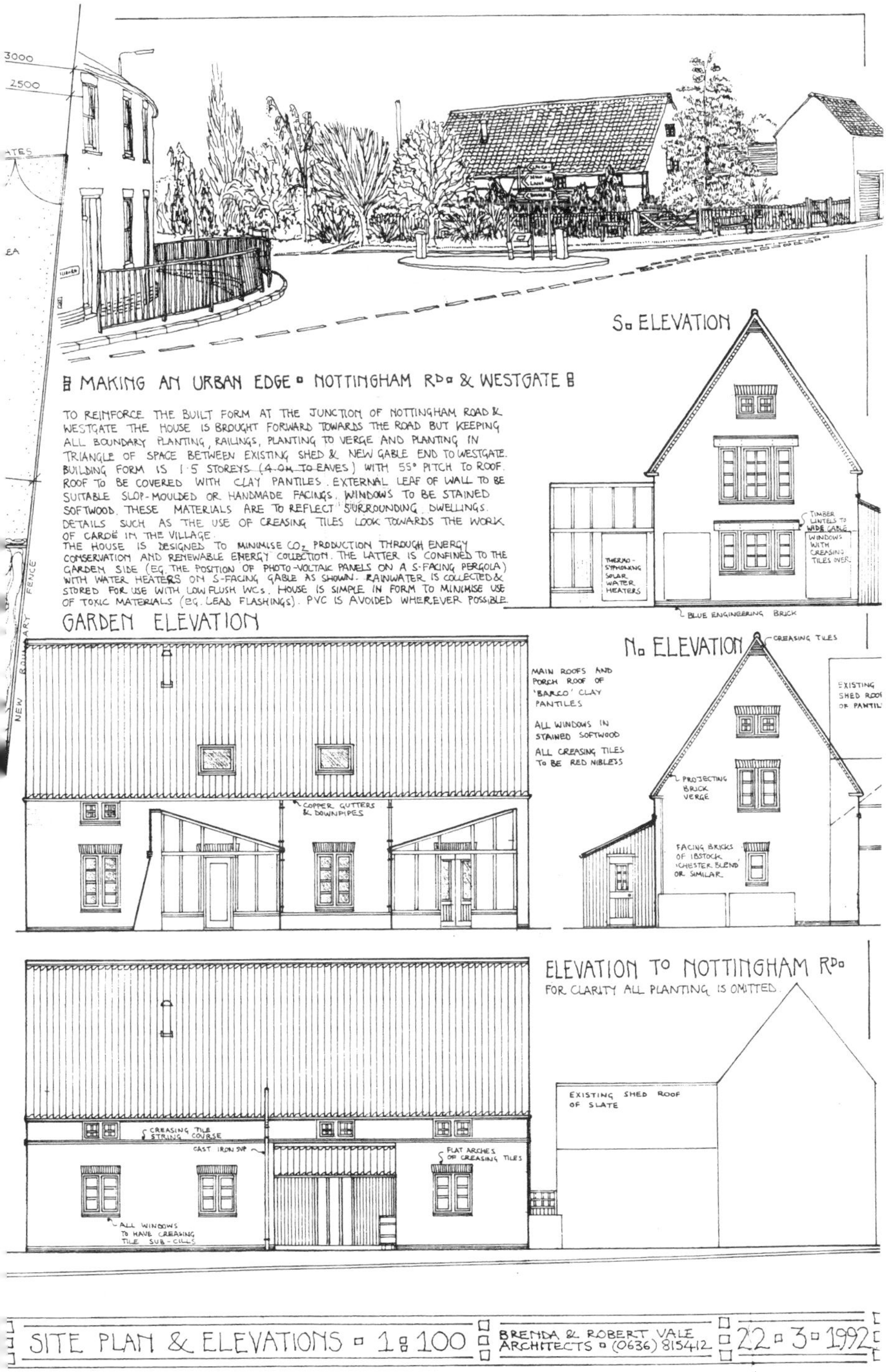

Fig. 5
*The planning
application drawing
(drawing by
Brenda Vale)*

3000
2500

⊞ MAKING AN URBAN EDGE ▫ NOTTINGHAM RD▫ & WESTGATE ⊞

TO REINFORCE THE BUILT FORM AT THE JUNCTION OF NOTTINGHAM ROAD &
WESTGATE THE HOUSE IS BROUGHT FORWARD TOWARDS THE ROAD BUT KEEPING
ALL BOUNDARY PLANTING, RAILINGS, PLANTING TO VERGE AND PLANTING IN
TRIANGLE OF SPACE BETWEEN EXISTING SHED & NEW GABLE END TO WESTGATE.
BUILDING FORM IS 1·5 STOREYS (4·0M TO EAVES) WITH 55° PITCH TO ROOF.
ROOF TO BE COVERED WITH CLAY PANTILES. EXTERNAL LEAF OF WALL TO BE
SUITABLE SLOP-MOULDED OR HANDMADE FACINGS. WINDOWS TO BE STAINED
SOFTWOOD. THESE MATERIALS ARE TO REFLECT SURROUNDING DWELLINGS.
DETAILS SUCH AS THE USE OF CREASING TILES LOOK TOWARDS THE WORK
OF CARDE IN THE VILLAGE.
THE HOUSE IS DESIGNED TO MINIMISE CO_2 PRODUCTION THROUGH ENERGY
CONSERVATION AND RENEWABLE ENERGY COLLECTION. THE LATTER IS CONFINED TO THE
GARDEN SIDE (EG THE POSITION OF PHOTO-VOLTAIC PANELS ON A S-FACING PERGOLA)
WITH WATER HEATERS ON S-FACING GABLE AS SHOWN. RAINWATER IS COLLECTED &
STORED FOR USE WITH LOW FLUSH WCs. HOUSE IS SIMPLE IN FORM TO MINIMISE USE
OF TOXIC MATERIALS (EG LEAD FLASHINGS). PVC IS AVOIDED WHEREVER POSSIBLE.

S▫ ELEVATION

- THERMO-
- STPHONING
- SOLAR
- WATER
- HEATERS

TIMBER
LINTELS TO
WIDE GABLE
WINDOWS
WITH
CREASING
TILES OVER.

BLUE ENGINEERING BRICK

GARDEN ELEVATION

COPPER GUTTERS
& DOWNPIPES

N▫ ELEVATION

CREASING TILES

MAIN ROOFS AND
PORCH ROOF OF
'BARCO' CLAY
PANTILES

ALL WINDOWS IN
STAINED SOFTWOOD

ALL CREASING TILES
TO BE RED NIBLESS

EXISTING
SHED ROOF
OF PANTILE

PROJECTING
BRICK
VERGE

FACING BRICKS
OF IBSTOCK
-CHESTER BLEND
OR SIMILAR.

ELEVATION TO NOTTINGHAM RD▫
FOR CLARITY ALL PLANTING IS OMITTED.

EXISTING SHED ROOF
OF SLATE

CREASING TILE
STRING COURSE

CAST IRON SVP

FLAT ARCHES
OF CREASING TILES

ALL WINDOWS
TO HAVE CREASING
TILE SUB-CILLS

SITE PLAN & ELEVATIONS ▫ 1⊞100   BRENDA & ROBERT VALE
                                    ARCHITECTS ▫ (0636) 815412   22 ▫ 3 ▫ 1992

Fig. 6
The final plan
(drawing by
Brenda Vale)

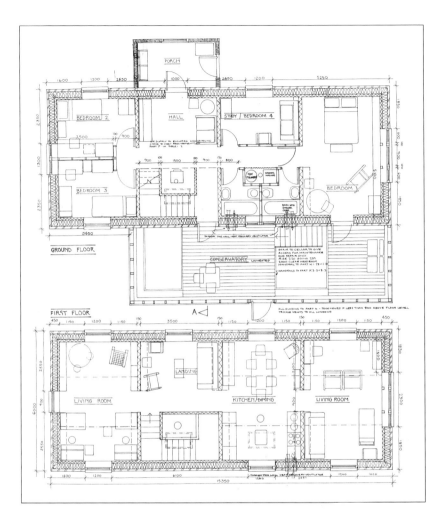

reputed to be 1,200 mm, would have necessitated deep excavation for conventional foundations. To provide access to the cellar, the originally projected conservatory and loggia were replaced by a single conservatory occupying the garden elevation of three of the four bays. It was not extended as far the fourth bay to avoid being too close to the neighbouring brick shed on the boundary. The conservatory would also have a cellar, spanned by wooden decks at ground level, with a stair to give access to the lower level, from where it would be possible to enter the main cellar under the house.

The desire to create a timeless building resulted in the decision to have as many spaces as possible planned in a simple axial manner, reflecting the basic internal planning of the Minster. The rather loose planning of the original version of the house was made more rigorous, and the size of the bays was tested against various requirements for furniture layout and circulation. The projected second staircase was removed as part of the revision of the design. The basic bay was assumed to have a central circulation zone, with room either side of this for a bed. It was intended that there should be a number of possible bed positions in each of the smaller bedrooms to allow for variety in the planning of the furniture layout of each room. The longer dimension of the bay was calculated as being a bed lengthways on (2,000 mm), plus a circulation space (900 mm) and another bed (2,000 mm). Adding 100 mm to each side of the circulation zone for a partition gave a bay dimension of 5,100 mm. The shorter dimension of the bay was dictated by the desire to be able to have two baths end-to-end (1,700 mm plus 1,700 mm) separated by a 100-mm partition to give a total dimension of 3,500 mm. This would allow the house to have relatively simple plumbing and hot-water arrangements, with the water services concentrated in a single bay containing the two bathrooms. The proposed use of a waterless sewage composting system sited in the cellar as part of the autonomy strategy had a powerful organizing influence on the plan, as there was a real need to concentrate the two bathrooms and, more particularly, the two toilets above the composting chamber.

It was during the period of redesign for autonomy that a number of basic decisions were confirmed. The house was for a family of two adults and three teenaged children, and it had been decided at the start to have two bathrooms, one en-suite to the parents' bedroom, to reduce the pressure on a single bathroom at the start of the day. "'Maybe we'd better cut out *one* bathroom," said Mr. Blandings, pleased with himself now that he had the water-supply problem well in hand. "I will not hazard the children's health in a house with three bathrooms," said Mrs. Blandings.'[33]

In the revised design, there were to be four bedrooms, one for each child and one for the parents. There would be a living room, a combined kitchen/dining area, and a room that would serve as a studio or additional living area. It was also decided that the living areas would be upstairs, with the bedrooms at ground level. There were a number of reasons for this decision. The first was that thermal stratification would suggest that the upper floor would be warmer than the ground floor, and it was desired to have the living rooms warmer than the bedrooms. The second was that the retention of the planting at the Nottingham Road edge of the site, and the presence of dense planting in the garden of the adjoining bungalow, meant that the ground floor rooms could be quite overshadowed, particularly in the winter, as much of the planting was non-deciduous. Living rooms on the upper floor would have more light and the possibility of long views over the adjoining bungalow and planting to the fields beyond the town. The roof could also be used to bring more light into the upper

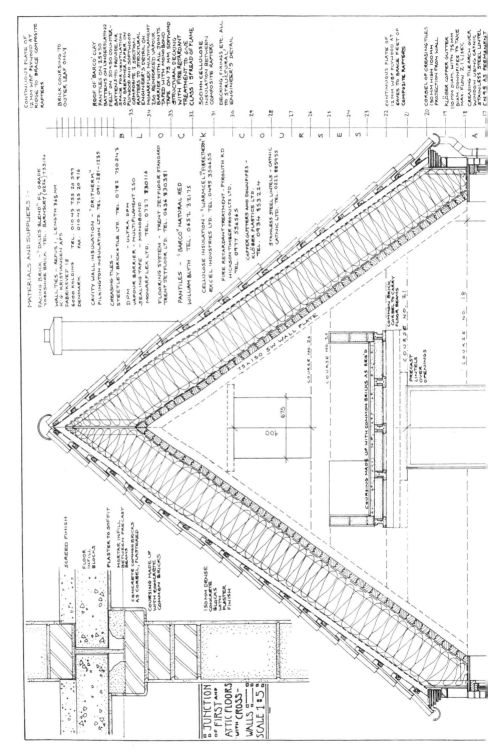

Fig. 7
The final section (drawing by Robert Vale)

MATERIALS AND SUPPLIERS:-

FACING BRICK - "DALES BLEND" FL GRADE
YORKSHIRE BRICK. TEL. BARNSLEY (0226)733114

WALL TIES - REFUS 1, LENGTH 345 MM
K-G KRISTIANSEN APS
FABRIKSVEJ 18   TEL. 010 45 755 20 599
6000 KOLDING   FAX. 010 45 755 20 916
DENMARK

CAVITY WALL INSULATION - "DRITHERM"
PILKINGTON INSULATION LTD. TEL. 091-281-1235

CREASING TILES -
STEETLEY BRICK ATLIE LTD. TEL. 0782 750243

DPM - ULTRA DPM
VAPOUR BARRIER - MULTIFILAMENT 250
SEALING TAPE - MONOBOND
MONARFLEX LTD.   TEL. 0727 830116

FLOORING SYSTEM - TRENT JETFLOOR STANDARD
TRENT JETFLOOR LTD. TEL. 0636 830381

PANTILES - "BARCO" NATURAL RED
WILLIAM BLYTH TEL. 0652 3Z175

CELLULOSE INSULATION - "WARMCEL" "FIBRETHERM"K
EXCEL INDUSTRIES LTD. TEL. 0495 350655

FIRE RETARDANT TREATMENT- PYROLITH KD
HICKSON TIMBER PRODUCTS LTD.
TEL. 0977 556565

COPPER GUTTERS AND DOWNPIPES -
KLÖBER PLASTICS LTD.
TEL. 0934 853224

STAINLESS STEEL LINTELS - CATNIC
CATNIC LTD. TEL. 0222 885455

B — CONTINUOUS PLATE OF
12 MM WBP PLYWOOD AT
RIDGE TO BRACE COMPOSITE
RAFTERS

L — BRICK COURSING TO
OUTER LEAF ONLY

35 — ROOF OF "BARCO" CLAY
PANTILES ON 25 x 50
BATTENS ON 38 x 50 COUNTER-
BATTENS TO PROVIDE AIR
SPACE FOR VENTILATION
ON BREATHER PAPER ON
PLYWOOD AND SOFTWOOD
COMPOSITE I SECTION
RAFTERS TO STRUCTURAL
ENGINEER'S DETAIL

34 — 250 REINFORCED VAPOUR
BARRIER WITH ALL JOINTS
TAPED WITH MONOBOND
TAPE ON 13 MM SOFTWOOD
STRUCTURAL DECKING

33 — STRUCTURAL DECKING
TREATMENT TO GIVE
CLASS 1 SPREAD OF FLAME
WITH FIRE RETARDANT

C — 500 MM CELLULOSE
INSULATION BETWEEN
COMPOSITE RAFTERS

32 — 500 MM CELLULOSE
INSULATION BETWEEN
COMPOSITE RAFTERS

31 — 500 MM CELLULOSE
INSULATION BETWEEN
COMPOSITE RAFTERS

30 — DECKING, FIXINGS ETC. ALL
TO STRUCTURAL
ENGINEER'S DETAIL

29 —

28 —

27 —

26 —

25 —

24 —

23 —

22 — CONTINUOUS PLATE OF
12 MM WBP PLYWOOD AT
EAVES TO BRACE FEET OF
COMPOSITE RAFTERS

21 — CORBEL OF CREASING TILES
150 MM HIGH 100 MM
PROTECTION FROM WALL

20 — KLÖBER COPPER GUTTER
100 MM DIAM. WITH 75 MM
DIAM. DOWNPIPES TO TAKE
MAX DISCHARGE 2.1 L/SEC

19 —

A — CREASING TILE ARCH OVER
WINDOW USING CATNIC
STAINLESS STEEL LINTEL
CNX90/100 AS PERMANENT

COMMON BRICK
CORBEL TO CARRY
PRECAST
FLOOR BEAMS

PRECAST
LINTELS
OVER
OPENINGS

COURSE NO. 26

COURSE NO. 25

COURSE NO. 21

COURSE NO. 18

COURSING MADE UP WITH COMMON BRICKS AS REQ'D

900

675

75 x 150 SW WALL PLATE

SCREED FINISH

FLOOR
INFILL
BLOCKS

PLASTER TO SOFFIT

MORTAR INFILL
BETWEEN PRECAST
BEAMS

CONCRETE COMMON BRICKS
AS CORBEL, PLASTERED

COURSING MADE UP
WITH CONCRETE
COMMON BRICKS

150 MM DENSE
CONCRETE
BLOCKS
WITH
PLASTER
FINISH

B — JUNCTION
OF FIRST AND
ATTIC FLOORS
WITH CROSS-
WALLS
SCALE 1:5

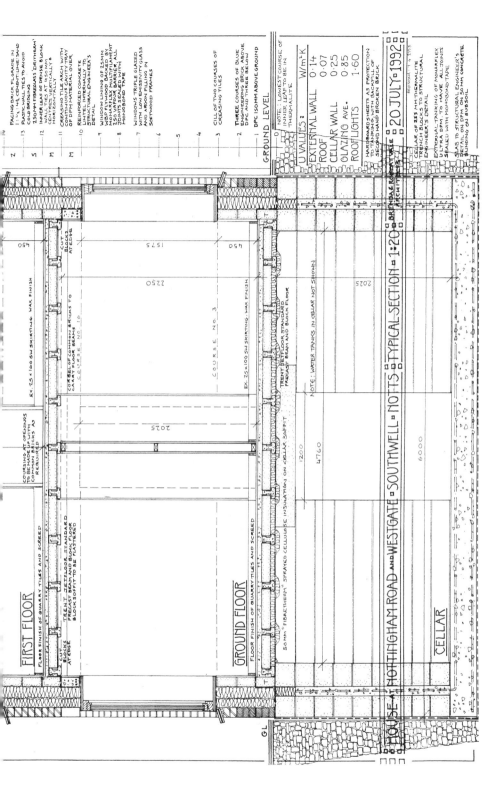

rooms, whereas bedrooms did not necessarily require such good light.

These result of these decisions was the following room arrangement: on the ground floor, one bay at the north end would be two children's bedrooms; the next would be the circulation bay, containing entrance hall and staircase; the next the services bay, containing the bathrooms and laundry area; and the one at the south end would be the parents' bedroom, its distance from the first two bedrooms lessening the potential for problems resulting from noise. The bathroom and laundry would occupy the space to one side of the circulation zone only, allowing a fourth bedroom on the other side of the corridor. On the first floor there would be four equal open bays, with no connecting doors. The cellar would contain the sewage composter and the rainwater tanks.

The re-thought planning of the bays gave a much simpler circulation arrangement, always on the axis of the space, and a clear distinction was made between loadbearing and non-loadbearing walls. The loadbearing masonry cross-walls were designed to have openings in them only on the centre line of each bay. Doors were never placed in these openings, but were set in separate wood-panelled partitions (wooden to differentiate them from the loadbearing masonry structure). The doors opened either to the side or in front of the openings in the walls, so that the occupants of the house would pass through the walls and appreciate their massivity, an important part of the house's thermal design, as will be explained in Chapter 4.

The design in Figure 6 was submitted for Building Regulations approval, following discussion with the building inspectors at Newark and Sherwood District Council. The house was shown in the first detailed section with timber floors, but these were later changed to concrete to give additional thermal mass, and to increase the possibility of airtight construction. (Concrete floors built into concrete-block walls would move less than timber joists, reducing the likelihood of unwanted air movement through the cracks created by such movement.) The attic-level spaces were designed originally with timber floors spanning between the crosswalls, creating complete separation between the attic and the living areas below, but these were changed with the introduction of the concrete floors into mezzanine platforms suspended between the crosswalls and separate from the roof, to give an impression of a larger space. Discussions with the structural engineer also confirmed that the use of concrete floors throughout would provide a considerable increase in overall structural rigidity.

The detailed design of the thermal insulation and of the technical elements of the house will be described in the following chapters. The purpose of providing a description here is to give an understanding of the basic design of the house in architectural and physical terms.

4 | *Theoretical Analysis of the Technical Options*

A METHODOLOGY FOR DESIGN

Designing a house is a complex process of juggling a large number of interacting factors: site, orientation, budget, materials, etc. In order to make comparisons between different approaches, a simplification of the design process is needed, so as to filter out complexities and throw the essential differences into relief. For discussion of the design decisions that might be appropriate for an autonomous house, it is proposed that in this chapter a hypothetical room be considered, which will serve as a model for the whole house. To approximate the bay dimensions that were used in the final design of the house, this room can be assumed to be 3.5 × 5.0 m on plan, and 2.3 m high. It is assumed also that this room has a single south-facing window (for solar gain) which is 1.2 metres square, inserted in the wall on the narrower plan dimension, and a door on the corresponding north side, 1.0 × 2.0 m. These dimensions give the surface areas enclosing the space listed in Table 4.1 overleaf.

This room will be used as the vehicle for discussion and comparison of various design options, particularly with regard to thermal performance. The results obtained from any calculations made involving the hypothetical room are not intended to be simulations of reality, but to demonstrate tendencies and point the way towards appropriate design decisions.

STRUCTURE

The degree of mass

The first decision in the design of an autonomous house is whether the building should be thermally lightweight or thermally heavy. The advantage of thermally lightweight construction is that it allows a house to be heated quickly when heat

Table 4.1: Surface areas of enclosing surfaces of hypothetical room in m²

south wall (net of window)	6.61
north wall	6.05
east wall	11.50
west wall	11.50
window	1.44
door	2.00
floor	17.50
ceiling	17.50
(volume	40.25 m³)

is applied. A typical lightweight construction would be a timber frame with insulation between the studs and an inner lining of plasterboard. Because little heat is stored in the materials of which the house is made, the building will heat up quickly; as the thermal capacity is low, the majority of the heat input will go into warming the space. When the heat input ceases the space will cool rapidly as there is no stored heat to temper it. Furthermore, the lightweight house can tend to overheat if it admits too much solar radiation on account of its design, or if the gains from occupants or appliances are excessive, as there is no spare thermal capacity to absorb the surplus gains, and the effect of the heat input is to raise the temperature of the space.

In a thermally heavy house, typically constructed (in the United Kingdom) with a dense-concrete-block inner leaf to the wall, cavity insulation and a masonry outer skin, the blockwork acts as a heat reservoir, with the capacity to absorb considerable heat gains without raising the temperature of the space. When the heat source is applied, the structural mass surrounding the space takes a considerable time to heat up, and the space is slow to warm. When the heat source is removed, the mass cools down slowly, releasing heat which maintains the temperature of the space it encloses. Sizemore et al. define the thermal mass of a building as follows: 'The heat storage or thermal capacity of the materials in the building envelope determines how much energy is required for a wall to change temperature.'[1] It follows that the thermally heavy space is better able to make use of solar and other passive heat gains than the thermally light space. As Goulding et al. say: 'The building needs thermal mass to store heat during the day and to re-emit it at night.'[2] Similarly Szokolay, referring to design strategies for cold climates, states:

> With continuous occupancy (e.g. in a family dwelling) and continuous heating the thermal inertia [i.e., the thermal mass] does not influence the indoor temperatures of the building. With intermittent heating a massive building will retain its high temperature for a long period, it will be slow to cool down. Conversely the heating up period will be longer. The indoor conditions will be more stable than in a thermally lightweight building.[3]

An autonomous house will not have the luxury of Szokolay's continuous heating powered by fossil fuels, and its heating will be, inevitably, intermittent. This suggests that it will need thermal mass to make the best use of the intermittent heat gains that it receives.

The effect of thermal mass on the overall space-heating energy demand of a house can be significant. A study of 28 houses in New Zealand, where the predominant method of house construction is timber frame with a timber floor, found that the simple addition of a concrete ground-floor slab in place of the usual timber floor would reduce the space-heating energy demand by 40%.[4] In the 1970s in the United States the two approaches adopted towards the design of low-energy houses were referred to as 'mass and glass' (a house that was thermally heavy in order to store heat gains, with deliberate use of passive solar techniques through the use of large south-facing windows) and 'light and tight' (a low-mass airtight house with careful air/vapour barrier sealing to control ventilation heat loss, and windows sized to avoid excessive solar heat gains). Olivier, describing the low-energy houses of northern Europe, points out another advantage of massive construction apart from the ability to store heat:

> ... this progress [in energy-efficient design] occurs within a building tradition which is based on heavyweight construction methods; that is masonry and in-situ concrete ... cavity masonry walls in the Netherlands and north Germany, solid walls in most of Germany, and a mixture of the two in Switzerland ... these countries' experience proves, if it were necessary, that it is much easier to construct draughtproof buildings from masonry and concrete than when using lightweight forms of construction.[5]

Olivier's comment would appear to create a new category of low-energy house, at least in Europe, the 'tight and massive' house.

The need for massive construction, particularly in relation to a house which attempts to avoid the use of any conventional heating system, is borne out in an extreme example by Lund, who has said that a superinsulated house with no solar components in Scandinavian latitudes needs 100 m³ of concrete to provide sufficient thermal mass to meet a zero space-heating demand.[6] To make sense of this statement, some definitions are needed. Olivier gives the following table of the insulation levels and air infiltration rate needed for various elements to meet a 'superinsulated' standard.

Table 4.2: Typical minimum superinsulated building practice

element	U value (W/m²K)
roof	0.15
exterior walls	0.20
floors above unheated basements	0.30
walls of heated basements	0.30
floor slabs on ground	0.30
windows	1.50

Note: air leakage/infiltration taken to be 2 ac/h at 50 Pascals; ventilation taken to be whole-dwelling mechanical ventilation, normally with heat recovery.[7]

Lund's paper assumes a house with an internal temperature varying on an annual basis between 17°C and 27°C. Lund's thermal-mass figure for a normal (rather than superinsulated), house is 1000 m³ of concrete. Assuming that Lund's lower thermal-mass figure (100 m³ of concrete in a superinsulated house) is the only one that has any practical chance of realization, what would be the effect if this amount of thermal mass were applied to an English house of conventional size (assuming superinsulation)? If a typical house has a floor area of 90 m², and a ceiling height of 2.3 m, it will have a volume of 207 m³, so Lund's requirement would represent a mass that was approximately half the volume of the house it serves. If this house had two storeys, with plan dimensions of 9.0 × 5.0 m and a floor-to-ceiling height of 2.3 m, it would have a total internal surface area (walls, floors, first-floor ceiling) of roughly 270 m². To meet Lund's requirement of 100 m³, this house would need walls, ground floor, first floor and first-floor ceiling to be of concrete nearly 370 mm thick, before considering the insulation and external cladding, and excluding any allowance for windows and doors. The problems posed by the incorporation of Lund's proposed mass in a real house are obvious, when it is considered that the thickness of the conventional inner leaf of a masonry cavity wall is only 100 mm, and a ground-floor slab is not usually more than 150 mm thick. Lund's paper does not state what the insulation levels would need to be in his example, other than to speak of 'superinsulation', but Olivier's figures, based on Dutch, Swiss and German examples, can be assumed to be appropriate minima.

As an example of the difference that can be made by more modest, and therefore more realizable, thermal mass to the thermal properties of a space, the hypothetical room described above, with dimensions as shown in Table 4.1, can be used. For the purposes of the consideration of thermal-mass effects, two rooms (one of low-mass timber-frame construction and one of high-mass masonry construction) with the following constructional properties can be considered.

Table 4.3: Construction of the hypothetical low-mass and high-mass rooms

element	low-mass (timber-frame)	high-mass (masonry)
walls	12.7-mm plasterboard	100-mm dense-concrete block
ceiling	12.7-mm plasterboard	150-mm reinforced-concrete slab
plaster	3-mm skim coat finish	12-mm sand cement render
floor	25-mm softwood boarding	150-mm reinforced-concrete slab
flooring	5-mm carpet on underlay	12-mm clay quarry tiles

To give a preliminary idea of the differences between the two constructional approaches, one can look at the volumes of materials available for the storage of heat in each room. The low-mass room has the following volumes of material available for storing heat.

Table 4.4: Volumes of materials in low-mass room in m³

plasterboard	0.68 (walls and ceiling)
plaster	0.16 (walls and ceiling)
carpet	0.09
underlay	0.09 (thickness assumed as carpet)
total	**1.02 m³**

The figures for thermal-storage volume given in Table 4.4 assume that only the surfaces on the warm side of the insulation are available for the storage of heat. In the thermal-mass calculations for the Saskatchewan Conservation House in Canada, one of the first 'superinsulated' houses, the mass of the timber framing is included, but the house has a double-stud construction to reduce cold bridging, so the inner set of studs can be considered as being on the warm side.[8] The low-mass room described above is assumed to have a conventional single-stud timber frame, so only the plasterboard inner lining to the studwork is assumed to be part of the usable thermal mass. The floor boarding is assumed to be insulated from the interior space by the carpet and underlay. The high-mass room has the following volumes of material available for storing heat.

Table 4.5: Volumes of materials in high-mass room in m³

concrete block	3.57 (walls)
plaster	0.64 (walls and ceiling)
reinforced concrete	5.25 (floor and ceiling)
quarry tiles	0.21
total	**9.67 m³**

The calculations for the high-mass room assume again that only the inner leaf of the cavity wall is available for the storage of heat, as it is on the warm side of the insulation.

The total volume of thermal-storage material (excluding the window and door, which are the same in each case and therefore do not enter into a demonstration of the relative differences between the two strategies) is 1.02 m³ in the case of the low-mass room, and 9.67 m³ in the case of the high-mass room. It can be seen, even ignoring the different heat capacities of different materials, that the high-mass room has more than nine times the volume, and hence potentially nine times the thermal capacity of the low-mass room. The difference between the low-mass room and the high-mass room is magnified if the mass per cubic metre of the various materials is added into the calculation. Data for the density of the various materials in kg/m³, and for their specific heat capacity in J/kg/K (where K is a degree Kelvin, the same as a degree Celsius) were obtained from Page[9] and are as shown in Table 4.6. Using these values it is possible to calculate the mass of the various materials in the two rooms as shown in Table 4.7.

Table 4.6: Material densities and specific heat capacities

material	density (kg/m³)	specific heat capacity (J/kg/K)
plasterboard	950	840
gypsum plaster	1,120	1,000
carpet	190	1,360
wool felt underlay	160	1,360
dense concrete	2,100	840
sand-cement plaster	1,570	1,000
quarry tiles	1,900	800

Table 4.7: Mass of materials used in the two hypothetical rooms

LOW-MASS ROOM material	area (m²)	volume (m³)	density (kg/m³)	mass (kg)
plasterboard	53.16	0.68	950	646
plaster	53.16	0.16	1,120	179
carpet	17.50	0.09	190	17
underlay	17.50	0.09	160	14
total				856 kg

HIGH-MASS ROOM material	area (m²)	volume (m³)	density (kg/m³)	mass (kg)
blockwork	35.66	3.57	2,100	7,497
plaster	35.66	0.43	1,570	675
concrete	35.00	5.25	2,100	11,025
quarry tiles	17.50	0.21	1,900	399
total				19,596 kg

The difference between the two rooms has gone from roughly 9:1, in the case of materials volume, to nearly 23:1 in the case of mass. Palz and Steemers[10] give the following table of thermal mass (measured as building mass [in kg] divided by building volume [in m³]) for 18 solar houses that they studied in Europe.

Table 4.8: Building mass/building volume in European solar houses

building mass/building volume	number of houses
0–150	7
150–250	5
250–	6

As a comparison, the high-mass room used in the examples above has a mass/volume figure of 487, and the low-mass room has a figure of 21.

If the specific-heat capacities of the materials of which the rooms are made are calculated, rather than just the masses of the materials, the results are those shown in Table 4.9.

Once the specific-heat capacities are taken into account, the high-mass room is seen to have nearly 22 times the thermal-storage capacity of the low-mass room. This suggests that mass alone gives a reasonable guide to the thermal capacity of buildings that use normal building materials, since it was shown above that the mass of the high-mass room was about 23 times that of the low-mass room. The thermal-storage capacity of the high-mass room can also be compared with the extreme situation represented by Lund's 100 m³ of concrete. Using the same data for the density and thermal capacity of concrete as used above (2,100 kg/m³ and 840 J/kg/K respectively, based on the values for dense concrete), 100 m³ of concrete would have a mass of 210 tonnes and would store 176 MJ/K. Reduced *pro rata* from the capacity for a notional 90-m² house to that of a 17.5-m² room, Lund's 100 m³ of concrete would become 19.4 m³, which would store about 34 MJ/K. This is double the capacity of the so-called high-mass room, giving a thermal-storage capacity of nearly 2 MJ/K per square metre of floor area, representing over 1.1 m³ of concrete per square metre of floor area. It is interesting to note that the high-mass room is significantly closer in its thermal-storage capacity to Lund's specification (a ratio of roughly 2:1) than it is to the low-mass room (a ratio of roughly 22:1), although its structural elements are no thicker than the same elements would be in a thermally light, all-timber, construction. No attempt has been made to increase the thermal mass beyond the dimensions that would be necessary in normal construction. This use of

Table 4.9: Specific heat capacities of the two hypothetical rooms

LOW-MASS ROOM material	mass (kg)	specific heat (J/K)	heat capacity (MJ/K)
plasterboard	646	840	0.54
plaster	179	1,000	0.18
carpet	17	1,360	0.02
underlay	14	1,360	0.02
total			0.76 MJ/K

HIGH-MASS ROOM material	mass (kg)	specific heat (J/K)	heat capacity (MJ/K)
blockwork	7497	840	6.30
plaster	675	1,000	0.68
concrete	11025	840	9.26
quarry tiles	399	800	0.32
total			16.56 MJ/K

conventional constructional component sizes to achieve thermal mass is the major difference between the high-mass room described here, and the theoretical approach suggested by Lund, which bears little relation to the practicalities of construction.

A comparison can be made between the low-mass room and the thermal mass of the timber-frame Saskatchewan Conservation House: 'The Saskatchewan Conservation House is generally regarded as the first superinsulated demonstration house built in Canada. Conceived as a research project by the National Research Council, the house was built to test the theories of superinsulation, air tightness, mechanical ventilation with heat recovery and the use of passive solar radiation.'[11] The thermal mass of the Saskatchewan House is quoted by Shurcliff as 18.5 MJ/K, comprised of 5.5 MJ/K for the gypsum board and 13.0 MJ/K for the timber framing, based on 'the components that are thermally isolated from the outdoors by the thick insulation and are in direct contact with the rooms'.[12] The given floor area of the house is 187 m^2 (2,016 ft^2),[13] so the total thermal mass works out to nearly 0.1 MJ/K/m², which gives, for the same floor area as the hypothetical low-mass room above, a *pro rata* value of about 1.73 MJ/K. The difference between the low-mass room, whose heat capacity, at 0.76 MJ/K, is half that of the Canadian example, and the Saskatchewan house is due to the fact that the timber framing of the low-mass room used here has not been considered as part of the thermal mass in the calculation, whereas the inner layer of framing in the Saskatchewan House is assumed to contribute to the available mass, as described above. It is also worth noting that an allowance of 10% of total mass, or 2.0 MJ/K for the whole house, has been calculated as the thermal mass of the furniture and appliances included in the Saskatchewan house.[14]

The low-mass room used in the above calculations is of timber-frame construction, in which the mass of the room is formed largely of the plasterboard internal lining to the timber frame. It can be seen from the calculations that thermal mass could be added easily to this room by giving it a concrete floor slab, which would add 5,513 kg and 4.6 MJ/K (150-mm-thick dense concrete, with values as above), but it would be necessary for this slab to be non-carpeted if it were to function as a thermal mass. As Tucker and Watt state: 'The problem of the very detrimental effect on slab storage which overlaid carpet causes can be overcome to a large extent through the use of alternative floor finishes such as slate or tiles.'[15]

The typical UK house, with a carpeted concrete ground-floor slab, aerated-concrete-block inner leaf to cavity walls and timber/plasterboard first floor, could be described as a mid-mass house. It would be expected to fall between the low-mass timber-frame and high-mass masonry examples. Using the same calculation basis as the high- and low-mass examples above, it can be seen that a mid-mass room has the following characteristics.

Table 4.10: Properties of a mid-mass room

walls	100-mm aerated-concrete-block walls with 12 mm of gypsum plaster
ceiling	12.7-mm plasterboard, 3-mm skim coat of plaster
floor	carpet on underlay
total mass	2,563 kg
total specific heat capacity	2.55 MJ/K

Note: calculated using values from Page, as before.

Again, 4.6 MJ/K could be added by the use of an uncarpeted concrete ground-floor slab. In calculating the thermal storage capacities for a room and a house, Littler and Thomas write as follows:

> There is, of course, a certain amount of thermal mass in any construction. For example, even an insulated timber-framed room lined on the inside with 15 mm plasterboard has a heat capacity of about 24 kJ/(m^{2}K), that is, a room with 60 m^2 of wall and ceiling has a heat capacity of 1.4 MJ/K in its plaster alone. Furnishings might add a further 0.4 MJ/K. For the whole house this adds up to about 10 MJ/K of thermal storage. For a house with an insulated brick and block cavity and solid floors downstairs, this value might be about 70 MJ/K.[16]

(Note that Littler and Thomas' calculation of the thermal-storage potential of 60 m^2 of plastered surface must have been calculated on the basis of an 18-mm thickness of dense sand-cement plaster to achieve the quoted figure of 1.4 MJ/K. However, in practice it is more common in timber-frame construction to use 9.5-mm or 12.5-mm thick gypsum plasterboard, both thinner and less dense .)

The values given by Littler and Thomas, if assumed to be for a house of 90 m^2, can be adjusted *pro rata* for the hypothetical room area of 17.5 m^2, giving a figure of 1.94 MJ/K for their timber-frame house, and 13.61 MJ/K for their brick and block house. The examples used above are set out in Table 4.11 overleaf to demonstrate the range of thermal capacities that can be achieved using different methods of construction.

Lund's work cited above seems to suggest that thermal mass is essential for a building with a zero-space-heating requirement. A high-thermal-mass strategy would appear to have advantages for an autonomous house, as it makes best use of all available heat gains; any gains contribute to the heating of the mass, which retains them for later use in heating the space. The mass makes it less likely that the space will overheat and need to be vented to control its temperature. In a conventional house, the need to husband heat in this way is less critical, as the heating system can always be used to provide heat when none is available from storage, but in an autonomous house the use of back-up heating in this way may not be available. Mass construction (brick and block cavity walls) is also the commonest form of house construction in the United Kingdom, although modern timber-frame house designs tend to use a concrete ground-floor slab,[17] which will provide a useful thermal benefit, as is suggested by the work of Breuer in New Zealand, described above.

The familiarity of UK contractors with masonry construction should mean that the high-mass house might prove to be a more practicable building option, leading to lower tender prices for the construction. In 1993, 174,100 houses were

Table 4.11: A comparison of the different thermal capacities of the different approaches

	thermal capacity based on area of hypothetical room (MJ/K)	thermal capacity (MJ/K/m²)
low-mass room	0.76	0.04
Saskatchewan Conservation House	1.73	0.10
Littler and Thomas' timber-frame house	1.93	0.11
mid-mass room	2.55	0.15
low-mass room with uncarpeted concrete floor	5.36	0.31
mid-mass room with uncarpeted concrete floor	7.15	0.41
Littler and Thomas' brick house	13.61	0.78
high-mass room	16.56	0.95
Lund's superinsulated house	34.22	1.96

completed in the United Kingdom, of which 8,200 were timber frame, representing only 4.7% of the total.[18] This claim of practicability is given support by a series of superinsulated moderately high-mass buildings built for public clients in Sheffield, which were designed by Brenda and Robert Vale and constructed between 1985 and 1992. These included the Heeley Green Surgery,[19] the Woodhouse Medical Centre,[20] the Industry Road houses[21] and the Cresswell Road houses.[22] The buildings were designed on the premise that a masonry cavity-wall construction would be the most familiar to a contractor, and the tender submitted would then not be inflated by an additional sum to cover the contractor's unfamiliarity with a novel form of construction. This assumption was borne out in practice; in each case the buildings were constructed within a budget that would be reasonable for the construction of a conventional building. As far as setting the budgets was concerned, the client for the two medical buildings was the National Health Service, through the Sheffield Family Practitioner Committee, and the client for the housing was the government's

Fig. 8
*The Heeley Green
Surgery, Sheffield:
a superinsulated
masonry building*

Housing Corporation, working through North Sheffield Housing Association. In all cases the building costs were required to fall within a permitted budget figure which was intended to cover construction of a conventionally insulated building. For all the buildings the quantity surveyors were Gordon Hall, Grayson and Co. of Sheffield, and the structural engineer was Allott and Associates, also of Sheffield.

Table 4.11 demonstrates one advantage of high thermal mass when compared to the example of the low-mass room: its ability to store considerably more heat in the fabric of the building. For a house which is intended to operate without space heating, any method of retaining heat is valuable, so that all gains can be used without the need to vent heat because of overheating. However, mass construction has other advantages, including its robustness and impact resistance in a domestic environment; its ability to take fixings for shelves, kitchen cupboards and the like over the whole of its surface; its sound-reducing qualities with respect to external noise; and, if internal partitions and intermediate floors are also massive, its potential for reducing internal sound transmission. On the other hand Table 4.7, which shows the actual, rather than thermal, mass of materials in the low-mass and high-mass rooms, highlights one of the potential disadvantages of thermal mass, which is its mass. The energy required to bring materials to a site should be taken into account in the overall energy design of the building, and it is worth pointing out that the materials of the high-mass room will need, all other things being equal, 23 times as much

y

THEORETICAL ANALYSIS OF THE TECHNICAL OPTIONS | **79**

energy to transport to the site as the materials for the low-mass room. Although mass has an important rôle to play in the thermal strategy of the autonomous house design, it is considered here, together with structure, since the choice between lightweight or heavyweight construction is the most fundamental aspect of a building's construction. It is the choice from which all other considerations must flow.

Frame structure or loadbearing structure?

The two common options for building a house are to use a frame and infill this to form walls, or to use loadbearing walls to provide support and enclosure in the same element. There are other possibilities such as a monocoque shell or an excavation in the ground, but loadbearing walls and frame construction represent the two modes of construction usual in the United Kingdom. Towards the end of the 1970s, timber-frame construction accounted for 'as much as 25% of new housing',[23] although this percentage fell considerably, from a high point of 48,000 houses (in 1977) to 8,200 (in 1993), and it declined steadily throughout the 1990s.[24] Almost all the timber-frame houses that are built in the United Kingdom make use of a brick external cladding for aesthetic/planning reasons, but the purest example in Britain of the frame house is probably the work of the late Walter Segal. Segal's houses used both a lightweight frame of carefully sized timber members, and a lightweight cladding of timber, plywood or Eternit (glazed-asbestos cement sheets, later fibre cement sheets). The relevance of Segal's work to this discussion is that it has been taken up, following Segal's death, by the London-based architectural practice Architype, as a way of designing low-energy housing that could be constructed by its users. The simplicity of the Segal method lies in its use of simple joints which need little in the way of carpentry or building skills, whereas masonry construction requires some expertise if it is to be carried out satisfactorily.

It is interesting to note that a Segal-type house is likely to be more expensive than a masonry house of the same size if constructed by a contractor rather than being built by an individual. A self-build scheme for two-storey Segal-type houses designed by Architype at Cat Lane in Sheffield was costed in April 1990 at a notional contract value (i.e., assuming that the houses had been built by a contractor) of £46,044 per house, including external works. The houses had a floor area of 80.6 m^2 (measured to internal faces of external walls) giving a cost, if contractor built, of £571.27/m^2. The houses had three bedrooms, a ground-floor toilet, first-floor bathroom, and built-in wardrobes in two of the bedrooms. Thermal insulation was extruded polystyrene, 50-mm Styrofoam in the walls and 100-mm Styrofoam in the roof; there was no insulation on the ground floor, but there was double glazing in timber-framed windows.[25] The rate of flow of heat (in watts) through 1 m² of a constructional element enclosing a space (such as a wall, floor, roof or window) for each degree Kelvin of difference in temperature between the inside and the outside is that element's U value. The U values for the construction just described are as follows.

Table 4.12: Constructional and thermal data for the Cat Lane houses

element	construction	U value (W/m^2K)
ground floor	19 × 125-mm softwood tongued and grooved boards on joists	0.71
external walls	5-mm Glasal fibre cement cladding, 50-mm Styrofoam IB insulation, 12.7-mm plasterboard	0.42
roof	Eternit fibre cement slates on battens on felt, 100-mm Styrofoam IB insulation, 12.7-mm plasterboard	0.25
glazing	standard sealed double-glazing units in timber frames	3.00
external doors	standard softwood glazed doors	not known

Note: ventilation achieved by opening windows; data for calculations from Page, as above.[26]

A pair of superinsulated houses designed by Brenda and Robert Vale were constructed in 1991 at 85–89 Industry Road, Darnall, Sheffield, for North Sheffield Housing Association. These were two-storey three-bedroom houses, with a ground-floor toilet and first-floor bathroom, like the Cat Lane houses. They had built-in wardrobes in all bedrooms and a whole-house mechanical ventilation system with heat recovery. Unlike the Cat Lane houses, the pair at Industry Road used a brick and lightweight-concrete-block cavity-wall construction, incorporating 150-mm-thick insulation, a superinsulated roof, triple-glazed low-emissivity argon-filled windows and insulated external doors. Floor area per house was 88.4 m². The final contract sum for the construction of the houses, including external works, was £91,106.67, giving a cost per house of £45,554.34, which is £515.31/m².[27] Had the Industry Road houses been built at the same cost as the Cat Lane houses, each house would have been £4,945.93 more expensive, an increase of 10.9%. The construction and U values of the various elements are shown in Table 4.13 overleaf.

Fig. 9
The Industry Road
houses, Sheffield

Table 4.13: Constructional and thermal data for the Industry Road houses

element	construction	U value (W/m²K)
ground floor	150-mm concrete slab on 150-mm Jablite expanded polystyrene	0.20
external walls	100 mm of concrete facing brick, 150 mm of Fibreglass Dritherm insulation, 100 mm of Thermalite aerated-concrete block, 12 mm of plaster	0.20
roof	Redland concrete tiles on battens on 8-mm 2L2 foil-faced plastic bubble film, on 50-mm Jablite expanded polystyrene, 200 mm of Fibreglass between rafters, 12.7-mm plasterboard	0.13 (allowing for thermal bridging through rafters)
glazing	Swedhouse triple-glazed low-emissivity argon-filled windows with timber frames	1.20
external doors	steel-faced polystyrene with gas-filled low-emissivity double glazing	1.00

Note: ventilation is a mechanical whole-house ventilation system with heat recovery and pollen filtration.

It is worth noting that the masonry houses are not only cheaper than the timber-frame Segal houses, they are also of a much higher thermal performance in terms of the U values of the various elements. As the Industry Road houses were built a year after the report on the Cat Lane houses had been written, at a time when construction prices were rising, and as there are only two of them, giving few economies of scale, the cost comparison is likely to be, if anything, biased in favour of the timber-frame houses. The great advantage of the Segal method of construction lies in its suitability for being built by the non-specialist individual – masonry is a more difficult construction method for unskilled builders but, in the United Kingdom at least, the Segal method is an expensive method if a contractor is employed.

The use of a timber frame and cladding results in a lightweight construction, as seen in the Cat Lane houses, with their Glasal external skin and plasterboard internal linings. For a house that was attempting to follow a high-mass strategy, for the reasons set out above, the use of a frame could seem problematic, particularly if the frame itself were expected to contribute to the thermal mass. The frame might need to make use of precast concrete elements to provide the necessary mass, and the making of moulds to cast such parts for a single dwelling would seem inappropriate and wasteful in material terms, as the formwork would be re-used infrequently. There would be a similar problem of waste of shuttering if an *in situ* concrete frame were used. One example of a high-mass framed low-energy, if not autonomous, house design in the United Kingdom is the 'Survivor' house built by David Stephens in Wales. This has a massive steel portal frame, designed for a life of 500 years. The external claddings, in the form of tiles and slates on a timber frame with insulation in it, are lightweight, and the mass of the first floor is increased by incorporating bottles of water into the floor construction.[28] The thermal capacity of water is 4,180 J/kg/K,[29] over four times better than that of dense concrete (840 J/kg/K), and this technique provides a way of adding effective mass to a lightweight building without having to transport the mass, provided that the house is connected to a convenient water supply.

The transport energy penalty of a high-mass construction was described above. If the use of mass is to be considered because of its thermal benefits, one way to reduce the transport penalty is to ensure that the mass can perform as many tasks in the building as possible. Stephens' solution of using water as applied mass in a frame structure is one way round this, allowing the water's mass to work purely as mass. Traditionally, mass, in the form of masonry or even soil, has been the way to build the walls of houses in many parts of Britain. If the thermal mass can also be the structure, it is performing more efficiently, and if it can provide in addition sound insulation and impact resistance, these will be further benefits.

The implicit result of these deliberations is a clear link between the thermal-mass strategy of a house and its constructional strategy. A thermally lightweight house is likely to use a frame construction, a thermally heavyweight one a loadbearing wall construction, which makes multiple use of the mass. These two scenarios do not cover all eventualities: it is quite possible to build a thermally lightweight house using masonry construction. The majority of timber-frame houses built in Britain are designed with an outer skin of a single (100-mm) leaf of brickwork tied back to the timber frame.[30] This is used for two reasons: it complies with the aesthetic strictures of many planning authorities, where a brick finish is required so as to be in keeping with existing properties; and it provides a maintenance-free exterior finish. The more logical cladding for a timber-frame construction would seem to be timber, but timber claddings require quite frequent maintenance. In the United States of America, where timber is a common exterior cladding for timber-frame construction, the recommended times between redecoration vary between 'two to three years' on planed timber, and up to ten years can be achieved 'when two coats are applied to a rough or weathered surface'.[31] These are the recommended times that may be allowed to lapse before reapplication of a penetrating pigmented stain finish recommended by the US Department of Agriculture.[32] The stain, developed by the Forest Products Laboratory of the USDA in Madison, Wisconsin '… has a linseed oil vehicle; a preservative, pentachlorophenol, to protect the wood from mildew; and a water repellant, paraffin wax, to protect the wood from excessive penetration of water.'[33]

The Canada Mortgage and Housing Corporation states that if one prefers to avoid the use of pentachlorophenol: 'Good quality house paint properly applied will usually last for four or five years.'[34] Howard Liddell of the Scottish practice Gaia Architects claims that with careful detailing to keep the wood dry, untreated timber can be used successfully as external cladding in the UK climate, provided that a naturally durable species such as Douglas Fir (Scottish grown to minimize transport) is employed.[35] He also states that the maintenance of timber is second nature in countries such as Norway, where there is a long tradition of timber construction. Problems have arisen with timber claddings in the United Kingdom, since the practice is not common. Hall gives the elements of buildings where the use of timber preservatives is required in the United Kingdom; these are listed in Table 4.14.[36]

Hall appears to bear out Liddell's views on the external use of untreated timber:

Untreated wood exposed outside, however durable it may be according to the classification, will soon lose its colour and develop surface checking. If continued for months and years, such exposure will result in soiling of the wood surface and gradual loss of fibre. It usually follows that some form of protection is required to prevent this weathering, although this erosion is said to occur at a rate of only 6 mm every one hundred years, and untreated wood components have performed satisfactorily without finishes for decades.[37]

Table 4.14: Categories of need for preservation for different building components

categories of need for preservation	building component examples
preservation unnecessary	interior joinery, floorboarding, interior wall studs
preservation optional	roof timbers (pitched), ground-floor joists, tile battens
preservation desirable	external wall studs, timbers in flat roofs, cladding
preservation essential	sole plates, loadbearing joinery, timber in contact with ground or concrete below damp-proof course

Note: for full specification guidance see BS 5268: Part 5 and BS 5589. Building components are assumed to be of timber with low natural resistance.

Sulman, a fellow contributor of Hall's to the book *Timber in Construction* provides a table of the properties of a large number of timber species.[38] Douglas Fir, *Pseudotsuga menziesii*, recommended by Liddell for use untreated as external cladding, is listed as 'moderately durable.'[39] Western red cedar, *Thuja plicata*, the best known in the United Kingdom of the timber claddings that can be left untreated, is in the 'durable' category, but comes only from North America.[40] Sulman defines durability with respect to timber as follows:

> *Durability is expressed by one of five classes based upon the average life of a 50 × 50 mm section of heartwood in ground contact. This is a particularly hazardous situation and timber used externally, but not in contact with the ground, will have a longer life than that indicated, even without treatment. These ratings refer to the heartwood only ... The classes used are*

very durable	*more than 25 years*
durable	*15–25 years*
moderately durable	*10–15 years*
non-durable	*5–10 years*
perishable	*fewer than 5 years*[41]

The use of brick as external cladding to a timber frame avoids the problems of durability, treatment and maintenance described above, but it also means that the brick is not performing the multiple rôle described above, one way in which the transport energy penalty of high-mass materials could be reduced. A more logical way of using masonry with timber would be to use the masonry wall as the inner structural element of a wall, with external cladding on a timber frame carrying insulation. This would eliminate the use of external brickwork used solely as cladding, but the wall might then require maintenance if the timber frame were to be timber clad. Planning pressures in the United Kingdom mean that timber cladding, in areas where brick is the norm, is unlikely to be accepted for many years to come. Timber cladding also requires the householder to perform regular maintenance, as described above. Maintenance can be avoided by the use of naturally durable timber, such as Western red cedar, that does not need preserving or finishing, but the fact that the United Kingdom imports at least 90% of its timber[42] makes the cedar a potentially higher-energy material than might have been thought at first.

BUILDING ENCLOSURE

Thermal insulation

Thermal insulation, particularly in the climate of the British Isles, is a key factor in the design of an autonomous house. Using the hypothetical room that formed the basis of thermal-mass calculations earlier, it is possible to look at the effects of insulation level on the thermal performance of three hypothetical rooms with low, medium and high levels of insulation. Table 4.15 shows the results of these calculations.

The East Pennines Region, where the autonomous house is located, has 2,373 degree days annually, to a base temperature of 15.5°C.[43] Base temperature is the exterior temperature above which no space heating is assumed to be needed in the building. The fact that this is lower than the generally accepted required indoor air temperature takes account of the fact that internal heat gains from occupants and appliances and the effect of solar gain through the windows combine to raise the internal air temperature, rendering additional space heating unnecessary, at least in theory, above the base temperature of 15.5°C. The three rooms have the annual fabric heat demands given in Table 4.16, based on the figure of 2,373 degree days.

Table 4.15: Thermal insulation effects in the low-, medium- and high-insulation hypothetical rooms

element	area (m²)	U value (w/m²K) for low-/ medium-/ and high-insulation rooms	heat loss (W/K) for low-/ medium-/ and high-insulation rooms
south wall	6.61	0.45/0.20/0.10	2.97/1.32/0.67
north wall	6.05	0.45/0.20/0.10	2.72/1.21/0.61
east wall	11.50	0.45/0.20/0.10	5.18/2.30/1.15
west wall	11.50	0.45/0.20/0.10	5.18/2.30/1.15
ceiling	17.50	0.25/0.10/0.05	4.38/1.75/0.88
floor	17.50	0.60/0.20/0.10	10.50/3.50/1.75
door	2.00	1.00/0.55/0.55	2.00/1.10/1.10
window	1.44	5.00/1.60/0.95	**7.20/2.30/1.37**
total fabric heat loss			**40.13/15.78/8.68 W/K**

Note: the U values for the low-insulation room represent a 1990 house with single glazing; the medium-insulation room uses the values used in the superinsulated masonry buildings in Sheffield; the high-insulation room uses values half those of the medium room where possible, and the best available technology elsewhere. For example, the high-insulation window is the value produced by a Swedish window manufacturer in an experimental window designed in an attempt to achieve a U value of 1.0 W/m²K or better,[44] and the door is the best on the market, also made in Sweden.[45] Ventilation rates, and their effects on the heat loss of the room, are discussed later.

Table 4.16: Annual fabric heat loss in kWh from the three hypothetical rooms

low-insulation	2,285
medium-insulation	899
high-insulation	494

Note: these calculations ignore the effects of ventilation heat loss.

Assuming a conventional UK heating season lasting from October to April inclusive, a total of 212 days, the annual demands can be reappraised as an average heating rate as follows.

Table 4.17: Annual heating rate in watts for the three hypothetical rooms (fabric only)

low-insulation	261
medium-insulation	103
high-insulation	56

Note: these calculations ignore the effects of ventilation heat loss.

The effect of the use of high levels of insulation is a reduction in the required heating rate by 79%. The heating rate is an artificial figure, as it will vary with external temperature and other factors.

Ventilation

The heat demand of the three rooms described above cannot be considered taking only the insulation levels into account: the rate of ventilation of the rooms will also have an important influence on the total heat loss. The volume of the hypothetical room used earlier as the basis for demonstrating the possible benefits of thermal mass in construction is 40.25 m^3. In Table 4.15 the effects of increasing insulation level were demonstrated, with the results that the total fabric heat losses in W/K of the three hypothetical rooms with low, medium and high levels of insulation were 40.13, 15.78 and 8.68 respectively. To these fabric losses can be added the heat loss due to the effects of ventilation, the bringing in of cold external air which must then be heated to room temperature. The ventilation heat loss from the room can be calculated by using the specific heat of air in the formula:

ventilation heat loss in W/K = volume × airchanges/hour (ac/h) × 0.33.[46]

A room with a volume of 40.25 m^3 has a ventilation heat loss rate of 13.28 W/K at 1 ac/h. It can be seen from Table 4.18 that while this is only 33% of the fabric heat loss of the poorly insulated room, it is 84% of the loss for the moderately insulated room, and a shocking 153% of the fabric loss for the well insulated room.

Table 4.18: The effect of ventilation heat loss on total heat loss for the three hypothetical rooms

	low-insulation	medium-insulation	high-insulation
fabric heat loss (W/K)	40.13	15.78	8.68
ventilation heat loss at 1 ac/h	13.28	13.28	13.28
total heat loss	53.41 W/K	29.06 W/K	21.96 W/K

The effect of the ventilation is to reduce the advantage of better fabric insulation from about 5:1 to little more than 2:1. This demonstrates that the reduction of ventilation rates is essential if low-energy performance is to be achieved. Once a reasonable level of insulation is provided in the building fabric, ventilation becomes the largest element of heat loss. However, a certain rate of ventilation is necessary to provide air for the occupants of the room. The CIBS *Building Energy Code* of 1980 says that in a mechanically ventilated building air should be provided at the rate of 5 l/sec for each occupant.[47] This represents a per-person rate of 18 m^3/h which, in the hypothetical room, would give an air change rate of 0.45 ac/h. A typical UK house with a floor area of 90 m^2 and a ceiling height of 2.3 m will have a volume of 207 m^3. If the house is occupied by five people, each needing air at a rate of 5 l/sec, the necessary air demand is 90 m^3/h, which gives a whole house ventilation rate of 0.43 ac/h, very close to the 0.45 value for the hypothetical room on its own. This ventilation rate can be used with the heat losses calculated above to see the benefit of a lower rate of air exchange on the overall heat losses of the three hypothetical rooms with different levels of insulation.

Table 4.19: The effect of reduced ventilation on overall heat loss in the three hypothetical rooms

	low-insulation	medium-insulation	high-insulation
fabric heat loss (W/K)	40.13	15.78	8.68
ventilation heat loss at 0.45 ac/h	5.98	5.98	5.98
total heat loss	46.11 W/K	21.76 W/K	14.66 W/K

Ventilation now represents 13%, 27% and 41% of the total heat losses respectively, and the total heat loss of the high-insulation room has been nearly halved by reducing the ventilation from 1 ac/h to 0.45 ac/h.

Some authors suggest that lower rates of ventilation than 0.45 ac/h may be used; Marshall and Argue, working in Canada, state the following:

> A conventional house will have an air change rate (the rate at which the entire volume of air in a house is replaced) of about one change every two hours (0.5ac/hr). Sealing a house well may reduce this rate to as low as one change every 10 hours (0.1ac/hr). By comparison, some new houses are being built with an air change rate as low as one air change every few days. Air quality suffers at such low air change rates.
>
> Potential problems of poor ventilation include accumulation of contaminants from household products; pollution from smokers, gas stoves and furnaces; accumulation of radon gas emitted by some construction materials; build-up of lingering odours; and depletion of oxygen in extreme cases, such as a smoldering fire that feeds on the oxygen supply. The most serious problems are caused by excessive humidity.
>
> Most potential air-quality problems disappear when the air change rate is 0.2 ac/hr and greater. However, humidity control requires a rate of 0.3 ac/hr or more.[48]

It may be appropriate to remain with the CIBS rate in view of the tendency for houses in Canada to be considerably larger than those in the United Kingdom, leading to greater air provision per occupant. As reported by Lowe et al.,[49] the more recent CIBSE *Guide* of 1986 calls for a per-person ventilation rate of 8 l/sec, but in view of the fact that the autonomous house is not intended to be occupied by people who smoke, it is proposed to continue here with the lower rate.

Achieving the controlled air change rates that are necessary for the accurate control of heat losses will necessitate mechanical ventilation as suggested by the CIBS *Code*. Once this is used, there is potential for considerable reduction in the energy penalty due to ventilation by the use of heat-recovery techniques in the mechanical ventilation system. Heat-recovery ventilation systems take the heat from the air leaving the building and transfer it to the incoming cold fresh air, so that the amount of energy used to heat the incoming air can be reduced. One of the earliest domestic uses of heat-recovery ventilation was in the Danish Zero Energy House, which had a heat-recovery system that was tested in the laboratory as giving a heat-recovery efficiency of 90% when supplying air at a rate of 100 m³/h, and 83% at a supply rate of 200 m³/h. The system was designed to work at the lower rate for twelve hours, and at the higher rate for twelve hours.[50]

In 1980, Amory Lovins spoke of the low-cost ventilation heat exchanger used for the Saskatchewan Conservation House: 'Besant, Dumont and van Ee (Department of Mechanical Engineering, University of Saskatchewan at Saskatoon) have published details of a very cheap (about $30 material cost) counterflow recuperator made from plastic sheets and giving an average efficiency around 80% in a cold climate.'[51] More recently, Nieminen reported on the Finnish International Energy Agency Task 13 solar house, which had two heat-recovery systems; one for the whole house, with a thermal efficiency of 80%, and one for the kitchen with an efficiency of 60%.[52]

Using a reasonably conservative figure for heat-recovery efficiency of 70%, and a ventilation rate of 0.45 ac/h, in line with the CIBS recommendations, the heat loss due to ventilation from the hypothetical room could be reduced, using heat recovery, from 5.98 W/K to 1.79 W/K. Taking the figure of 2,373 degree days, the annual saving attributed to the use of heat recovery in the room in this case is 239 kWh. The technique of heat recovery is valid only if the amount of electricity needed to operate the mechanical ventilation system is significantly less than the heat recovered. This is of even greater importance if the house has a fossil-fuel back-up heating system, as there might be a situation in which electricity (assuming that it is being generated from fossil fuels), with its high carbon dioxide penalty, was being used to provide heat recovery to offset the use of natural gas (which has a much lower carbon dioxide penalty) in central heating. The Building Research Establishment give the following figures for the emission of carbon dioxide per kilowatt hour for different energy sources.

Table 4.20: Relationship between primary fuel use and carbon dioxide emission (kg/kWh delivered) in the United Kingdom[53]

fuel	1991	1996
electricity	0.75	0.59
solid fuel	0.31	0.31
petroleum products	0.28	0.27
gas	0.21	0.19

The improvement in emissions for electricity is due to the increasing replacement of coal-fired generators by natural-gas generators in the 1990s. It is clear from these figures that any heat-recovery system will need to have a performance advantage of over 3:1, in terms of heat recovered versus electricity consumed, if the heat is being provided by gas. Although this calculation does not take into account the detailed efficiency of either the heat-recovery unit or the heating system, it does make clear the nature of the problem.

Esbensen and Korsgaard reported the following energy balance in the Danish Zero Energy House: 'The heat recovery equipment in the ventilating system reduces the heat requirement in the house from 5,760 kWh to 2,300 kWh. To obtain this reduction the ventilators need an electric energy supply of about 210 kWh.'[54] This is a heat saving of 3,460 kWh/year for an electrical consumption of 210 kWh, i.e., the electrical demand represented just over 6% of the recovered energy, a ratio of nearly 16.5:1. Applying this ratio of heat recovered to electricity consumed to the hypothetical room suggests that it should be possible to recover 239 kWh of heat with an electrical consumption of 14.5 kWh. Over the 212 days of the heating season (October to April), assuming that opening windows are used for ventilation during the rest of the year, this is an electricity consumption of 68 Wh/day, or a continuous rate of 2.85 W. The volume of the room is 40.25 m³, or 40,250 l; at a ventilation rate of 0.45 ac/h the system will need to supply 18,113 l/h, or about 5 l/sec.

The 12-V 5-W fan supplied for the Clivus Multrum residential sewage composter used in the autonomous house can supply air at 44.8 l/sec, giving a performance of 9 l/sec/W,[55] so the provision of one tenth of that amount of air with the consumption of half the power seems feasible. The table below shows the performance of a number of 12-V fans marketed by the Real Goods Trading Corporation, an American supplier of low-energy equipment.

Table 4.21: Performance of a range of 12-V fans

model number	ft³/min	amps	l/sec	watts	l/sec/W
64-221	650	0.70	307	8.4	36.5
64-222	550	0.50	259	6.0	43.2
64-213	105	0.55	50	6.6	7.6
64-212	32	0.25	15	3.0	5.0
64-211	15	0.24	7	2.9	2.4

Note: the ft³/min and amps data were provided by the supplier; other figures have been converted.[56]

The Model 64-211 meets almost exactly the requirement of the room (5 l/sec and 2.85 W), although in terms of the amount of air delivered per watt of power, it is the least efficient of the fans listed, delivering air at a rate of only 2.4 l/sec/W – the most efficient in the list delivers it at a rate of 43.2 l/sec/W. Heat-recovery systems generally need two fans, one for air intake and one for extraction, so the performance of each fan would need to be twice as good as the Model 64-211 to meet the theoretical requirement of 5 l/sec/W: this would suggest the Model 64-212, which provides more air than is required, but could therefore be used to supply more than just a single room.

The reason for this detailed examination of 12-V fans is that the Real Goods Corporation makes the point that DC motors are generally more efficient than their AC equivalents.[57] This is borne out by the performance of the 'Electric Air-brick' through-the-wall heat-recovery unit made by ADM Indux, and designed to serve one room, like an extractor fan, rather than a whole house. On its low setting, the unit delivers 43,000 l/h (11.9 l/sec) while consuming 12 W of electricity at 230 V, giving a value of 0.99 l/sec/W.[58] However, this unit is a full heat-recovery system, with a heat-recovery efficiency of 70%, and has two fans. The corresponding electricity consumption of a purpose-made heat-recovery ventilator using two Real Goods Model 64-212 fans would be 6 W for a supply of 15 l/sec. The use of 12-V fans would halve the electricity needed to run the ventilator. Over a year, if the system were run for 24 hours a day, the difference would be worthwhile: the 230-V unit would use 105 kWh and the 12-V system half this. In a house designed to run on renewable energy such savings are significant, and must be sought, in order to avoid small individual loads building into a large total.

The effect of the use of heat-recovery ventilation (assuming a heat-recovery efficiency of 70%) on the heat loss of the three hypothetical rooms is shown in the table below.

Table 4.22: Heat losses from the hypothetical rooms with 70%-efficient heat recovery and ventilation at 0.45 ac/h

	low-insulation	medium-insulation	high-insulation
fabric heat loss (W/K)	40.13	15.78	8.68
ventilation heat loss (W/K)	1.79	1.79	1.79
total heat loss	41.92 W/K	17.57 W/K	10.47 W/K

Overall, the effect of the ventilation is reduced to a relatively trivial proportion of the total heat loss, even in the case of the highly insulated room. For this theoretical performance to be achieved in practice, it will be necessary for the house to be constructed carefully with regard to airtightness, as the controlled ventilation will be rendered ineffective by uncontrolled air movements within the building.

Heat gains

CIBSE[59] gives the heat emission from a seated adult male at rest, with a body surface area of 2 m², as 115 W. The following table shows the heat emission for other activities.[60]

Table 4.23: Heat generation in watts for various activities

typing	130
cooking	190–230
house cleaning	230–400
dancing, social	280–510
calisthenics/exercise	350–470
pick and shovel work	470–560

These figures suggest that the highly insulated room, with its heat-loss rate of 10.47 W/K (assuming heat-recovery ventilation), could possibly be heated by its occupant. A way to examine the situation is to multiply the heat-loss rate of the room by the likely maximum temperature difference (say 21K) to see what the worst case heat demand would be. This gives a figure of 220 W for the highly insulated room, which suggests that the room would need two occupants during the coldest part of the winter, or about 15 cats. The combined sensible and latent heat output of a 3.0 kg cat is listed by CIBSE as 14.8 W,[61] and cats have figured in literature in ways that suggest their use for space heating. The Countess of Groan in *Titus Groan*, the first novel of Mervyn Peake's *Gormenghast* trilogy, is described as moving about her castle surrounded by a sea of white cats:

> In the distance a vibration was becoming louder and louder until the volume seemed to have filled the chamber itself, when suddenly there slid through the narrow opening of the door and moved into the fumid atmosphere of the room an undulation of whiteness, so that, within a breath, there was no shadow in all the room that was not blanched with cats.[62]

This use of cats in Peake's bleak Gormenghast Castle may be more than merely an atmospheric description. A typical cat is about 450 mm in length (excluding the tail, which can be assumed to be underneath or otherwise out of the way) and less than 150 mm wide. (The particular specimen measured by the authors, Bessie, was in Geelong, Australia.) Taylor gives the weight of an average adult cat as lying in the range 2.75–5.5 kg,[63] suggesting that the CIBSE cat may be on the small side, with a correspondingly reduced heat output. The dimensions above suggest that 1 m² of floor space could contain, at the packing density described by Peake, about 15 cats, with a total heat output of 222 W. The hypothetical room, with a floor area of 17.5 m², would contain about 260 cats at this density, with a heat output of nearly 4.0 kW. This would be a useful heat gain even for a room in a cold castle, being nearly four times the maximum heat demand (at a temperature difference of 21K) of the low-insulation room with ventilation at 1 ac/h.

The use of the body heat of building occupants, whether feline or human, is a practicable proposition. The Director of the Office of Energy Conservation in Boulder, Colorado reports: '... Canada's two-storey Saskatchewan Conservation House in Regina is so well-insulated that according to its designer, it needs "only a single light bulb and two couples making love" to heat it.'[64] Using the data from Table 4.23 and taking making love as the average of the range for 'calisthenics/exercise', i.e., 410 W per person, gives a total heat output of 1,640 W. A 100-W light bulb would bring the total to 1,740 W.

Heat gains to a room also come from appliances, lights and from cooking and water heating. An alternative approach for assessing the appropriate insulation levels for an autonomous house might be to look at the total heat gains into a house and then use this figure on an area-weighted basis to derive a heat gain to the room which is being used for these initial calculations. The problem with this approach is that there are widely differing estimates of the heat gains to a typical house. Shurcliff, who has spent 20 years cataloguing various types of low-energy houses throughout the world, gives the data in Table 4.24 for what he calls 'intrinsic' heat gains. Over the 212-day UK heating season, Shurcliff's level of heat gains would produce 7,424 kWh of useful heat input at a rate of 1.46 kW. The problem with the Shurcliff figures given here is that they were established in the United States of America, where houses tend to be large and appliances are not necessarily the most efficient. It is also surprising that no allowance is made in Shurcliff's table for lights: five 100-W lightbulbs, in use for six hours a day would add 3 kWh to the table, or roughly 10% to the daily total.

The *Technical Requirements* of the Canadian Advanced Houses Program set out the design criteria for 'the next generation of energy-efficient and environmentally-friendly homes that are consistent with the long-term goal of

Table 4.24: Amount of intrinsic heat produced in a typical house on a typical 24-hour midwinter day

	Btu	kWh/day
human bodies (two adults and children)	29,000	8.50
cooking stove, microwave oven	18,600	5.45
heater for domestic hot water	4,100	1.20
clothes dryer	8,300	2.43
miscellaneous electrical equipment, including clothes washer, dish washer, refrigerator, TV and radio, hair dryer, blankets, toaster, coffee pot, blowers, fans	59,500	17.44
total	**119,500 Btu**[65]	**35.02 kWh/day**

Note: Shurcliff's data have been converted from Btus to make them more relevant to this discussion.

Fig. 10
A whole-house ventilation heat-recovery unit in the British Columbia Advanced House, Vancouver, Canada

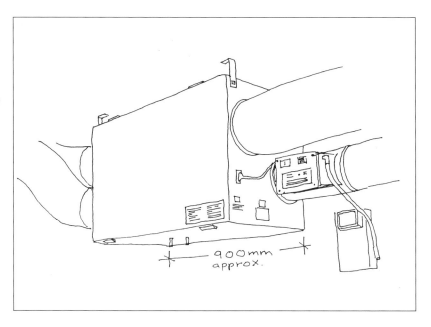

sustainable development'.[66] This document includes a list of appliances that must be included in each house design (so that all the houses submitted for the Advanced Houses Program have the same basis for comparison) and values for the energy consumptions that should be assumed if highly efficient appliances are installed. The appliances and quoted energy values are as follows.

Table 4.25: Required appliances and energy consumptions for advanced houses

appliance	kWh/year	(kWh/day)
refrigerator	240	0.66
cooking stove	780	2.14
clothes washer (excluding hot water)	144	0.39
clothes dryer	1,140	3.12
dishwasher (excluding hot water)	252	0.69
television	312	0.85
heat distribution system (furnace fan(s), water circulating pump(s), etc.)	1,512	4.14
heat-recovery ventilator fans and electric defrost units (if used)	631	1.73
vacuum cleaner	96	0.26
clocks (2)	96	0.26
iron	90	0.25
total	5,293 kWh/year (14.49 kWh/day)[67]	

This total is quite shocking when one realizes that it is meant to represent the most energy-efficient house designs in Canada, but it does highlight the national differences in energy use. It should be realized that this figure of 14.49 kWh/day refers only to appliances, and does not include lighting or occupants. Taking Shurcliff's figure for occupants (8.5 kWh/day) and the figure suggested above for lights (3.0 kWh/day) would make a total daily gain for the advanced houses of about 26.0 kWh/day, not a large saving compared with Shurcliff's figure for a conventional house. It should also be noticed that the advanced houses are assumed to use electricity at the rate of 172.5 W for the 'heat distribution system', and 72 W for the 'heat-recovery ventilator fans'. Canadian houses generally use ducted hot-air heating, so both these figures reinforce the comments made earlier about the inefficiency of AC mains-operated fans. The figure for heat distribution is the largest single electricity consumption in the list, and may be compared with a typical UK central-heating pump for pumping water through a system of radiators which has a consumption of only 40 W. The North American tradition of blown-air central heating is clearly leading to higher than necessary energy consumption: 1,512 kWh/year compared with a maximum possible 350 kWh for a water-based central heating system using radiators (assuming that the pump runs all year in a domestic hot-water mode). This demonstrates the importance of questioning the national traditions that exist in the servicing of houses, as other cultures may offer much more efficient ways of doing the same thing.

Schick et al. of the Small Homes Council of the University of Illinois[68] give a value for useful heat gains of 51,000 Btu/day (14.95 kWh), which may be more relevant to the United Kingdom as it refers to small homes. It can also be compared with the European value of 15 kWh established by Goulding et al. with data from nine different sources (a rate of 625 W).[69] They break this figure down as shown in Table 4.26.

Table 4.26: Heat gains in European houses

	kWh/day	(watts)
occupants	4.0	167
lighting	1.5	63
appliances and cooking	6.5	270
hot water	3.0	125
total	15.0 kWh/day	(625 W)

This list raises some interesting differences when compared with the figures given by Shurcliff and listed in Table 4.24. The gains from people in the European houses are half those from people in the American houses, and the hot-water heat gain of the European house is, surprisingly, twice that of the American one. In a survey of 31 solar houses in Europe, Palz and Steemers state: 'In addition, all activities of the occupants in the building generate some heat – estimated between 2,000 kWh/year to 8,000 kWh/year for single family houses.'[70] These figures give a range from 5.5 kWh/day to 21.9 kWh/day; the upper figure begins to approach that of the US data given by Shurcliff. The analysis of the data for heat gains from various sources makes clear that heat gains vary greatly, both geographically and within regions. Table 4.27 sets out the various heat gains given in the examples above.

Table 4.27: Heat gains to a typical house and adjusted pro rata *figures for the hypothetical room*

source of data	kWh/day to house	watts to house	kWh/day to room	watts to room
Palz and Steemers (low)	5.48	228	1.07	44
single male at rest	n/a	n/a	2.76	115
advanced houses	14.49	604	2.82	117
Schick et al.	14.95	623	2.91	121
Goulding et al.	15.00	625	2.92	122
Palz and Steemers (high)	21.92	913	4.26	178
Shurcliff	35.02	1459	6.81	284
(Gormenghast cats	474.95	19,790	92.35	3,848)

Note: the values from various sources have been assumed, arbitrarily, to apply to a house with 90 m² of floor area. The value for a single male has been assumed to apply only to the room.

Excluding the cats, the highest quoted gains are over six times greater than the lowest. Assuming the value of 15 kWh/day quoted by Goulding et al. to be appropriate for a typical European house, because three examples are around this figure, and a total house floor area of 90 m², the room used in these calculations will have casual heat gains of 2.92 kWh/day on a *pro rata* basis, or 122 W. It can be seen that, given sufficient insulation, it could be possible for the casual heat gains to meet the thermal requirements of the room, which were shown earlier to be 10.47 W/K for the highly insulated room. At a temperature difference of 21K however, the heat loss from the room becomes 220 W, which would give a figure for heating demand of 5.28 kWh/day. At first sight, the body heat from a seated male occupant (115 W), or the middle-range gains typified by the data from Goulding et al. (as well as the Advanced Houses Program and Schick et al.) are insufficient to meet the heat demand of the room when the temperature difference is 21K. This problem could be overcome in a number of ways; the single occupant could turn on a 100-W lightbulb, which would require electricity; or share the room with a friend (a total of 230 W, if both are male and at rest); or increase heat output by doing something more active (cooking or housework at least).

At this point the calculations of thermal mass made earlier come into play. Table 4.11 showed the conclusions that were reached about the thermal mass of various constructional options for the hypothetical room. It gave a range of thermal storage values from 0.21 kWh/K for the low-mass room to 4.60 kWh/K for the high-mass room, with Lund's theoretical house at 9.51 kWh/K. Taking the 10K temperature range mentioned earlier (that was suggested by Lund for his high-mass superinsulated house), over a range of internal temperatures from 27°C to 17°C, means that the high-mass room could store 46 kWh in its fabric. Based on 2,373 degree days, its heat loss would be 596 kWh over the heating season, and its heat gain, from a single male occupant with no lights or appliances (115 W) would be, over the same period of 212 days, 585 kWh, giving a thermal shortfall over the heating season of only 11 kWh. Of course, this assumes that the occupant never leaves the room, or else replaces absences by some more vigorous activity to add back the missing heat gain. The rôle of the thermal mass is to store the heat input from times when it is not needed for space heating (this could be referred to as charging the mass, analogous to charging a battery) and re-emit it at times when the gains are insufficient to meet the demand (discharging the mass). At an internal temperature of 17°C (Lund's low-point temperature) and an external temperature of 0°C, the heat loss from the room is 4,272 Wh/day; when the internal temperature is 27°C the heat loss from the room is 6,785 Wh/day. The mean of these two values is 5,529 Wh, which could be used as a very crude approximation of the effect of the changing temperature on the dynamic heat loss of the room as the thermal mass is discharged. If the heat gain from the occupant is 2,760 Wh/day, the shortfall of 2,769 Wh/day could be made up by discharging the mass, which would provide enough stored heat to meet the heat shortfall for slightly less than two days per degree of temperature drop of the storage. Discharging the mass over the full 10K range would provide heat for 17 days of freezing external temperature.

This admittedly crude calculation is also made without any allowance made for passive solar gains (which cannot be counted on in the United Kingdom in the middle of winter), or gains from any lights and appliances which might tend to offset the heat loss. The discussion here serves to clarify why mass is so necessary in the autonomous house; it is the element that enables the house to survive the coldest periods without recourse to external energy sources.

Some caveats with reference to heat gains

In an autonomous house, which attempts to use no fossil fuels, the availability of heat gains from lights and appliances may be limited, particularly since examples of ultra-low-energy appliances may be chosen to reduce the need for electricity generation and possibly electrical storage equipment. For example, the refrigerator for the Advanced Houses Program in Canada is assumed to use 240 kWh/year, giving a potential heat gain of 0.66 kWh/day (see Table 4.25) If an energy-efficient model, such as the Bosch KDR 3700 (364 l net capacity, 10/10 EU energy rating)[71] is used, the electricity required will amount to only 0.36 kWh/day, or 131 kWh/year. The halving of the electricity consumption will represent a useful saving in terms of the house's total energy consumption, which will reduce the cost of providing this electricity from non-fossil sources. However, it will also represent a reduction in the heat available for meeting the heat demand of the building.

A further caveat is necessary in considerations of heat gains from lights and appliances, since the essence of an autonomous house is to minimize total energy requirements, on account of its need to operate from diffuse income energy sources such as solar or wind power. The data quoted above for casual heat gains (summarized in Table 4.27) assume a house that is fully mains connected. This means that some of the space-heating energy demand offset by the casual gains is being made up by mains electricity – certainly that portion of it related to 'lights and appliances', and quite possibly the water heating and cooking as well. If this house were to have gas-fired central heating, the electrically derived component of the casual gains would have a higher carbon dioxide emission penalty than the space-heating energy that it displaces, as was shown above in Table 4.20. It is important in the case of the autonomous house to consider the total energy demand of the building, rather than selected sectors of that demand. One could, in theory, have a house which claimed 'zero-space-heating' energy demand solely on the basis of a high rate of electrical appliance use. Such a house could reduce its total primary energy demand and its carbon dioxide emissions by the apparently contradictory step of installing gas-fired central heating and high-efficiency appliances. The appliances would use less electricity and therefore create less casual gain, while the shortfall in casual gains would be made up by the installation of the central heating, with its lower carbon dioxide emission rate per useful kilowatt hour compared to electricity. This situation is summed up well by Abel:

> When low-energy buildings are planned and constructed and when
> demonstration projects in the low-energy building area are evaluated, it is
> important that the term 'low-energy' is clearly defined in each case. It should

be made clear whether the goal is to minimize the need for: heat only,
electrical energy only, or both heat and electrical energy. It should also be
made clear whether the goal is to minimize the amount of energy required for
the operation of the building, or to find solutions that make the building more
or less self-supporting from an energy point of view. It is also important to
verify whether energy costs are to be taken into consideration or if the financial
aspects are of less importance compared to other possible gains.

An analysis of discussions and papers about low-energy buildings, as well as
different low-energy building projects, indicates that the ideas behind
demonstration projects are often based on a few fundamental conditions.
Usually, however, these conditions are not accounted for explicitly, but,
nevertheless, they do exist. This can lead to misunderstandings and
conclusions which can be misleading. If, for instance, the low-energy
technology studied focuses on heat or fuels only, without taking into
consideration what happens with the electricity requirements, the results
obtained and the experience gained are questionable. This can be avoided if
the goal of the project and the conditions which form the basis thereof are
clearly defined in advance.[72]

A good example of this problem can be seen in the case of the Caer Llan Berm House in Gwent.[73] This is an extension to a field studies centre in Wales, and provides guest bedrooms and bathrooms in a single-storey earth-sheltered (or 'bermed') structure of relatively modest thermal mass. The Caer Llan house is described as 'probably the first domestic scale building in the United Kingdom to have achieved zero space heating demand'.[74] The building comprises a row of seven double bedrooms with en-suite bathrooms, plus a staff bed-sitter. The dimensions of the bedrooms, 2.4×5.4 m (including the bathroom areas), are not dissimilar to those used for the hypothetical room in this study, and give a floor area for each room of 13 m^2. The total floor area of the building is 363 m^2, but the area of the bedrooms and the bed-sitter, the 'heated' part of the building, is 115.6 m^2. Assuming that all rooms are fully occupied, there are 16 people in this area, giving a heating rate of 1,840 W. In a typical house with 90 m^2 of heated floor area there might be five people, or one person per 18 m^2. In the Berm House there is one person per 7.2 m^2 of heated space. Adjusted to the same area as the hypothetical room, this gives a heating rate of 279 W, well over the energy needed for the room. The mass of internal partitions and floor evens out the daily heat flows in the bedrooms, which show an annual temperature range of 17.5°C to 24.5°C. The access corridor is not intended to provide full comfort conditions, and has a low temperature of 14°C.

The problem of definition pointed out by Abel above is clear in the case of the Berm House. It is included in the *Review of Ultra-Low-Energy Homes* made for the Building Research Energy Conservation Support Unit (BRECSU); yet it is a quite different building from the other examples in that publication, being more analogous to a hotel. It has an occupancy rate considerably greater than that of a conventional house, giving potentially high thermal gains, and its cooking, domestic hot-water and appliance loads are provided by the adjacent field studies centre. The structure is claimed, in the BRECSU *Review,* to have a total electricity consumption of 14 kWh/m²/year, of which 5 kWh/m²/year is for ventilation. On this basis, a conventional house, assuming a floor area of 90 m², would have an electricity consumption of 1,260 kWh/year, but as this level of electricity consumption provides only the lighting and ventilation for the Berm House, a meaningful comparison with a normal house cannot be made. The *Review* also fails to make clear whether the electricity consumption data apply to the whole floor area, given as 363 m², or only to that part of the building, the bedrooms, which is kept at reasonable temperatures in the winter; the rest of the Berm House is corridor, workshop, toilet and storage. The *Review* makes clear that the temperature in the corridor is allowed to fall much lower than that in the rooms, and lower than any part of a normal house would be expected to reach.

The only way to test the performance of the Berm House is to make calculations based on the information given. Taking the notionally heated area of the Berm House, and assuming that each room contains two people for eight hours a day, plus the electrical demand for lighting of 9 kWh/m²/year (the total demand less the figure given above for the ventilation component of that demand), the total thermal gains, excluding solar, can be calculated as 17.57 kWh/day. This represents a heating rate of 6.33 W/m². Adjusted to the same floor area as the hypothetical room used earlier, this gives a rate of 111 W. Comparison with the values given in Table 4.27 shows that this is a relatively low value for heat gains, so the achievement of zero space heating claimed for the Berm House is an impressive achievement, and reinforces what has been said about the hypothetical room and the benefits of thermal mass. The Berm House is probably performing better than this calculation suggests, as it is unlikely that all the rooms are occupied by two people all the time, and the actual heat outputs from people asleep are likely to be lower than if they are awake. However, because of the differences between the Berm House and a normal house, no comparisons can be made in overall performance, since the Berm House does not provide many of the services (cooking, appliances, hot water) that are provided in a conventional dwelling. Any figures for its electrical consumption, for example, cannot be compared with any other house, as it is part of a much larger complex which is providing services by conventional means.

In energy terms, the goal of the autonomous house is to eliminate fossil-fuel use and the associated carbon dioxide emissions. This means that *all* energy consumption must be considered in the calculations, not just space heating. The autonomous house must supply hot water, cooking, lights and appliances from non-fossil-fuel sources, as well as maintaining thermal comfort for its occupants.

SERVICES

The various servicing options for an autonomous house will be analyzed in order of energy intensity, based on typical energy intensities for a conventional house in the United Kingdom. Those services that are not obviously based on energy, such as water and sewage treatment, are dealt with at appropriate points.

Space heating

Probably the most complex space-heating system of any 'autonomous' house that has been built so far is the one used in the Autonomous Solar House constructed by the Fraunhofer Institute in Freiburg, Germany. This uses photovoltaic panels to produce electricity, which in turn is used in an electrolysis cell to produce hydrogen and oxygen from water. The hydrogen is produced when the sun is shining and is used as the fuel for space heating when there is a demand in mid-winter that cannot be met by the passive solar design of the house.[76] Similar complexities are seen in the designs for active solar-powered space-heating systems such as those proposed in the apparently simple autonomous houses designed by Gerrard Crouch[77] and Brenda Vale[78] at the University of Cambridge in 1972. Studies made of solar houses in operation have also tended to show that many of these display considerable complexity in their systems (see, for example, Palz and Steemers).[79]

In spite of this tendency towards complexity, some authorities have suggested that a simpler approach may yield benefits. Bainbridge proposed that passive solar systems were preferable to complex active systems: 'This bias towards expensive and complex hardware is representative of a much larger problem that has diverted attention from passive solar systems to active solar systems and other more expensive energy alternatives such as nuclear power.'[80] Bainbridge suggests that social pressures lead designers to seek complex solutions to design problems: 'To be successful in academia and socially prominent one cannot study simple problems with simple solutions, for if everyone can understand them you are no longer an expert.'[81]

Given that the design of the autonomous house described here is intended to be based on the concept of alternative rather than advanced technology, it would seem that the simplest possible space-heating system should be employed. This will reduce both complexity and cost, as the problem with many solar houses in the past has been the need to incorporate an auxiliary space-heating system to provide heat when the solar input is insufficient. This adds to the cost of the project, as effectively the building is being provided with two separate heating systems, each with its own components. The cheapest heating system is none, and this was the intended design strategy.

The simplest way forward appeared to be that of minimizing the demand for heat through the use of high levels of insulation, as described earlier. In the United Kingdom, the passive solar approach of using the solar gain through south-facing windows appears to be marginal in terms of useful energy gains, compared to the energy savings that can be achieved by the use of adequate insulation. Simulations prepared for the large Pennyland passive solar housing demonstration project in Milton Keynes, and subsequent monitoring, clearly showed the effectiveness of insulation in a UK Midlands climate, and the small contribution that could be added by the passive solar measures (see, for example, Everett).[82] If an autonomous house requires some sort of back-up heating on top of what can be achieved by good insulation plus sensible passive solar design, a system that does not use any form of non-renewable fuel should be used; this means that the heating will have to be solar- or biomass-powered.

A solar-based system does not necessarily require solar collectors, which suffer from the obvious problem that the periods of maximum sunshine and maximum heat demand are six months out of phase. Another way to utilize solar energy is through wind, generated in the world's weather system, which is driven by the sun. A system installed by Brenda and Robert Vale in their highly insulated Cambridgeshire house in the 1970s (a Victorian house converted to low-energy operation) used a 5-kW three-bladed wind turbine to supply electricity to a number of domestic storage heaters, of the type developed for off-peak electric heating. This system had the benefit of a good match between periods of high heat demand and periods of electricity availability, and the heaters provided thermal storage over a period of about 24 hours.[83] The reliability of the aerogenerator, made by Elektro of Winterthur, Switzerland, proved to be the greatest problem, and it suffered two catastrophic failures, probably caused by vibration. This installation was in a rural area; the biggest problem with the use of such a system, assuming reliable equipment, might be its acceptability in a more urban environment. Although Montgomery claims that 'wind utilization at a domestic scale has no serious aesthetic disadvantages',[84] many planning officers in the United Kingdom would appear to disagree.

To allow an estimate of wind turbine size to be made, it is necessary to have an estimate of the power produced. At the early planning stage a simple estimate is adequate. Measured data from individual manufacturers would be required for detailed design, together with an on-site wind survey for at least a year, although many manufacturers use computer-based wind simulation software that they claim can give accurate forecasts of available energy from knowledge of site location alone (see, for example, Petersen et al.).[85] The amount of power that can be generated by a given wind turbine will vary according to the site and the particular machine specified, but some idea of the range of outputs can be found. Walker[86] gives a measured figure of 1,400 kWh of energy produced annually per kilowatt of installed wind turbine capacity in an area of low average windspeed (3.8 m/sec). This is based on trials of a 7.5-kW Allgaier machine at Cranfield in Bedfordshire. Gipe[87] gives values based on rotor diameter for the outputs of a range of wind turbines currently available. Using Gipe's additional table of wind turbine capacity versus rotor diameter, it is possible to construct a table of electricity outputs per kilowatt of wind turbine capacity for a range of domestic scale turbines as follows.

Table 4.28: Estimated energy output of wind turbines in kWh/year and (kWh/year/kW)

average windspeed	rotor diameter in metres – capacity in kW		
	1.0 m – 0.25 kW	3.0 m – 1.5 kW	7.0 m – 10 kW
9 mph (4.0 m/sec)	150 (600)	1,300 (867)	7,000 (700)
10 mph (4.5 m/sec)	200 (800)	1,800 (1,200)	10,000 (1,000)
11 mph (4.9 m/sec)	240 (960)	2,200 (1,467)	13,000 (1,300)

Gipe suggests considerably lower outputs than those measured by Walker, roughly half in the case of the lowest of Gipe's windspeed bands.

Costs for wind turbines will vary according to the individual manufacturer, but Akbarzadeh[88] quotes a price of $Aus 3,000/kW (approximately £1,050/kW, currency rates as at September 1998) for a machine with an output of 1–3 kW, plus $Aus 8,000 (approximately £2,800) for an 18-m high hinged tower to mount it on. A 13-m tower is only $Aus 2,900, but the high tower would be needed in a built-up area to get the turbine out of the disturbed airflow resulting from neighbouring buildings. This is clearly not a low-cost option, and experience with operating a wind generator of modest size[89] has shown that maintenance requirements may become quite excessive. More recent machines are claimed to need less maintenance; Schaeffer et al. say of the Bergey range of wind turbines: 'Recommended maintenance is this: once a year on a windy day, walk out to the tower and look up. If the blades are turning, everything is OK.'[90] This was confirmed on a visit to the rural campus of the Melbourne Methodist Ladies' College, MLC Marshmead, made on 27 May 1995. This school, which is off-the-grid and off-the-road, has an electrical system powered partly by an Australian built 10-kW Bergey/Westwind wind turbine. The machine had been in use for five years with no maintenance at all, and appeared to be in perfect condition.

It appears then that a wind generator is not an option for space heating on account of planning restrictions; active solar heating seems not to make sense because of the mis-match between supply of energy and demand for heat, while passive solar heating shares the disadvantage of active, plus the inability to supply a useful amount of energy. The fall-back position is probably to make use of some sort of biomass-derived fuel. The Forestry Commission in the United Kingdom[91] states that the growing of managed coppice as a fuel produces 30 kWh of energy for the input of 1 kWh in the form of fuel, fertilizers, the energy needed to make the tools and tractors, the fuel to run them, etc. Vale[92] found that a hectare of hazel coppice could yield 25,000 kg/year of air-dried wood, of sizes down to 10–12mm in diameter, on a ten-year rotation. A hectare of mixed English woodland by comparison, will produce 7,400 kg of wood.[93] As another comparison, a eucalyptus plantation in a tropical climate like Brazil can produce 30 tonnes/ha/year, and may even produce as much as 70 tonnes/ha/year on occasion.[94] The use of wood or other biomass as a fuel has the great advantage that it does not add carbon dioxide to the atmosphere. As Szokolay states: 'energy production (supply side) major improvements could be achieved by the substitution of biomass fuels, such as firewood ... The use of these will have no net effect on the atmosphere, as the CO_2 produced in combustion is the same quantity as that used in photosynthesis, in plant growth.'[95] The same conclusion is reached by the New Zealand Ministry of Commerce:

> ... biomass is likely to provide a carbon cycle neutral energy system. The carbon dioxide produced during combustion can be considered to be re-absorbed by new trees or the coppice regrowth that replaces the harvested fuel. The amount of fossil fuel needed to run a biomass system is thought to be around 5% of the calorific value of the biomass used (based on work at FRI [Forest Research Institute] in 1980).[96]

The figure for the energy consumed by a biomass energy system is close to that quoted above from the United Kingdom's Forestry Commission. The New Zealand Ministry of Commerce also sees the growing of fuel biomass as a way of handling sewage effluent, as the trees would be able to use the nutrients in the sewage, and the system would avoid the possible pathogen problems that might occur if sewage were to be used on food crops.[97]

Fig. 11
*The 10-kW
Bergey/Westwind
turbine at MLC
Marshmead*

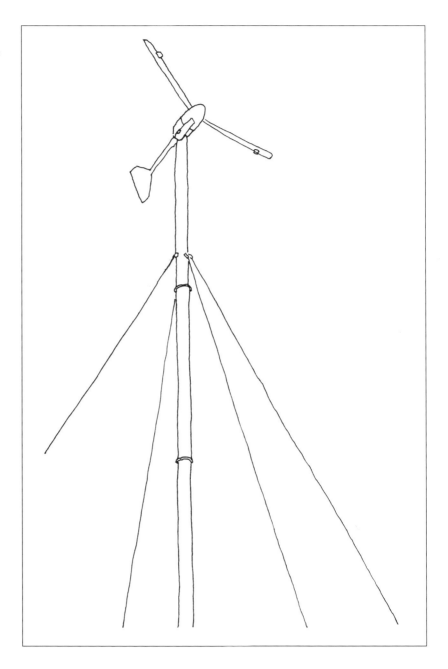

Wood is still widely used as a fuel in some developed countries. In New
Zealand in the domestic sector, wood is the second largest source of energy after
electricity, satisfying 34.9% of space-heating energy demand, compared with
39.8% from electricity. Electricity provides 71% of the total domestic-sector

energy consumption, and wood 14%, with the domestic sector representing 13% of total New Zealand energy use (– 1991 data from Massey University).[98] The 1986 census in New Zealand reported that 50% of houses used wood as a heating fuel.[99] For a single house the simplest method of using biomass fuels is in a wood-burning heating stove, but larger-scale installations have the possibility of creating a source of zero carbon dioxide electricity for back-up heating. Newark and Sherwood District Council in north Nottinghamshire is investigating the possibility of building small-scale local power stations, fired by coppiced timber, to supply electricity free of any possible future carbon tax to Council housing tenants. The scheme is based on power stations small enough to be within tractor-and-trailer range of the farms where the coppice would be grown, so that farmers can make use of their existing equipment to transport the fuel. The intention is to provide not only clean electricity, but also locally based long-term employment in energy production, following the demise of the local coal mines.[100] However, even if one does not have access to locally generated biomass electricity, the simple wood-burning stove offers quite good conversion efficiency from fuel to useful heat for an autonomous house: '... modern airtight wood stoves have seasonal efficiencies up to 65 percent.'[101]

The biggest problem of burning wood, which is particularly ironic considering its natural origin, is that of pollution. Todd[102] says that approximately 25% of households in Australia were using wood as space-heating fuel in 1988, consuming 4.4 million tonnes of air-dried wood annually, and he estimates that this figure has risen to 4.7 million tonnes. This is resulting in an annual emission of 50,000 tonnes of particulates, and has caused measurable atmospheric pollution in parts of Tasmania and elsewhere. Pollution can be cleaned up in a wood-fired power station by the use of conventional flue-gas cleaning technology, but on a small stove the problem is more difficult, and has led to the fitting of exhaust catalysts by some American manufacturers. In Australia the response has been to apply a new Australian Standard, AS4013, which has led to a design change in which the air supply to the stove cannot be turned off completely, as it has been found that emissions of particulates are highest when a stove is burning at its lowest setting. Todd's advice for the correct use of a stove is as follows:

Improving user behaviour, however, offers the best opportunity for a rapid decrease in smoke emissions ... telephone surveys have shown most people do not follow all the best practices in operating a woodheater. The most common failing is to set the combustion control for a medium or slow burn immediately after reloading the heater. This usually leads to a period of high smoke emissions as the stove smoulders away for hours. A far better approach is to leave the combustion air inlet on fast burn for 20 minutes or so and turn it down only when the new load of fuel is burning well. Overloading the heater so that there is no space left in the combustion chamber for gas and air to mix and burn is another common fault, but there are many others as well. Changing user behaviour can halve emissions.[103]

If the stove is being used as the back-up heating for a more or less zero-energy house, the pollution problem is reduced, compared with the use of a wood burner to replace the total heating of an uninsulated house, as the stove will be running for a far smaller amount of time in the autonomous house.

The conclusion from this discussion of space heating for an autonomous house is that the easiest and cheapest option is to aim to design for no space heating, other than what can be provided by heat gains from the occupants, coupled with simple direct passive solar energy through the glazing. This approach reinforces the idea of a very high level of insulation, coupled with high thermal mass. As a fall-back position, a wood-burning stove seems the most appropriate way of providing small amounts of renewable energy for heating on an intermittent basis. The wood stove would have the added advantage that it could be used on a more regular basis for drying out a high-mass structure – masonry construction inevitably has a high moisture content, from the mortar, the plaster, and rainfall absorbed in walls and slabs before the roof is in place – during its first year or two of operation.

Water and sewage treatment

One side of the argument for autonomous servicing is financial: the cost of many normal services is now considerable. For example, in the United Kingdom '... since 1989–90 average bills for water and sewerage have risen by 77 per cent and 70 per cent respectively, more than three times the rate of inflation.'[104] Water, once supplied for a fixed charge unrelated to use, is now metered like electricity, and is becoming an expensive commodity. The other side of the argument for autonomous servicing is the question of whether the environment can sustain the demands made on it by conventional servicing. Examples of water shortages are seen in the United Kingdom fairly regularly, in spite of the country's traditional rainy reputation.[105] Other industrialized and densely populated countries have similar problems. For example, Japan increased its rate of domestic water consumption from 169 l/head to more than 300 l/head in the period from 1965 to 1991, and the increased extraction of groundwater has resulted in increasing water shortages.[106] In the United Kingdom, the announcement by the managing director of the then recently privatized Yorkshire Water that he had not taken a bath or shower for three months during the drought of summer 1995 was even the subject of an editorial in *The Times*.[107]

One way to reduce domestic water consumption would be to reduce the use of water for flushing the toilet. In a typical four-person household in the United Kingdom, about 35% of the total daily water consumption of 440 l is used for flushing the toilet.[108] The use of a Swedish toilet, the Ifö Aqua, which flushes with 3.75 l of water rather than the 9 l of a typical UK cistern, can reduce the consumption of this hypothetical household by 90 l/day or 32,850 l/year. (35% of 440 l is 154 l; at 9 l per flush this represents 17.1 flushes/day, which would be 64 l/day using the Swedish technology.) The reduction in water consumption represents a saving of about 20% of total consumption. These toilets have been used in a pair of Housing Association houses designed by Brenda and Robert Vale at Cresswell Road in Sheffield, and have been operating successfully for several years.[109] The use of Swedish toilets in these houses has been combined with the provision of rainwater collection and storage to provide water for gardening, to show an overall saving of 114 l/day, or nearly 42,000 l/year (calculated saving based on data from Table 2.10 in Wise).[110] The financial savings to the tenants are small, as water costs are still relatively low in comparison with other utilities, but with a typical household in the Yorkshire Water region being charged £200 per annum for water (according to the table of water costs from Nicholson-Lord),[111] the reduction of this cost by 26% might show a saving of roughly £1/week. For a low-income household this is a useful cash saving that can be achieved at little or no cost by careful design.

Conventional systems for the disposal of sewage have two principal drawbacks. The first is that they waste the potential fertility contained in the sewage. Western agriculture in the 20th century has been based on the use of fertilizers made from oil and natural gas, with the result that the energy provided to the consumer by food is considerably less than the energy put into the food in the form of non-renewable resources. For example, Chapman gives the thermal energy required to produce a loaf of bread as 5.6 kWh,[112] whereas the quoted calorific value to the consumer of an 800-g Sainsbury's medium sliced wholemeal loaf is 896 kJ/100 grams, giving a value for the whole loaf of 7.168 MJ, or 1.99 kWh.[113] A loaf of similar size and type from the Co-op quotes a value of 912 kJ/100 grams, to give an energy content per loaf of 7.296 MJ, or 2.03 kWh.[114] It can be assumed then that the average loaf of commercial bread provides the consumer with around 2.0 kWh of food energy. Chapman breaks down the energy used to produce a loaf as shown in Table 4.29 overleaf.

If sewage were to be available as fertilizer, it could reduce the energy content of the loaf by 11.6% by replacing the fossil-fuel-based fertilizer. For less processed foods, such as fruit and vegetables, this percentage should be higher, as the fertilizer would represent a larger proportion of the total energy needed to supply the foods to the consumer. The largest single component of the energy content

Table 4.29: Energy breakdown of a standard white loaf of bread

farm	fertilizer	11.6%
	tractor fuel	7.3%
	other	0.4%
mill	transport	1.4%
	other	2.0%
	milling fuel	7.4%
	packaging	2.2%
bakery	transport	5.0%
	other ingredients	9.4%
	baking fuel	23.6%
	packaging	8.3%
retail	transport	12.2%
	shop heat and light	8.6%[115]

of the loaf is the energy used to bake it. Leach[116] gives 'energy ratios' (energy out to energy in) for a number of crops grown in the United Kingdom, as well as details of the total energy input to the crop, and from these it is possible to work out the inputs of manufactured fertilizers as shown in Table 4.30.

It should be borne in mind that these figures are for produce to the farm gate (or the factory gate in the case of sugar), and that the figures for the farm crops, if not the allotment, will be altered by transport and packaging. Even some fresh vegetables (peas and Brussels sprouts) use more energy to grow than they give to those who eat them, as shown by Leach's energy ratios. A figure less than 1.0 shows that it takes more energy to produce the crop than it provides to the consumer; winter lettuce is clearly an energy disaster. Leach has also calculated the energy ratio attributable to 'all food supply, UK, 1968' as 0.2.[118] This means that the overall embodied-energy content of the UK diet is five times the energy that it contains as food, energy that is derived from non-renewable resources. This figure is likely to have increased since 1968 due to the increase in production of processed, and therefore more energy-intensive foods, and is applicable to any country operating a modern system of agricultural production.

Table 4.30: Fertilizer as a percentage of total energy in a crop

crop	energy ratio	total energy input GJ/ha	kWh/ha	fertilizer as % of total
field beans, spring 1971	4.50	11.69	3,250	39%
sugar beet, 1968–72	4.20	27.39	7,614	56%
(sugar from beet	0.67	124.40	34,583	12%)
average potatoes, 1968–72	1.57	36.15	10,050	52%
carrots, 1971	1.10	27.59	7,670	33%
fresh peas, 1971	0.94	10.93	3,039	11%
Brussels sprouts, 1971	0.19	47.94	13,327	57%
winter lettuce, 1971–72 (in heated greenhouse)	0.0023 −0.0017	4550 −6060	1,264,900 −1,684,680	0–0.2%
allotment garden, 1974	1.30	46.00	12,788	70%[117]

In an environmentally conscious world it should be possible to regard sewage as a resource to be used rather than as a waste to be disposed of, as it is clear that its use could provide significant energy savings as a replacement for manufactured fertilizers. Leach quotes the following values for the energy content of typical fertilizers, bagged and delivered to the farm.

Table 4.31: Energy content of manufactured fertilizers in MJ/kg (kWh/kg)

nitrogen	80 (22.2)
phosphate	9 (2.5)
potash	2 (0.6)

Whereas the other two fertilizers are mined from natural deposits, nitrogen is manufactured from natural gas, a use which is in conflict with the use of the gas as a fuel.[119]

The second disadvantage of conventional sewage treatment, after the waste of its potential value as fertilizer is that it relies on purified drinking water for the transport of the 'wastes' from their point of production to the place of treatment. As discussed earlier, the water consumption for this purpose alone may account

Fig. 12
*The Clivus Multrum
compost unit in the
cellar of the
autonomous house*

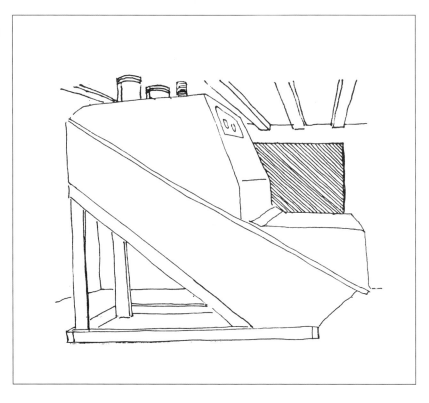

for 35% of the total water consumption of a typical UK household. As a comparison, the percentage of domestic water use for flushing the toilet reported for Germany is 32% (46 l/head/day out of a household total of 145 l/head/day).[120] There is no reason why this water needs to be of drinkable quality.

Options exist for replacing the water-borne sewage disposal system with a method that both avoids the need for water (thus reducing the need for water collection and storage) and enables the nutrients in the sewage to be retained for use as fertilizer. One of these is the Swedish Müllbank toilet, which was tested by the Royal Agricultural College of Sweden in 1975.[121] The toilet uses a 140-W electric heater, combined with a 21-W ventilation fan to accelerate the aerobic decomposition of the wastes that accumulate within it, and the output was deemed safe to use on garden plants and edible crops. The advantage of the Müllbank and similar units is that they are comparable in size to a conventional toilet, although taller and bulkier, and will thus fit in a bathroom. The BioLet, a similar device, is approved by the National Sanitation Foundation in the United States of America. The approved version, the Model XL, uses 370 W, but only 323 W continuously: the remaining 47 W operates the mixer motor that stirs the contents automatically.[122] For the designer of an autonomous house, the disadvantage is that these toilets need electricity to operate the heater that allows the toilet to be of smaller physical bulk by artificially speeding the decomposition of the wastes. The heater and fan of the 161-W Müllbank will need an electricity consumption of 3,864 Wh/day, or 1,410 kWh/year, a not insignificant load. The 370-W BioLet will use correspondingly more, although the heaters in it are controlled by a thermostat, which should reduce the consumption to some degree. Some manufactures offer 'non-electric' versions of their standard model. The BioLet NE (not NSF-approved) needs a drainage system for urine; alternatively, the urine can be allowed to collect in a container and then emptied onto a compost heap.[123]

The other contender in the waterless toilet options is the aerobic bulk-composting system, typified by the Clivus Multrum,[124] which avoids the need for electric heating by using a very large waste container, about the size of a small car, directly below the toilet seat. This allows a large enough volume of waste to be gathered together that conventional aerobic composting will take place over an extended period, as in a garden compost heap. The problem of electrical demand is exchanged in this device for the problem of space, as the unit will not fit in a conventional bathroom. Even with the Clivus, although it does not have a heater element, it is recommended that an electric fan be installed for continuous ventilation (although this is a 5-W DC version,[125] with an annual electricity consumption of 44 kWh).

The treatment of sewage is only part of the water cycle that must be provided for a domestic situation. An autonomous house which uses a waterless toilet will need a supply of water for drinking, washing and all other household needs. If a well is unavailable (and a well is a solution that would be very site-dependent), this supply will have to come from collected rainwater. There is little literature on the use of rainwater for domestic water supply in industrialized countries, but a Canadian report states that '... the quality of water draining from roofs and gutters of acceptable materials was well within the limits set by Health and Welfare Canada in *Guidelines for Canadian Drinking Water Quality*.'[126] A UK study by Fewkes and Turton at the Nottingham Trent University looked at the collection of rainwater in the Nottingham area, initially as a source of water for toilet flushing. Surprisingly, they found that '... the physical and chemical characteristics of the roof waste from both tanks, excepting turbidity, complied with the minimum WHO [World Health Authority] standards for drinking water.'[127] This would appear to suggest that the use of rainwater for purposes other than toilet flushing might be a reasonable proposition, even in the United Kingdom's East Midlands, where the presence of a number of coal-fired power stations concentrated in the Trent Valley might lead to an expectation of high levels of water pollution.

On Waiheke Island in the Hauraki Gulf of New Zealand's North Island, 35 minutes commuting time from central Auckland by fast ferry, there is a community of people (the population was given in the 1991 census as 5,391)[128] who have no mains water supply at all, and who rely on water collected from their roofs, or from boreholes. The annual rainfall is about 760 mm, and each house typically has a 25,000-l storage tank. These used to be made of reinforced concrete but the more recent ones are moulded polyethylene, with a wall thickness of 10mm. The concrete tanks, which cost the same as the plastic ones, are still popular on the island, although they can crack. The plastic tanks carry a 25-year guarantee.

The cheapest tanks available are made on the island by rolling corrugated galvanized-steel sheets to form a cylinder of the required size, soldering on a flat galvanized-steel base and lid, and soldering a number of cylinders end-to-end to achieve the required capacity.

No attempt is made to keep the water cool, and the majority of the tanks stand outside at the side of the house, on the ground. The only Local Authority regulations for the systems are concerned with the size of individual tanks; no single tank may be over 5,000 gallons (approximately 25,000 l) without a permit, to ensure the structural integrity of the tank. Obtaining a permit is an expensive and time-consuming process, and most permanent residents on Waiheke Island (which also has many holiday homes, or 'baches') use one or more 25,000-l tanks. The corrugated tanks are popular with bach owners because their appearance is part of the traditional New Zealand vernacular, but they must be carefully sited to minimize rusting. The tank should sit on tarpaper on a Tanalized wooden platform, i.e., one where the wood has been treated with Tanalith, a copper chrome arsenate (CCA) preservative. Between the tank and the platform is a layer of tarpaper to prevent the Tanalith from rusting the steel. Rainwater only should be used with steel tanks as bore water is corrosive on account of its iron content.

Because tanks are classed as non-permanent structures they can be sited only 400 mm from a site boundary, whereas the usual limit for buildings is 1,500 mm. The 25,000-l tanks weigh about 300 kg, and are transported to site on a purpose-made trailer. Waiheke is extremely hilly, and many of the driveways to houses have a slope of 1 in 4, but no difficulty seems to occur with the installation of tanks where required. The water is collected in guttering in the normal way, with PVC being the most popular guttering material. The island has some areas which are heavily wooded, and various types of leaf grids are employed to keep leaves out of the gutters and hence out of the water supply. The water is fed to the house (or restaurant, hotel, supermarket, etc.: the tanks are not only used in domestic situations) by one of two types of pumping system. These employ

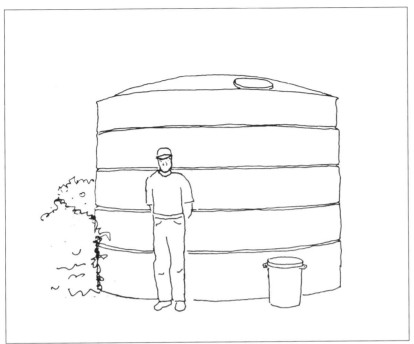

Fig. 13
Dr David Leifer of the Department of Architecture, University of Auckland, standing by his 25,000-l plastic water tank on Waiheke Island

Fig. 14
Making galvanized tanks on Waiheke Island

SIZE	DIAMETER	HEIG...
5000	3.43	2.44
3000	3.43	1.55
2000	2.20	2.4...
1000	1.83	1.08

Fig. 15
A water tanker
service

either a pressure pump which is activated as soon as a tap is turned on, and supplies water direct, or a header tank at high level, fed by a pump and ball valve. The header tank, where the design of the building permits its use, was the more popular method, as the island used to have electric power cuts of 20 minutes duration about once a month. The recommended head for showers is 3.6 m, and the pumps have a life of 10–15 years in use.

People on the island are used to the idea that water is a scarce resource, and make attempts to control their consumption, by the use, for example, of dual-flush toilet cisterns. However, if a household runs out of water, there are three water suppliers on the island, all of whom have boreholes to obtain their water supplies. They carry the water in stainless-steel articulated tanker lorries and in 1995 charged $NZ52.00 for a load of about 5,500 l. This is a cost of $NZ9.45 (approximately £3.20 in 1995) for one cubic metre of water, considerably more than the cost of a cubic metre of mains water in the United Kingdom.

Filtration or any other form of treatment of the water is often not considered necessary; 99% of systems are used without filtration. The island is free of possums (imported into New Zealand from Australia in the past) which are a serious pest, because they eat the native trees and the newly planted forests. Their droppings are a common hazard for users of rainwater systems in other parts of New Zealand, as is the finding of a dead possum in the water tank. The only perceived problem on Waiheke is seagulls (particularly *Larus novaehollandiae scopulinus*),[129] which sit on roofs and leave their droppings. Mosquito larvae can also be a problem sometimes, but this is usually due to badly designed installation with exposed areas of water surface in the tank. The tanks have access lids, and are cleaned by sucking out the sediment at the bottom with a swimming-pool vacuum cleaner. The supply of tanks, pumps, filters (if wanted), gutters and leaf grids, a cleaning service and the other components of an autonomous water system has led to the establishment of a small local industry on the island, and elsewhere in New Zealand, where similar systems are very common away from urban areas.[130]

The use of unfiltered water collected directly from roofs (particularly roofs frequented by seagulls) might be expected to give rise to health problems. To ascertain if this were the case, interviews were conducted with a number of health workers, both on Waiheke Island and in the city of Auckland. Yvonne Maguire, the New Zealand Registered Nurse at the Red Cross Medical Centre in Oneroa, which is the largest settlement on Waiheke, had been working there for ten years at the time of the interview. She said that she could not attribute any recognizable health problems to the water systems; most intestinal problems were related to campylobacter which is found in infected food. There were about six cases every year of giardia, a disease which can be related to bird droppings and dead animals. This has been considered hard to diagnose in the past, but can be treated successfully once diagnosed. It is now more widely recognized, leading to earlier diagnosis. It is caused by an organism that is not flushed from the body by the diarrhoea the organism causes (unlike many similar diarrhoea-causing organisms), so it tends to erupt at intervals until diagnosed and treated.[131] Jim Graham, the Health Protection Officer for Auckland Public Health Office, said that no specific data had been collected, but that very few cases of disease could be attributed to roof-collected water, although it might be suspected in some cases. There were cases of giardia in the Gulf Islands (which include Waiheke), but these were thought mostly to have been caused by person-to-person infection. On a personal basis, he preferred that rainwater systems used in-line filters to remove disease organisms where possible, but said that there was no legislation that controlled the use of rainwater. His personal view was in favour of rainwater systems, as they were often cheaper for the user, but official policy was that reticulated (mains supply) water was the better alternative wherever possible.[132]

For the United Kingdom some form of water filtration might be considered necessary, because of the greater population density and the consequent risk that the rainwater might be contaminated by atmospheric pollution. However, data collected by Fewkes and Turton suggest that this may be an unnecessary refinement. The United Kingdom does not have the robust tradition of backyard water tanks that makes unfiltered water supplies apparently acceptable to the

New Zealand public. In the United Kingdom it seems to be tradition that dictates the use of mains water, perhaps on account of the high urban densities and the outbreaks of cholera that occurred in the 19th century.

Domestic hot water

At first glance, the obvious choice for hot-water provision in an autonomous house would seem to be some form of solar panels. The United Kingdom's Building Research Establishment estimated over 20 years ago: 'A collector of roughly 6 m^2 in area positioned on the roof of a house will heat sufficient water to satisfy a household during most days in summer and over the year, assuming a mean efficiency of collection between 40 and 50 per cent, will provide about 7 GJ [approximately 1,950 kWh] of energy.'[133]

The problem with a solar hot-water system in the United Kingdom, as with solar space heating, is that the supply of solar radiation varies so widely from summer to winter. A south-facing roof in Manchester at a slope of 45° will receive a daily total (direct beam plus diffuse radiation) of 4.80 kWh/m^2 in June, but only 0.85 kWh/m^2 in December.[134] In spite of this variation, daily hot-water demand will remain more or less constant. This suggests, for an autonomous installation, the use of a large area of collectors, of the highest possible efficiency, and a considerable amount of storage, because the system has to be sized to meet a constant hot-water demand (estimated by the Building Research Establishment [BRE] in 1975 as 12 GJ/year, which works out to over 9 kWh/day)[135] during the least sunny month of the year. For the rest of the year the system is considerably over-sized. One way round this might lie with a combined wind/solar water-heating installation, but the use of two energy sources potentially doubles the cost. There can be a hidden energy penalty in the operation of a solar water heating system, and that is in the pump. As Wozniak explains: 'In a typical domestic solar system the requirement [for energy to pump the heat transfer fluid round the system] will be about 2 W, but a suitable centrifugal accelerator pump will consume about 30 W of electricity.'[136] In Manchester there are an average of 3.65 hours of sunshine per day, varying from 1.21 in December to 6.37 in June.[137] If the pump works only when the sun is shining, it will operate for 1,332 hours per year and consume 40 kWh of electricity.

Given that the use of a solar water-heating system will require the installation of a thermal store (to provide hot water when the sun is not shining); solar panels; a pump and interconnecting pipework; and a temperature controller (to ensure that the pump is turned on only when there is enough energy to be worth collecting), it may be worth looking at other, potentially simpler ways of producing hot water. One alternative would be to power the pump directly from a photovoltaic panel: it will then only pump when there is enough solar radiation.

Fig. 16
*Solar water heaters
in Cook, on the
Nullarbor Plain,
Australia, an ideal
setting on account
of high radiation*

It might be simpler, for example, if not cheaper, to use photovoltaic panels plus a conventional electric immersion heater for hot-water production, as this would avoid the need to pump a heat transfer fluid between the panels and the storage tank, and would eliminate the control system. The panels could then be sited wherever was convenient, as the only connection between the panels and the hot-water store would be a cable. The approximate annual yield from 1 kW of photovoltaics in the United Kingdom is quoted as 1,000 kWh.[138] To meet the BRE's target for domestic hot water supply of 12 GJ/year (3,336 kWh), one would need a photovoltaic system of roughly 3.34-kW capacity. A cost of £5,000 per kilowatt[139] means the system would be extremely expensive at £16,700, and would still suffer from the problems of seasonal mis-match that affect thermal solar-panel installations.

The seasonal performance might be improved to some extent by using a wind turbine as the energy source. The data for monthly wind speeds show that the variation is much less over the year than for solar energy; using Manchester again as the example, the average wind speed in December (the windiest month) is 5.1 m/sec, while in August (the least windy month) it is 3.8 m/sec.[140] Whereas the variation in sunshine hours is in a ratio of 1:5.3, the wind speed ratio is only 1:1.3. As shown above in Table 4.28, the annual yield from a turbine (assuming a relatively low wind speed area) could lie in the range 600–867 kWh/kW, meaning that a machine with a capacity of roughly 5 kW would be necessary, at a cost of at least £5,000 plus the tower on which it stands. It should also be realized that the output from a solar collector is directly proportional to the number of hours of bright sunlight, whereas the output from a wind turbine is proportional to the cube of the wind speed, which lowers the ratio of the worst month to best month to 1:2.4, and reduces the advantage of a wind system when compared to a solar-based system.

Both the photovoltaic and wind power systems for domestic hot-water provision would be even more effective if linked to a heat pump. Heat pumps for domestic hot-water supply have been manufactured in Australia for many years, and a current model has been tested as having an annual coefficient of performance (the ratio of electricity put in to useful heat taken out) of 3:1.[141] The use of such a device would reduce the hot-water energy demand of a typical household to 3 kWh/day, or 4 GJ/year. In recent times, a hot-water heat pump has not been commercially available in the United Kingdom, but EA Technology at Capenhurst has been working on an air-to-water heat pump for domestic hot-water supply, using air from a whole-house ventilation system as the heat input; the company reports coefficients of performance of between 3 and 4 in practice.[142] The use of a heat pump would reduce the cost and size of the photovoltaic or wind energy system by a factor of three, leading to a photovoltaic cost of perhaps £5,600 and a wind turbine cost (excluding tower) half of this amount.

Electricity

The concept of an autonomous house might seem at first to preclude a choice between mains- or battery-supplied electricity. Logically, an autonomous house cannot use mains electricity. However, if one considers the reasons for building the house, rather than the house as abstract concept, the question of electricity supply appears in a different light. The point of building an autonomous house is to eliminate reliance on non-renewable resources, and to minimize pollution; the use of mains electricity therefore becomes a possibility that must be considered.

The generation of electricity from renewable sources is a relatively straightforward process, using either a wind generator or photovoltaic panels (or both together) as the power source. The problem with these sources is that they do not generate continuously: the wind must blow and the sun must shine. Both

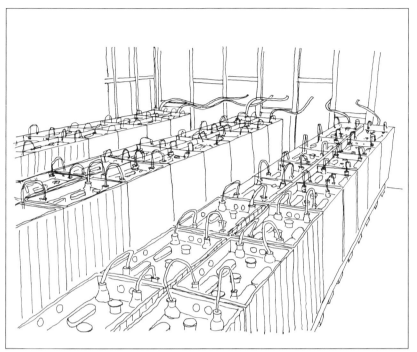

Fig. 17
A large Remote
Area Power System
battery bank at the
Methodist Ladies'
College (MLC)
Marshmead,
Australia

technologies need a method of storing the electricity for periods of no
generation, so that a continuous supply can be maintained, comparable with that
obtained from the mains. For a house in an urban setting in the United Kingdom,
wind power is probably out of the question as planning authorities would not
permit it. Of photovoltaics, the other possibility for generation, Rotchie et al. say:
'1 kg of pv [photovoltaic] cells will produce as much electricity in 20 years as 1 kg
of refined uranium fuel would in a nuclear power station.'[143]

Figures quoted earlier in Table 4.26 for a typical European house show a
demand of 6.5 kWh/day for appliances and cooking, and 1.5 kWh/day for lighting
– both of which might be provided by electricity in an autonomous house –
making a total demand of 8.0 kWh/day. Allowing for a period of zero energy
input to the system of 10 sunless days, a battery-based system will need to
provide storage of 80 kWh, or 67 100-Ah batteries at 12 V. However, battery
systems are more complex than this. The State Electricity Commission of
Victoria, Australia, and Energy Victoria produced guidelines for what are called
Remote Area Power Supply (RAPS) systems. These are defined as 'power
supplies for homes not connected to the State electricity system, or "grid"...
although many of these power supplies are not necessarily operating in areas
remote from towns.'[144] They recommend that batteries, to prolong their life,
should not be discharged beyond 50% of their capacity. This effectively doubles

the required size of the battery bank, and a typical European house would thus need a capacity of 160 kWh, or 133 batteries. It is also necessary to add in a loss factor for losses of energy in cables and in the inverter that produces alternating current to operate conventional domestic appliances from the batteries. These figures form the basis of the following calculation for battery capacity.

Table 4.32: Calculating battery capacity[145]

daily energy use	8,000.0 Wh
days of storage	10.0
loss factor	1.5
discharge depth factor	2.0

battery bank capacity = daily energy use × days of storage × loss factor × discharge depth factor
= 240,000 Wh

If the battery voltage is 240 V, the battery capacity will be 1000 Ah; if the voltage is 12 V, the battery capacity will be 20,000 Ah. In practice, the largest possible voltage would be used, and the battery would be assembled from a number of individual cells.

A 100-Ah 12-V gel electrolyte lead-acid battery costs roughly £100,[146] so the necessary capacity, excluding connections between the batteries would cost £20,000. There might be some reduction in cost for buying a large set of batteries, but the appropriate deep-cycle stationary batteries are more robustly constructed (thicker plates, space for sediment collection, etc.) than typical car starter batteries, and are less widely available; as a result, they tend to be expensive, even in quantity.

The other problems with batteries, apart from their price, are their maintenance; the materials from which they are made; and their life-span. The State Electricity Commission of Victoria is noticeably coy about battery life in its publication, limiting its comments to the following: '... it is not possible to give a definite period for the overall life of a RAPS battery. The experience of many RAPS owners has shown that battery lives have been many years in the majority of properly engineered and maintained systems.'[147]

Describing an operating domestic RAPS installation, Nguyen and Bolzon state the following: 'The battery system comprises 48 series connected BP PVSTOR 2-V 425-Ah capacity (C100 rate) lead-acid batteries which are housed in a separate enclosure. Cycle life as indicated by the manufacturer is 2,500 to 50 percent discharge. A warranty period of five years has been supplied by the

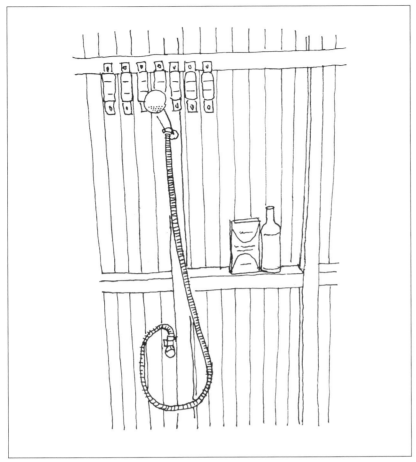

Fig. 18
A well-organized
battery room, with
spare fuses, shower
and bicarbonate of
soda for acid burns

manufacturer.'[148] If the batteries go through a cycle in a day (this will vary depending on both the system design and varying weather conditions), 2,500 cycles will represent something less than seven years. Even if the batteries have a life of ten years, the cost of replacing them per annum will be £2,000, irrespective of any consideration of the loss of income on the money that could be invested elsewhere. It is suggested that some types of batteries have a lifespan considerably in excess of ten years. The Real Goods Trading Corporation in the United States of America gives a life expectancy of '15 to 20 years or more' for steel-cased Pacific Chloride industrial batteries;[149] this figure was also quoted during visits to a number of RAPS installations in Australia. The installations tended to use very large banks of batteries that were operated generally at cycle depths of only about 20% of total capacity. Telecom Australia quotes a battery life of up to seven years on their solar-powered rural and transcontinental telephone lines, which are powered by over 2 MW of installed photovoltaic capacity.[150]

Clearly it would be possible to design a system where the electrical demand was reduced, so as to lessen the load to be met from battery storage, but there is still the inherent problem that the batteries are made of lead (other types are much more expensive), which is a toxic metal in terms of production and eventual disposal. Pratt makes the following comment on the problems of worn-out batteries:

> Batteries wear out, and when they do, they must not be disposed of carelessly. The active ingredients in these batteries, lead and sulfuric acid, can be highly toxic and dangerous and need to be handled with great respect.
> Every stream on the Hawaiian island of Maui, for example, has been found to contain certain trace poisons which can only result from the improper dumping of lead-acid batteries. In addition to posing a danger if it enters the water cycle, lead is considered a strategic metal, and has salvage value, so it should be recycled. Turn in old batteries for recycling at auto-parts stores or recycling centers. A majority of the lead in new car batteries comes from recycled batteries.[151]

Lave et al. take a less sanguine view of the wisdom of using large quantities of lead-acid batteries. Their paper in *Science* looked at the implication of increased use of electric cars (with lead-acid batteries) as a result of US 'zero-emissions' legislation in certain states. They concluded that the use of electric cars and the corresponding need to manufacture lead-acid batteries would result in considerable increases in lead emissions into the environment, from the mining, processing and recycling of the lead:

> A 1998 model electric car is estimated to release 60 times more lead per kilometer of use relative to a comparable car burning leaded gasoline. The United States banned TEL [tetra ethyl lead, the lead additive in leaded petrol] in large part for health reasons. Electric vehicles would introduce lead releases to reduce urban ozone, a lesser problem. These lead discharges would damage ecology as well as human health. Even with incremental improvements in lead-acid battery technology and tighter controls on smelters and lead reprocessors, producing and recycling these batteries would discharge large quantities of lead into the environment.[152]

The next day an article appeared in the *New Scientist*[153] saying that Lave et al. had grossly over-estimated the amount of batteries that would be used in a 1998 model electric car, and citing General Motors' experimental Impact model (later marketed as the EV1) as an example. Leuthold and Rossetti claim that 94% of the ingredients of a lead-acid battery in a polypropylene case can be recycled, as is shown in Table 4.33.

Table 4.33: Recycling of a lead-acid battery

component	% of total battery
metallic lead	28
lead oxide	22
lead sulphate	17
sulphuric acid	21
polypropylene	6
total	94%[154]

What is not made clear is whether there is significant loss of lead in this process, as claimed by Lave et al., and whether this lead enters the environment.

Finally, there is the question of maintenance and management of battery systems. In RAPS systems these are onerous in terms of space, first aid provision and additional safety clothing and equipment (see Appendix 4).[155]

In 1994, the following announcement appeared in a leaflet on RAPS issued by Energy Victoria: 'Electricity Services Victoria (formerly State Electricity Corporation Victoria) offer the Remote Area Power Supply Incentive Scheme (RAPSIS) to eligible applicants about to connect power to a home. An incentive payment of up to $3000 (1993) may be made ... The RAPSIS is currently under review, contact Energy Victoria regarding its availability.'[156] Williams reported a similar scheme in New South Wales:

> ... the NSW Government in 1987 introduced the Remote Area Power Assistance Scheme (RAPAS) which provides grants to assist residents in remote areas of NSW to either be connected to the grid or to purchase a RAPS system.
>
> From the commencement of the Scheme to May 1992, 1820 grants to the value of $11.4 million have been given. Of these, 1035 with a value of $5.2 million have been provided to purchasers of RAPS systems. A large proportion of these systems incorporate renewable energy technologies. [Some are diesel.]
>
> Apart from assisting remote residents of NSW to obtain an adequate domestic electricity supply, RAPAS has assisted the development of the commercial RAPS market and a viable industry in NSW.[157]

The announcement showed a desire to encourage the take-up of RAPS systems in spite of their apparent complexity. However, it was Robert Vale's impression, visiting Australia in May and June of 1995, that many of the RAPS grant schemes were either in decline or had been terminated as part of a general cutting-back of state and federal expenditure. A country like Australia with its huge areas of very low-density habitation is an appropriate place to use systems based on batteries, because of the cost in money and materials of bringing mains electricity to remote households.

It may be that where the system is not remote from the existing grid, as in the United Kingdom, mains electricity is a better option; this apparently contradictory idea will be discussed below. It should be pointed out, however, that many UK boat owners, particularly on Britain's canal network, operate battery-based systems similar to those used in Australia with few problems, using the boat's engine to charge the batteries when cruising, and the batteries to supply power when moored. These systems often incorporate inverters to provide 230-V alternating current, and may operate microwave cookers, toasters, hairdryers, televisions, computers, etc. The number of appliances installed is increasing, leading to the description 'floating cottages', and blurring the distinction between shore-based and water-based accommodation. The following description of the electrical installations of the winner of the trophy for best amateur fitted-out canal narrowboat at the 1994 National Waterways festival is typical:

> Engine is a brass-encrusted Russell-Newbery DM2 ... The DM2 drives two 24 Volt alternators – the higher voltage greatly reduces the problem of voltage drop over long cabin lengths ... The cabin alternator supports a large capacity of traction battery power via an electronic alternator controller. These batteries run a microwave oven and automatic washing machine via a Victron 2.5 kW inverter ... a Zeisse diesel-powered generator is installed under the boatman's side bench; and a Victron marine battery charger recharges the batteries from generator or landline.[158]

The alternative to batteries for the autonomous house is to use a system linked to the electricity grid. This is not necessarily as 'un-autonomous' as it might at first appear, as it is possible to use renewable energy systems to produce electricity which can be fed to the grid in times of surplus, and drawn from the grid in times of need. Provided that the total system generates at least as much power in a year as is consumed in the house, the system can be said to be in 'energy balance', as the power fed in offsets the use of conventional fuels which would have been used to generate that amount of power. The use of such systems is widespread in Germany, where the government has been running the

'Thousand Roofs' programme to encourage, with the use of financial incentives, the fitting of grid-linked photovoltaic systems onto domestic roofs.[159] The system has three major benefits; two practical and one more philosophical. In practical terms, the first advantage is that the necessary inverter to make the grid link costs approximately £2,000,[160] which could be the price of one year of battery life (see above), and is likely to have a longer life than batteries, as it is an electronic, rather than chemical, device. With photovoltaics costing, in the United Kingdom, about £5,000–£6,000 per installed kilowatt, the cost of the photovoltaic system and inverter could be less than that of the batteries alone for a fully stand-alone system. The second advantage is that there is no limit to the use of appliances in the house. A battery-based system will be limited by the capacity of its inverter (DC from batteries to 230 V AC) to supply a load, so the user must be careful to manage the loads to keep them within the capacity of the inverter. Some makes of inverter can be coupled together to increase capacity, but the costs of them are directly related to the power output required. The grid-linked system automatically makes up the demand as required from the mains, once the capacity of the photovoltaic generator is exceeded at any moment. This provides a seamless power supply, and means that appliances such as electric cookers, which create large loads for short periods, can be used with no problems. The final advantage of the grid-linked system is more theoretical. In the early days of autonomous house research, critics were concerned that such houses would encourage a degree of selfishness by their occupants, who could retreat from society into their self-sufficient dwelling, and ignore the rest of society. This attitude was summed up in the drawing on the cover of volume 46 of the journal *Architectural Design* for January 1976, which showed a stern-faced elderly couple in front of their Alexander Pike house, with a large sign reading 'Autonomous Property, Keep Out'. The grid-linked autonomous house is symbolically putting something back into the community, by supplying renewable energy to the local electricity grid. At the same time, it is making use of the community's services to supply its power when the renewables are not operating.

The biggest disadvantage of the grid-linked system is its very existence. By making the grid link, the system is no longer autonomous, as it is linked to mains services. However, it may be argued that the net result of eliminating fossil-fuel use is achieved as effectively by grid-linking as by using batteries, if looked at over a whole year on a national basis. If the environmental impacts of the manufacture of the batteries are taken into account, the grid-linked system is likely to appear even more favourable (since the grid already exists, it has already made its impact), so the only additional input to the system is that required to produce the grid-linking inverter.

Cooking and cookers

A typical house in the United Kingdom, if using electricity for cooking, is reputed to use it at a rate of 5 GJ/year. The figure for gas is higher, because of the lower efficiency of gas cookers; the electricity figure represents the basic energy input to the cooking process, and its use is appropriate here.[161] This represents nearly 1,400 kWh, or 3.8 kWh/day, or a continuous rate of 160 W. The UK figure given here may be an over-estimate. In New Zealand for example, the situation is somewhat different, according to the published figures: 'Around 75% of energy use in the kitchen is by the electric range. This amounts to about 630 kWh per house, or 2% of total New Zealand power consumption.'[162] The New Zealand household therefore needs only 1.7 kWh/day. It is not entirely clear from the references, both from the Building Research Establishment and the New Zealand Ministry of Energy, whether this is the energy use of the cooker alone or if it includes other appliances, which may be quite energy-intensive, either because of high ratings (kettles, toasters) or long usage (refrigerators). However, it probably does refer only to that part of the energy that is consumed by the cooker itself, and is assumed to do so here. More detailed data are given in a relatively recent paper that reported on the cooking energy use of 106 households in Cardiff. The data measured are summarized in Table 4.34.

Table 4.34: Electricity consumption of kitchen appliances in kWh/week

hob	2.432
main oven	3.543
top oven	1.505
grill	0.403
total for cooker	**7.883 (410 kWh/year)**
microwave oven	0.882
kettle	2.461
toaster	0.331
coffee maker	0.793
deep fat fryer	0.683
total for other appliances	**5.150 (268 kWh/year)**

Not all households had all the appliances, but the reported weekly energy consumption relates to the appliance if possessed by the household. The figure for 'top oven' did not differentiate between gas and electric, all others did.[163] This gives a total electricity consumption, for a household with all these appliances, of 678 kWh/year, which is less than half the BRE's figure, and represents a daily energy demand of only 1.86 kWh.

Cooking is probably the biggest problem for the off-the-grid house that is trying to use only renewable-energy sources. Most other domestic-energy needs can be handled by the use of small energy inputs over extended periods: the 3 kWh/day calculated for the heat pump hot-water system earlier, for example, represents an energy input on a continuous basis of only 125 W. This level of power could be fed into a hot-water storage cylinder to produce the appropriate quantity of hot water, as the system includes storage. Cooking, however, requires the use of higher energy rates. Table 4.35 shows the power consumptions for the component parts of cookers manufactured by the German appliance maker AEG.

Table 4.35: Power consumption of electric 'slot-in' cookers made by AEG

Key: N – normal solid ring, F – fast ring,
A – automatic ring (thermostatic control),
A/H – automatic halogen ring

HOBS cooker model	hob type	ring type	diameter (mm)	load (W)
3200F	solid	N	145	1000
		F	145	1500
		F	180	2000
		A	220	2000
total load				**6.5 kW**
5730 V	ceramic	A	145	1200
		A/H	145	1200
		A/H	180	1700
		A	210	2100
total load				**6.2 kW**

OVENS all models	heating-up time	heating-up	continuous operation*	heating-up plus one hour
main oven	13 min	0.4 kWh	0.4 kWh/h	0.8 kWh
second oven	12 min	0.5 kWh	0.6 kWh/h	1.1 kWh

*These values are given here in kWh/h, as the operation of the oven thermostat means that the energy required will vary over the hour.[164]

total connected load for Model 3200 F: 11.6 kW; total connected load for Model 5730 V: 12.3 kW

It seems surprising, in view of the fact that the second oven is often used for small cooking tasks because its smaller size is assumed to use less electricity, that the main ovens of these cookers are more efficient in their energy use than the second ovens. This may be due to the fact that the main oven on each of the AEG models is fan assisted, which is described as 'very energy efficient', whereas the second oven has conventional heating elements. The volumes of the main and second ovens are 54 l and 30 l respectively, so the electricity consumptions in use (heating-up plus one hour, to represent a typical cooking operation) are 14.8 Wh/l for the main oven, and 36.7 Wh/l for the second oven.

The installation of sufficient inverter capacity to allow the simultaneous use of all the hob plus an oven on a RAPS system would be a very expensive option.[165] The use of an inverter might perhaps be easier than creating a special low-voltage DC cooker. An Australian study of houses using RAPS systems found the following percentages of users using their RAPS for cooking.

Table 4.36: Percentage of RAPS users using cooking devices with RAPS system

microwave	> 30%
oven	5%
cooktop (i.e., hob)	0%

Note: the data are based on a survey of 700 RAPS users, of whom over 300 replied. The figures given above are interpreted from a three-dimensional graph in a paper by MacGill and Watt, who say: 'Household services and appliances with high energy demands, including cooktops, ovens, hot water and, to a lesser extent, refrigeration are rarely run off RAPS systems. RAPS consumers will, instead, usually satisfy these needs with other energy options, notably solar, wood and LPG.'[166]

Recent projects for zero-energy houses have tended to give up when it comes to cooking. The 'Energy Showcase', for example, a house proposed by David Olivier, is to use bottled propane for cooking.[167] Perhaps the only project to date to take the culinary bull by the horns is the Fraunhofer house, where the cooking is done on photovoltaically generated hydrogen, using an estimated 700 kWh/year, very close to the New Zealand domestic average.[168] The high cost of a prototype hydrogen generator means that this option is not yet available to the designer of an autonomous house in the real world, although recent work in New Zealand has resulted in a commercial portable hydrogen generator for welding, using water and electricity as the inputs. This would allow the possibility of small irregular inputs of energy from a photovoltaic array or a wind turbine, with the resulting hydrogen being stored for intensive use in cooking. If the efficiency of conversion of electricity to hydrogen can be improved sufficiently, the hydrogen generator may be the future solution to many of the energy-storage problems in an autonomous house.

The use of hydrogen, which produces water when burned, would also eliminate the great problem of gas for cooking, which is that its combustion results in the creation of a number of undesirable products, such as carbon monoxide, oxides of nitrogen, etc., which have to be removed by ventilation. Given the care with which gas boilers, often with total thermal outputs of less than 10 kW, are room-sealed and fitted with balanced flues, it seems surprising that a gas cooker, with an output comparable with that of a modest boiler, especially if it is cooking a Christmas dinner, can discharge its products of combustion into the house with little concern from the authorities. The problem is exacerbated in a low-energy house, as there is a desire to minimize ventilation and the associated heat loss. Indeed, as Shurcliff comments on this problem: '... in superinsulated houses, electric stoves should be used – not gas stoves.'[169] The problem has been tackled by the Canadian Gas Research Centre with their design for a room-sealed balanced flue gas cooker, used in the experimental Waterloo Region Green Home, an advanced house near Toronto. The cooker has a glass top and the gas flames burn underneath this, just as the electric elements do in a ceramic top cooker. Combustion air is supplied, and products of combustion removed, through the sealed space between the underside of the glass and the top of the cooker itself.[170]

Another way to handle the intermittent energy production from renewables might be to use a thermal storage cooker. The famous Aga cookers, originally designed to burn coke at very high efficiency, can now be obtained in an electric version, which is intended to be heated up at night using off-peak electricity, the stored heat then being used for daytime cooking. There are two problems with this approach, which seems attractive initially. The first is that the size of the renewable-energy system required (which would have to incorporate wind energy, as solar alone would be too seasonally unbalanced) would be considerable, needing to supply 25–30 kWh/day as a minimum, or 9,000–11,000 kWh/year.[171]

Fig. 19
Room-sealed gas
cooker in the
Vancouver
Advanced House

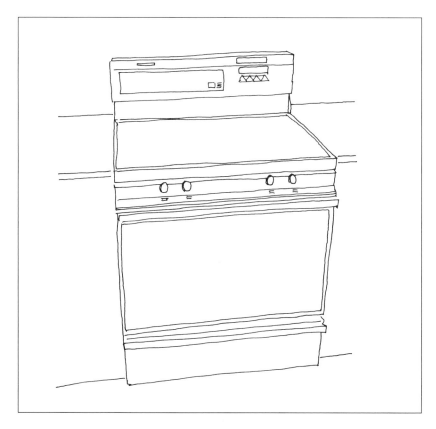

With a wind turbine output of 700 kWh/kW (see Table 4.28), this would require a turbine of up to 16 kW just to run the cooker, whereas the actual energy used for cooking in a typical house, 410 kWh (figure for a cooker alone – see Table 4.34) could be met by a 0.6-kW wind turbine, a much more practicable proposition, if only a way could be found to store and release the energy at will. The second problem is that the heat output from the cooker, about 1,000 W, while welcome in winter would be an embarrassment in summer, and might render the house uninhabitable unless it could be vented away, which would be wasteful. The electric Aga is an attractive possibility, but its energy balance seems extravagant, although the basic idea of a thermal storage cooker, able to use trickle inputs of electricity as and when available, would seem to have great possibilities for further development, both for autonomous houses and for load spreading on the National Grid.

The closest analogy to the autonomous cooker to be found currently in the United Kingdom is in canal boats, as described above in the discussion of RAPS systems, but there is little of any help here. Canal boats are more relevant to this study than yachts and similar sea-going craft, because they are not subject to the same amount of movement, since the water of canals is not rough. For most purposes the floor of a canal boat may be considered stable, like that of a domestic interior. There may be some connections with caravans, but again, the canal boat offers more space, and therefore a greater range of options for appliances, and there is no weight penalty; indeed, as most boats carry several tonnes of ballast, the use of heavy appliances may be seen as an advantage, provided the weight can be kept reasonably low in the hull. Some boats use battery-powered microwave ovens, electric kettles and toasters, operated through a 12-V DC to 230-V AC inverter, but the bulk of cooking is performed using bottled gas, with occasional use made of solid fuel or wood. The trend is gradually moving away from gas (which, being heavier than air, collects in the bilges if a leak occurs, and may cause an explosion) towards diesel-fired cookers and hotplates, but at present these are expensive and rare. A fan-assisted diesel cooker is shown in Burnett, where it is described as providing 'cooking temperature within minutes from tickover'.[172] A diesel ceramic hob, able to bring two pints of cold water to the boil in six minutes is also available from Japan.[173] The advantage of these devices to the autonomous house designer, interested in zero carbon dioxide performance, is that a diesel cooker could probably be powered by 'bio-diesel':

> The conversion of animal fats and vegetable oils into triglyceride esters (bio-diesel) is well understood following research undertaken in the mid 1970s to mid 1980s. Such fuel, based on oilseed rape, is commercially available in Austria, Germany and France but only economically feasible due to incentives. Production of rapeseed oil esters in New Zealand would cost approximately double current diesel prices ... Environmental and health reasons for using liquid bio-fuels include:
>> Minimum oxygenate levels to reduce air pollution (for example, CO, HC)
>> Reduction of aromatics (for example, benzene)
>> No sulphur compounds present
>> Less sooty particulates emitted
>> Reduced CO_2 emissions
>> C neutral if crops replanted[174]

This route might provide a potentially zero carbon dioxide cooking fuel (because it would be biomass-derived), as an alternative to liquid petroleum gas (LPG), assuming that fully autonomous cooking were not possible.

The canal boat example points to another possible route that would allow the use of a RAPS system to provide power for cooking. Many boat owners use microwave ovens, toasters, electric kettles, etc., none of which has a power rating greater than about 1,500 W. If the cooking, instead of being concentrated into one cooker, were to be disaggregated into a number of separate appliances, each with its own in-built heating element, it might be possible to achieve greater efficiency of use, as well as better load control. Sunbeam make a range of electric frying pans with power ratings ranging from 600 W for a small omelette pan to 1500 W for a large roasting pan with a domed cover,[175] and they also produce a 300-W slow cooker for stews. These power ratings are lower than those for the hotplates on a conventional cooker at full power, but the hotplates are usually turned not kept on full in use. Studies carried out by the authors on a solid-ring Husqvarna Culinar electric cooker found that with a ground base pan that makes good contact with the cooking surface, a pan of water can be kept boiling on the lowest power setting (150 W for a solid plate 150 mm in diameter, with maximum power setting of 1,550 W). Other parts of the cooker are rated as follows.

Table 4.37: Electricity consumption of Husqvarna Culinar cooker at various settings

	minimum setting (W)	maximum setting (W)
150-mm ring	150	1,550
225-mm ring	200	1,900
190-mm thermostatic ring	0	2,000
upper oven	upper and lower elements together	1,500
	start setting (for use no longer than 8 minutes)	3,500
	lower element only	650
	grill	2,000
lower oven		1,500[176]

One possible advantage of pans with in-built heating elements is that there might be better heat transfer between the element and the pan than if a separate pan is used on top of a cooker. The lack of significant differences in the power ratings of these appliances compared with conventional hobs (at least in terms of the hob in use, rather than its maximum rating), added to the inconvenience of trailing flexes makes them seem more useful as an adjunct to a conventional cooker (which is how they are marketed), rather than as a replacement for it.

However, the use of disaggregated appliances might change cooking habits so that they are more appropriate for the achievement of an autonomous life-style. Instead of filling the oven to make the best use of the fuel, one might do one-pan cooking, single-batch baking and so on, putting each appliance to maximum use to minimize the overall load, and using only one appliance at a time. An Australian survey of the efficiency of various types of hot plates for cooking gave the following results.

Table 4.38: Measured efficiencies of different types of hot plates for cooking

hot plate type	efficiency (%)	manufacturers' tests (%)
coil	70	
solid	60	40
ceramic	50	47
halogen		51
induction		74
gas		43[177]

Note: data in first column have been taken from Choice *for 1987;* Choice *is a consumer testing magazine.*

The coil type hot plate, used on the cheaper types of cooker, is the most efficient, approaching the performance of the induction hot plate, which is not yet readily available for domestic use, and is described by Harris et al.[178] as costing three times as much as a halogen hob, itself already more expensive than other types. The problem of cleaning the fixed-coil hot plates used on UK-manufactured cookers seems to have been solved by New Zealand manufacturers of electric cookers, which have rings that unplug or swing aside for cleaning, and which sit on removable supports over drip bowls in the cooker top.

The same report by Harris et al. also discusses ovens, and states: '[fan] Convection ovens have a 5 to 15% energy efficiency advantage over conventional ovens, as well as having other advantages.'[179] Harris et al. also give the following quotation from Wilkenfield on the subject of microwave ovens:

Their advantage is greatest in cooking or heating small portions, and it decreases with the size of the cooking task: doubling the mass will double the microwave energy required, whereas a conventional oven will do twice the mass at only marginal increase in energy. For this and other reasons, their impact on

cooking energy is unclear, and will vary with the habits of each individual household. In 1991 as in 1980, one major use of microwaves is in defrosting food. If this would otherwise be done leaving food out or in the refrigerator, then the microwave actually adds to energy use. Another of the most popular and successful uses is for cooking vegetables. As this would have been done on the hotplate, which is far more efficient than the oven, the net saving may be less than expected.[180]

This points to one way of reducing energy demand for cooking: make more use of the top of the cooker and less of the oven.

A section on cooking should not be left without a consideration of the potential of the methane digester. Isaacson of the Gas Research Institute in Chicago writes enthusiastically of the potential of this particular technology in the United States:

SNG [substitute natural gas] from biomass and wastes is not a fossil fuel but is renewable energy. Burning this SNG results in no net gain to the global carbon dioxide budget, another decided advantage. Ironically, after more than a decade of 'benign neglect' or more often being totally ignored, renewable energy presently accounts for 13% (biomass alone accounts for 50% of this) of the nation's electric power or nearly 10% of the US primary energy demand, roughly 23% more energy than nuclear power which continues to be highly subsidised. It has been estimated that this renewable energy reduces carbon-dioxide emissions in the USA by more than 500 Mtonnes ... or roughly equal to the output of 138 typical coal-fired power plants.[181]

Methane digesters figured in several early autonomous house designs[182] and the technology was even tried out in practice in Graham Caine's 'Street Farmhouse' in London.[183] More recently, Spargo[184] gave details of a small-scale methane digester that will produce enough gas to allow 20–30 minutes of cooking per day. A daily input of slurry, consisting of 6 l of fresh cow or pig manure mixed with water is required. It is obvious from this that a family's solid wastes will not be adequate to meet their cooking needs. Smith[185] found that a household of three people, using all their sewage and garbage to feed a methane digester, could produce 0.8–1.2 kWh/day, or 292–438 kWh/year, which is well below the average requirement for gas cooking. Danish experience with farm scale methane production plants suggests an energy yield of 7 kWh/day from one cow.[186] Rosenburg[187] gives a table of the manure production from a range of farm animals, expressed in 'livestock units'; a cow is 1. On the same scale a man is rated at 0.02 livestock units, the same as a weaner pig, a goose or a turkey. On this basis, the methane from the excrement of a family of five adults would provide 700 Wh/day, or 256 kWh/year, hardly enough for cooking. As the keeping of a cow to provide enough methane to be useful is not a viable prospect in an urban or suburban setting, methane can be disregarded as a realistic source of energy for an autonomous house.

5 | *The Technical Options Implemented*

SAVING ENERGY

The autonomous house was designed to make the maximum use of insulation in order to eliminate (at best) or to minimize (at worst) the demand for space heating. To this end, insulation levels were specified that were well in excess of the Building Regulations requirements that were current in the United Kingdom at the time the house was designed.

Table 5.1: U values in W/m²K required in UK Building Regulations 1991[1]

roof	0.25
external walls	0.45
ground floor	0.45
glazing	5.60

Note: the regulations are slightly more complex than this, for example, in terms of permitted areas of single glazing. The values quoted are the lowest that were allowed to be used.

The insulation values that were used for the autonomous house reflected the availability of components, rather than a performance-driven approach. It was part of the design strategy that the house should make use of off-the-peg components. This strategy was adopted for two reasons: the first was that it would serve to demonstrate that an autonomous house was a feasible and realistic concept, because all the technology needed to build it was already available (– if the house worked, it would show that in principle any builder could obtain the components that were needed to build such a house); the second reason was that it was likely to be cheaper to make use of existing components rather than having items made specially for the house. The high cost of similar dwellings such as the Fraunhofer Institute's Autonomous Solar House (which uses a large amount of highly experimental equipment, such as a photovoltaic hydrogen generator), demonstrates the importance of this argument.[2]

STRUCTURE

External walls

It was already determined that the autonomous house would be a brick building, because of the highly sensitive nature of the site in visual terms, on the corner of the main road into Southwell from Nottingham, and the fact that the Local Council intended to include the site in a conservation area. The desire to incorporate a large amount of thermal mass (as discussed in Chapter 4) dictated that the most appropriate construction would be a conventional masonry cavity wall (the commonest form of construction in the United Kingdom) with an inner leaf of dense-concrete blockwork to provide the wall's contribution to the internal mass. It was then a case of finding a way to incorporate the largest possible thickness of insulation within the wall. The Code of Practice for masonry cavity walls in the United Kingdom, BS 5628 Part 3,[3] allows a maximum cavity width of 150 mm. If this is fully filled with a suitable insulating material, such as resin-bonded glass fibre, it will give a U value of about 0.20 W/m^2K (with an aerated-concrete-block inner leaf), or about 0.22 W/m^2K (with a dense-concrete-block inner leaf).

To achieve better insulation performance, there are several possibilities. The first is to adopt a double-cavity construction by building a third leaf, so that the wall, from outside to inside, is brick/cavity/block/cavity/block/plaster. This would give potentially a U value of 0.11 W/m^2K (assuming dense blocks were used to reduce the cost and maximize the thermal mass). The disadvantages of this method of increasing the insulation value are threefold: there would be an increase in cost; there would be an increase in wall thickness (it would be 600 mm overall if both leaves of blockwork were 100 mm thick, and both layers of insulation 150 mm thick); and the thermal mass of the central leaf of the wall would be of little or no relevance to the thermal performance of the building. This is perhaps the most telling criticism, as in the normal cavity wall, the inner leaf performs both structural and thermal-mass functions, an efficient use of the material. In the double-cavity wall there is potentially a 200-mm thickness of mass, but only 100 mm of it are connected to the building interior and able to participate in the internal thermal environment, as described in Chapter 4.

Another possibility for improving the insulation of the wall is to make the inner leaf of a wall with a single 150-mm cavity (the maximum allowable under the Code of Practice) out of a better insulating product, such as hollow concrete blocks with a polyurethane foam core. Polyurethane has a good thermal conductivity (k) value, 0.026 W/m°C, compared with 0.036 W/m°C for glass fibre,[4] which makes a significant improvement to the overall thermal performance of the hollow block. The use of such blocks could raise the U value of the whole wall, but the replacement of the concrete with insulating material inevitably decreases the available mass.

Another possibility, although with similar thermal-mass problems, is to use an inner lining of insulated plasterboard on the inner leaf in order to upgrade the thermal insulation. This has the further disadvantage of adding to the sequence of operations needed to build the wall. If a cavity wall is being constructed, the bricklayer needs to do nothing extra whether the insulation is 50 mm or 150 mm thick; as soon as another layer is added to the construction there is additional labour and hence additional cost. There is also some doubt whether the use of plasterboard and similar dry linings on masonry walls can achieve the degree of airtightness necessary for ventilation control. The use of traditional plaster on the inner leaf of a masonry wall provides an excellent air seal, as it is a wet product that fills all the inevitable cracks and gaps in the mortar of the blockwork of the inner leaf.[5] When dry lining is used, often fixed on plaster or adhesive 'dabs',[6] a cavity is created between the wall face and the back of the plasterboard, and air may circulate in this cavity having passed through any gaps in the masonry. As this air will be at close to external temperature, it can have the effect of lowering the overall U value of the construction. For maximum airtightness, the use of a traditional wet plaster finish on masonry is preferable, as stated by Lowe et al.: 'Airtight construction appears to be considerably simplified by the use of wet construction, and in particular the use of wet plaster instead of plasterboard.'[7]

Failing the use of wet plaster, deliberate steps, such as edge sealing of the dry lining, must be taken, which will add to the labour cost of installing the dry lining. This is how Redland Plasterboard recommend that their material be installed: 'Apply a ribbon of Bedding Compound, either horizontally or vertically as required, around all wall perimeters, junctions with partitions and door and window frames. This will help to control the circulation of air behind the plasterboards, which might otherwise reduce the thermal performance of the dry lining.'[8] The recommended edge-sealing technique will also tend to increase the difficulty of supervision of the work on site, as it is easy to see if plaster has not been applied to a wall, but not easy to check the edge sealing behind a sheet of plasterboard once the latter is in place. The apparent decline in the number of skilled plasterers in the UK is a cause for concern.

Fig. 21
*The 250-mm
insulated brick and
block cavity wall*

It seemed clear from the consideration of the alternatives given above, that the most appropriate solution for the exterior walls of the autonomous house would be to use a conventional cavity wall construction with a wider than normal cavity to give as much additional insulation as possible. In Denmark the Danish Building Research Institute's Code of Practice allows cavities in loadbearing masonry walls of up to 300 mm in width, provided that eight wall ties are used per square metre of wall. The ties may be plastic, to reduce the thermal bridging effect.[9] It was decided to make use of Danish wall ties for the autonomous house to allow the construction of a wide cavity with a single leaf of masonry on each side. The ties were obtained from K.G. Kristiansen APS of Kolding, and are made of glass-reinforced plastic, which minimizes thermal bridging. The largest size that could be obtained was the 'Refus 250', suitable for a cavity width of 250 mm. Calculations and performance data were also supplied by the manufacturer; these were used by the structural engineers for the house, E.J. Allott and Associates of Sheffield, to prepare calculations for submission to the Building Control Department of Newark and Sherwood District Council. A preliminary meeting with members of the Building Control Department before the designs were submitted for approval had confirmed that the Council would be prepared to consider the calculations on their merit, given that Denmark was a member of the European Union. The cavity was designed to be filled with resin-bonded glass-fibre insulation to give an overall U value of 0.14 W/m^2K. Calculating from the data used in Chapter 4, the thermal mass of 1 m^2 of the wall is 0.20 MJ/K; had it been made with an inner leaf of aerated-concrete blocks (using Thermalite or similar for example), the thermal mass would have been 0.06 MJ/K.

The facing bricks used for the external skin of the house had to satisfy the normal architectural criteria of appearance, performance and cost, but, in addition, they were selected for their low environmental impact. It was intended to make use of bricks from a reasonably near source in order to reduce transport energy demand, as discussed in Chapter 3. It was also the aim to find bricks that had a low embodied energy from their manufacturing process. The selection of bricks was made by means of obtaining samples from a brick merchant in Nottingham, with particular emphasis being placed on bricks that were red/orange in colour, somewhat irregular in appearance, and of FL grade for frost resistance. The bricks that were chosen were 'Dales Blend' made by the Yorkshire Brick Company in Barnsley, South Yorkshire. This gave a transport distance (assuming the delivery truck were to drive along the A 635 from Barnsley to the A1(M); A1(M) to Newark and A617/A612 to Southwell) of 100 km (62 miles). The bricks were chosen partly on grounds of colour (an accurate match to the local bricks used on the 19th-century houses adjoining the site); texture (they are slop moulded, giving an irregular quality similar to that of hand made bricks); and cost (£260/1,000, price from Taylor Maxwell and Company Ltd, Brick Merchants, Nottingham, 30 March 1992). However, the final factor that weighed in favour of these particular bricks is that they were made in a brickworks which uses the gas from decomposing garbage to fire the kilns, offsetting the use of North Sea gas. The brick company removes the clay from the ground to make the bricks, and rents the resulting holes to Barnsley Local Authority for use as landfill sites for refuse. The brick company lays pipes in the excavation to collect the methane given off as the refuse decomposes, and this gas is then used to fire the kilns, reducing the use of fossil fuel by up to 50%.[10]

The cellar

The design of the autonomous house is unusual, at least for late 20th-century Britain, in that it incorporates a full cellar. The cellar walls were also designed to be insulated to a high standard, although not as highly insulated as the external walls. The initial design of the cellar was based on the rule-of-thumb that a retaining wall should have a thickness of one quarter of its depth below the ground. On this premise, the walls of the cellar were designed to be made of 600-mm thick Thermalite aerated-concrete blocks, as the depth below ground was to be 2,400 mm. Thermalite was specified since it is made using pulverized fuel ash from the coal-fired power station at Radcliffe-on-Soar (near Nottingham) as the aggregate,[11] which seemed a good use of a local waste material. Following consultation with the structural engineer, the design was changed to two leaves of Thermalite with a 100-mm cavity which was filled with reinforced concrete tied in to the reinforcement of the cellar-floor slab. This was proposed by the engineer to give better three-dimensional bonding of the various elements of the cellar into a coherent whole. The cellar floor is a simple flat slab of 300-mm-thick reinforced concrete. There is no insulation under the slab; it rests on a thin (50-mm) blinding layer of concrete, which is laid directly on the firm clay subsoil. On top of the blinding, which is there to provide a smooth surface, and under the

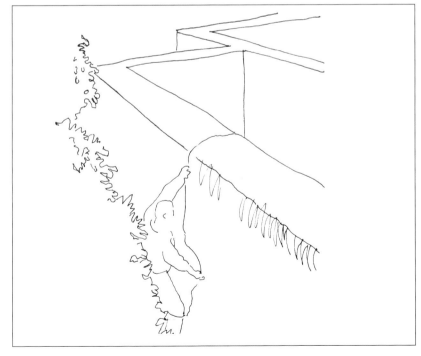

Fig. 22
Nick Martin, the builder, installing the cellar tanking membrane

main slab, is a damp-proof membrane of polyethylene reinforced with a nylon mesh (Monarflex Multifilament 250). This is also taken up the exterior of the cellar walls, and jointed with butyl tape where necessary, to act as a water barrier for the cellar. The design intention was to produce a cellar that would remain dry under normal conditions, but some water penetration was considered acceptable during periods of extreme rainfall. It was not intended to make a habitable cellar, which would have needed more elaborate tanking. Externally, the membrane was covered with sheets of oil-tempered hardboard as a mechanical protection, and the excavation was then backfilled with brick rubble from demolition sites, so as to reduce the need for freshly quarried material such as broken stone.

The cellar floor was left uninsulated as the temperature 3 m below ground is relatively stable, as described by Page: '... the amplitude of the annual variation is greatest near the surface and decreases with depth, becoming only about 3.5°C at 3.0 metres.'[12] It was intended that this would keep the cellar at a roughly constant temperature that would be appropriate for the storage of drinking water.

The calculation of the heat loss from structures in contact with the ground is a complex procedure. However, excluding any consideration of the effects of the surrounding soil (in other words, treating it as a normal external wall), the cellar wall has a U value of 0.31 W/m^2K. It might also be appropriate to consider the cellar as a ground-floor slab, by imagining the vertical walls, as it were, folded flat, to create a slab (excluding the ends) with dimensions about 12 × 15 m. If this were regarded as insulated with a 500-mm thickness of aerated concrete (a 600-mm thickness less the 100-mm reinforced concrete core), the U value could be calculated by taking the basic R value (1/U) of an uninsulated slab of these dimensions (assuming the basic U value for a slab of these dimensions is 0.48 W/m^2K,[13] giving an R value of 2.083), and adding the R value of the insulation (3.125). Treated as a ground-floor slab in this way, the cellar could be assumed to have a U value of 0.19 W/m^2K overall.

One part of the cellar wall has additional insulation: this is the section that separates the cellar under the house from the cellar under the conservatory, so it is strictly speaking a loadbearing partition rather than a cellar wall. This wall needs no reinforced-concrete core, as this is confined to the perimeter of the whole house/conservatory, so the 100-mm reinforced-concrete core in this partition wall is replaced by 100 mm of resin-bonded glass-fibre insulation, giving a U value of 0.17 W/m^2K. It made more sense to use the same block thickness and cavity width throughout the whole cellar, rather than to design a detail which would require different materials. There was also the thought that in the summer the conservatory might reach quite high temperatures, measurements of conservatory temperatures in the architects' former home, the Horse and Gate house in Cambridgeshire, in the 1970s having once peaked at 50°C.

As the cellar was to be used to contain the drinking-water tanks, and it was felt appropriate to keep these cool, it seemed important to try to limit possible temperature build-up in the main cellar area. In one bay of the cellar, that beneath the bathrooms, where the composting chamber for sewage treatment is located, there are air bricks in the wall between the cellar and the conservatory. These are necessary to provide an air supply to the composter, but they may compromise to some extent the attempt to keep the cellar at a relatively constant temperature.

If the air vents tend to raise the cellar temperature, the presence of the drinking-water tanks probably tends to moderate it. When full, the tanks hold 30,000 l, or 30 tonnes of water. With a specific heat of 1.16 Wh/kgK, the water stores 34.8 kWh/K. If the cellar is assumed to have a U value of about 0.19 W/m²K, the total heat loss from the cellar will be 27.1 W/K (assuming that no heat escapes into the house, which is deemed to be warmer than the cellar). The floor of the cellar is uninsulated; this suggests that the temperature of the cellar will be determined to some extent by the soil temperature beneath it, which will vary, according to Page, by about 3.5°C around an average of 10°C. The floor between the cellar and the house is a suspended concrete floor (like all the floors in the house, for reasons of thermal mass) using prestressed inverted T-beams with standard concrete blocks as infill between them. The soffit of this ground floor is insulated with 50 mm of sprayed-on cellulose insulation in a water-based binder. Again, this is to help maintain the cellar at a lower temperature than the house, by reducing the flow of heat from the dwelling space into the cellar. The thermal conductivity value of the insulation is 0.038 W/m°C,[14] which gives an overall U value for the ground floor between the house and the cellar of 0.63 W/m²K. The insulating material cannot be used at a greater thickness than 50 mm because its weight becomes too much for the adhesive binder, and it will not remain in place. The desire to keep the water tanks cool, which was one of the reasons for building the cellar in the first place, may have been unfounded, if the New Zealand approach to non-mains drinking-water supply is followed. As described in Chapter 4, the water tanks used in New Zealand for domestic water supply are invariably stood outside the house, and the water temperature is reasonably close to the ambient temperature.

Windows, doors and glazing
The house was designed with a considerable number of windows, the intention being to provide rooms with light from two sides where possible. The total window area is 19% of the total habitable floor area (ground floor, first floor and attic) but varies from 21% for each of the ground and first floor, to only 5.6% for the attic. The glazed door from the house into the insulated porch has also been

Table 5.2: Window areas in the autonomous house in m²

north wall	3.2
south wall	7.9
east wall	9.9
west wall	10.1
rooflights	2.9
total	**34.0 m²** (19% of total habitable floor area)
ground-floor windows	17.3 (21% of ground-floor area of 80.7 m²)
first-floor windows	15.5 (21% of first floor area of 73.7 m²)
attic windows	1.2 (5.6% of attic floor area of 21.6 m²)
south-facing windows	23% of total glazing area (4.5% of total floor area)
north-facing windows	9% of total glazing area (1.8% of total floor area)
east-facing windows	29% of total glazing area (5.6% of total floor area)
west-facing windows	30% of total glazing area (5.7% of total floor area)
rooflights (west)	8% of total glazing area (1.6% of total floor area)
total area of glass	**16.7 m²** (49% of total window openings area)

omitted from this calculation, as the presence of the porch is assumed to turn the door effectively into an internal partition door, rather than a glazing element. All windows between the house and the conservatory have been counted, as they are in a space that receives solar gain but is not well insulated.

The need to specify windows that were available, rather than those that might be theoretically preferable – Lowe et al. reported on windows available in Canada with an overall U value of 0.73–0.90 W/m²K[15] – led to the choice of Swedish MF windows from Swedhouse UK, a company which had been marketing them in the United Kingdom for a number of years. The company were asked for the best specification that they could offer, which was triple-glazed with two low-emissivity coatings and krypton gas filling. This they said would give a centre of glass U value of 0.95 W/m²K and an overall (frame and glass) U value for an opening window of 1.10 W/m²K. Other U values offered by Swedhouse are listed in Table 5.3.[16]

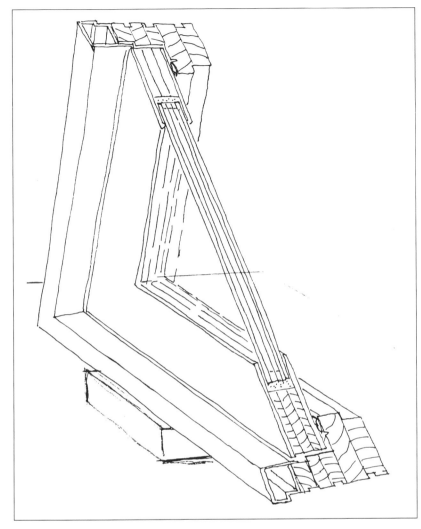

Fig. 23
Canadian 'superwindow'; quadruple-glazed with two low-emissivity films in the cavity, one low-emissivity coated pane of glass, krypton/argon fill and insulated glazing spacers, in a laminated wood frame

External doors were to be of a similar specification and fully glazed, while the front door was a Swedish Ekstrands Ekodoor composite unit insulated with CFC-free polyurethane, giving a U value of 0.55 W/m²K.[17] All doors and windows have built-in gaskets on the opening components to ensure airtightness, and were supplied factory-glazed and painted.

Rooflights were provided in the two middle bays of the four-bay plan to admit additional light into the centre of the house, since these bays could not take advantage of three external walls in which windows could be placed. The rooflights, made by Velux, are double-glazed, with one low-emissivity coating and argon gas filling. They are the poorest specification windows in the house, with a

Table 5.3: Window U values in W/m²K offered by Swedhouse UK (February 1993)

triple-glazed sealed unit T4-12 with one layer of Kappa energy glass, argon gas

glass unit only	1.2
whole window fixed light	1.4
openable window	1.5

triple-glazed sealed unit with two layers of Kappa energy glass, argon gas

glass unit only	1.05
fixed light	1.1
openable window	1.2

triple-glazed sealed unit T4-12 with two layers of Kappa energy glass, krypton gas

glass unit only	0.95
fixed light	1.0
openable window	1.1

U value quoted by Velux of 1.8 W/m²K.[18] In their report for BRECSU, Olivier and Willoughby state that the effective U value of these rooflights in practice may be as low as 3.3 W/m²K, based on Canadian studies of similar windows in practice and computer simulations.[19]

The roof

The roof was designed to have twice the insulation value of the walls. This is comparable to the situation that is seen in the U values required by the Building Regulations (as shown in Table 5.1), where the roof U value is close to twice that of the wall, and reflects the fact that the roof is losing heat to the night sky. The steep pitch of the roof of the autonomous house means that its surface area is relatively large compared to the floor area of the house and the area of the walls.

The roof insulation was potentially affected by two factors that would have led the design of the house in different directions: on one hand, the thickness can be as great as desired, because the dimension is not governed by the size of available components such as wall ties; on the other, a practical way had to be found to construct the roof with a high level of insulation incorporated in it. The

Table 5.4: Area of roof/ceiling in m² compared with floor and wall areas

area of ground floor	80.7
total habitable floor area	176.0
gross wall area	167.9
roof/ceiling area	128.3

house was designed to have the insulation in the plane of the roof as this would maximize the usable space within the building. Once the thickness of insulating material increases to more than 200 mm, it can no longer be incorporated between the rafters of a sloping ceiling, since the maximum easily (and economically) available size of timber in the United Kingdom for rafters is 200 mm in depth. The situation as regards the availability of timber at builders' merchants has arisen in spite of BS 4471, Part 1: 1978, which suggests that 225-mm deep timber should be readily available.[20] It is possible to use a layer of rigid insulation as a sarking above the rafters to increase the insulation value; this technique was used in the pair of semi-detached houses at Industry Road, Sheffield, designed in 1989 for North Sheffield Housing Association by Brenda and Robert Vale.[21] The intention at Industry Road was to design a roof which would give the maximum possible insulation value, with the insulating material contained in the plane of the roof covering, as outlined above. The construction that resulted had a plasterboard ceiling on a reinforced vapour barrier fixed to the underside of 50×200-mm softwood rafters at 600-mm centres. The spaces between the rafters were filled with 200-mm-thick glass-fibre insulation. Over the top of the rafters was a layer of 50-mm-thick expanded polystyrene, held down by 50×50 mm counterbattens running from eaves to ridge and nailed through to the rafters. The roof tiles were carried on softwood battens on 2L2 reflective bubble film insulation used as sarking felt. The U value of the whole roof, after making allowances for the reduced insulation at the rafter positions (due to the poorer thermal conductivity of the wood compared to the insulation) is 0.13 W/m²K. The thickness of the expanded polystyrene layer, which also has the useful effect of reducing the thermal bridging through the timber of the rafters, was limited to 50–75 mm because nails long enough to fix through a thicker layer were not available. The British Standard for nails (BS 1202, Part 1: 1974)[22] lists nails 200 mm long, but these are available to special order only, and must be purchased in bulk. Enquiries made to Messrs GKN at the Interbuild Exhibition in Birmingham in 1992 revealed that the reason for this is that the 200-mm nails are manufactured using a very old machine which is not used for modern production; it is only worthwhile operating this machine if there is a large order. This limitation on the thickness of insulation between rafters effectively means a maximum U value for this type of roof of 0.13 W/m²K, unless insulation materials with better thermal conductivity are used. These tend to be materials which have been made in the past using CFCs (for example, extruded polystyrene and polyurethane).[23] The long-term performance of the replacement, non-CFC, materials is not yet known, and it was decided to remain with familiar materials that were proven over some time, hence the use of expanded polystyrene.

It would be possible to have a greater thickness of roof insulation if a trussed rafter roof were used. Here the insulation can be laid on top of the ceiling and over the tops of the trusses. There are several problems with this approach, of which the first is that the thickness of the insulating material is reduced at the eaves by the descending roof slope, leading to a tailing-off of the U value at the perimeter of the house. This problem was solved in the Cresswell Road houses in Sheffield, designed by Brenda and Robert Vale in 1991, again for North Sheffield Housing Association, by the addition to the bottom horizontal chord of the trusses of a second chord of timber, supported by small timber hangers, to form a horizontal member to which the ceiling could be fixed. This extra truss member was designed to provide full thickness of insulation across the entire width of the house. The design does mean that the height of the eaves is raised relative to the window heads on the first floor, but this proved to be no problem in practice. The use of a modified truss has the additional small advantage that the original bottom chord of the truss is now not covered by the insulation, making it possible to have a boarded floor to the attic area. In the Cresswell Road houses the insulation is Warmcel cellulose fibre, made from recycled newspaper, with a thickness of 400 mm, giving a U value of 0.08 W/m²K.[24]

One problem with this approach, which is why it was not considered for the autonomous house, is that it leads to unusable space in the attic, as there is a space under the roof that is effectively at external temperature. Any tanks or pipework in this space will need to be insulated to prevent freezing. Furthermore, any pipes or wires passing through this space will have to penetrate the vapour barrier under the ceiling, and will need careful sealing at each penetration. This is part of normal practice in Canada and Scandinavia, where highly insulated construction is the norm, but is not yet part of the working vocabulary of UK builders. The problem was overcome in the Cresswell Road houses by fixing a ceiling of 6-mm plywood under the trusses, to which the vapour barrier was fastened. The vapour barrier was turned down the walls and fixed to them by nailing to the wall a galvanized-steel plaster stop bead to give a key for the wall plaster to meet the vapour barrier. 25 × 50-mm timber battens were then nailed through the plywood to the trusses above to give a space in which wiring could be run, and the electrician was told that no penetrations could be made of the plywood. Finally, a plasterboard ceiling was fixed to the battens. The pipe and tank problem was avoided by using a Yorkpark condensing combination gas boiler with a pressurized system, which meant that no pipework needed to run above the ceiling. However, the rising ducts for the humidity-sensing passive stack ventilation system had to penetrate the vapour barrier and pass through the attic space.

Because of the limitation on roof insulation thickness, and because of the desire to use the whole of the roof space, a new design approach was needed for the autonomous house. Part of the house's design philosophy was to use each material to its best potential, and to let each material appear in the house as itself, rather than disguised in any way. In the case of the roof, this led to the use of a roof construction of structural softwood decking which spanned between the concrete-block crosswalls at 3,650-mm centres, instead of conventional rafters. The decking is of 70-mm-thick double-tongued and grooved Russian pine, and its exposed underside forms the ceiling. On top of the decking, which is untreated, is a vapour barrier, of the same material as used round the cellar (Monarflex Multifilament 250), and this is sealed to the edges of the surrounding walls (to the outer face of the inner leaf of the cavity wall) with butyl tape to control air movement through the roof structure. The vapour barrier also served to protect the timber from rainfall during the time that the roof was being constructed. This was an important factor, as the timber is exposed to view in the interior as the ceiling, and any staining from rainwater would have detracted from its appearance. As it was intended to have no finish on the timber, there would be no chance of disguising any staining.

It should be explained here that the roof construction chosen for the autonomous house was a result of the architectural approach, and should not be considered as a necessary part of any autonomous house design. It is a construction that made sense for this particular house in this particular setting, incorporating particular ideas about space and materials. The choices behind the construction were the logical result of an attempt to achieve a combination of high insulation and a usable roofspace, but in terms of the attempt to design a house that required no space heating, any technique that provided an appropriately high U value could be used. In terms of low cost, the roof trusses with dropped bottom chord used at Cresswell Road provided a U value approaching that of the autonomous house, and the cost of each house was £3,000 less than the Housing Corporation budget for a conventional Building Regulations house.[25] The use of a truss with a dropped bottom chord would appear to be the cheapest way to design a roof with very high insulation levels, but it does not provide a habitable roof space.

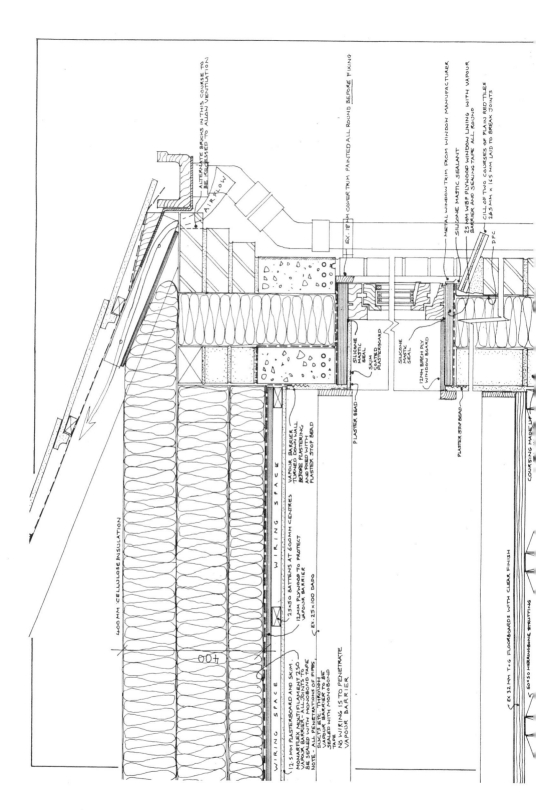

ALTERNATE BRICKS IN THIS COURSE TO BE RECESSED TO ALLOW VENTILATION

AIRFLOW

EX. 18 MM COVER TRIM PAINTED ALL ROUND BEFORE FIXING

METAL WINDOW TRIM FROM WINDOW MANUFACTURER

SILICONE MASTIC SEALANT

25 MM WBP PLYWOOD WINDOW LINING WITH VAPOUR BARRIER AND SEALING TAPE ALL ROUND

CILL OF TWO COURSES OF PLAIN RED TILES 265 MM x 165 MM LAID TO BREAK JOINTS

DPC

SILICONE MASTIC SEAL

SKIM COATED PLASTERBOARD

SILICONE MASTIC SEAL

12 MM BIRCH PLY WINDOW BOARD

PLASTER STOP BEAD

VAPOUR BARRIER TURNED DOWN WALL BEFORE PLASTERING AND FIXED WITH PLASTER STOP BEAD

25 x 50 BATTENS AT 600MM CENTRES

12 MM PLYWOOD TO PROTECT VAPOUR BARRIER

EX. 25 x 100 DADO

WIRING SPACE

400 MM CELLULOSE INSULATION

PLASTER BEAD

COURSING MADE UP

EX 32 MM T+G FLOORBOARDS WITH CLEAR FINISH

50 x 150 HERRINGBONE STRUTTING

WIRING SPACE

400

12.5 MM PLASTERBOARD AND SKIM. MONAFLEX/MONAFILAMENT 2.50 VAPOUR BARRIER - ALL JOINTS TO BE SEALED WITH MONOBOND TAPE. NOTE - ALL PENETRATIONS OF PIPES, DUCTS ETC. THROUGH VAPOUR BARRIER TO BE SEALED WITH MONOBOND TAPE. NO WIRING IS TO PENETRATE VAPOUR BARRIER

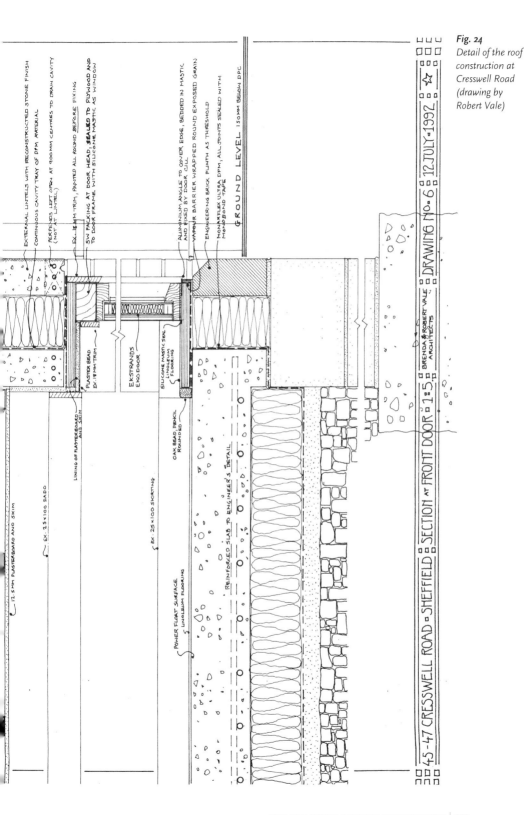

Fig. 24
*Detail of the roof
construction at
Cresswell Road
(drawing by
Robert Vale)*

EXTERNAL LINTELS WITH RECONSTRUCTED STONE FINISH

CONTINUOUS CAVITY TRAY OF DPM MATERIAL

PERPENDS LEFT OPEN AT 900 MM CENTRES TO DRAIN CAVITY (NOT AT LINTEL)

EX. 19 MM TRIM, PAINTED ALL ROUND BEFORE FIXING

SW PACKING AT DOOR HEAD, **SEALED** TO PLYWOOD AND TO DOOR FRAME WITH SILICONE MASTIC AS WINDOW

ALUMINIUM ANGLE TO COVER EDGE, BEDDED IN MASTIC AND FIXED BY DOOR CILL

VAPOUR BARRIER WRAPPED ROUND EXPOSED GRAIN

ENGINEERING BRICK PLINTH AS THRESHOLD

MONAFLEX ULTRA DPM, ALL JOINTS SEALED WITH MONO BOND TAPE

GROUND LEVEL 150 MM BELOW DPC

12.5 MM PLASTERBOARD AND SKIM

EX. 25 × 100 DADO

LINING OF PLASTERBOARD AND SKIM

PLASTER BEAD

EX. 19 MM TRIM

EKSTRANDS EKO DOOR

SILICONE MASTIC SEAL

LINOLEUM FLOORING

OAK BEAD PENCIL ROUNDED

EX. 25 × 100 SKIRTING

POWER FLOAT SURFACE

LINOLEUM FLOORING

(REINFORCED SLAB TO ENGINEER'S DETAIL)

45 – 47 CRESSWELL ROAD ▫ SHEFFIELD ▫ SECTION at FRONT DOOR ▫ 1 ∷ 5

BRENDA & ROBERT VALE ARCHITECTS

DRAWING N⁰ 6 ▫ 12 JULY 1992 ▫ ☆

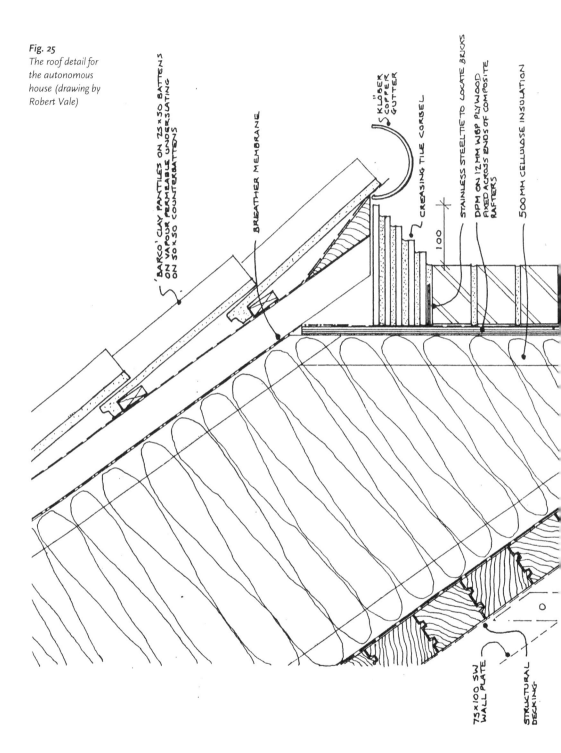

Fig. 25
*The roof detail for
the autonomous
house (drawing by
Robert Vale)*

'BARCO' CLAY PANTILES ON 75 x 50 BATTENS
ON VAPOUR PERMEABLE UNDERSLATING
ON 50 x 50 COUNTERBATTENS

BREATHER MEMBRANE

1¼" KLÖBER COPPER GUTTER

CREASING TILE CORBEL

STAINLESS STEEL TIE TO LOCATE BRICKS

DPM ON 12 MM WBP PLYWOOD
FIXED ACROSS ENDS OF COMPOSITE
RAFTERS

500 MM CELLULOSE INSULATION

100

75 x 100 SW
WALL PLATE

STRUCTURAL
DECKING

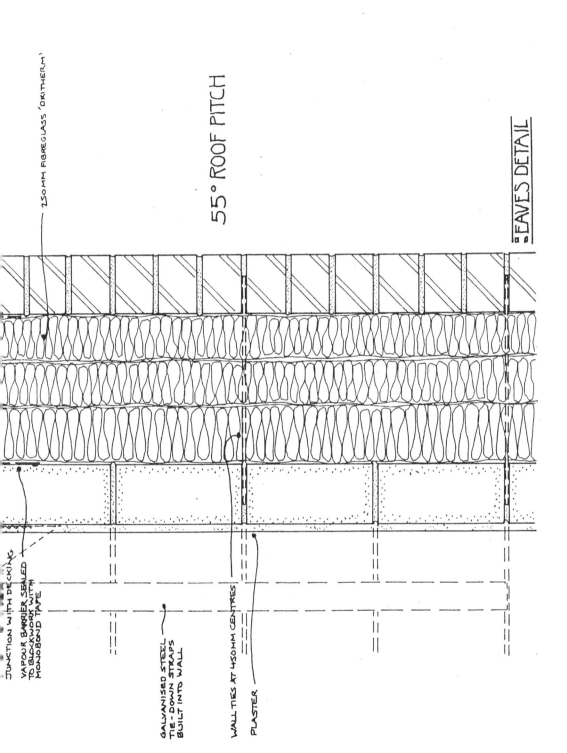

250MM FIBREGLASS 'ORTHERM'

55° ROOF PITCH

JUNCTION WITH DECKING

VAPOUR BARRIER SEALED TO BLOCKWORK WITH MONOBOND TAPE

GALVANISED STEEL TIE-DOWN STRAPS BUILT INTO WALL

WALL TIES AT 450MM CENTRES

PLASTER

EAVES DETAIL

It was decided, somewhat arbitrarily, that the roof insulation for the autonomous house should be twice as thick as the wall insulation. This decision was based partly on earlier work by Brenda and Robert Vale with superinsulated buildings, in which a similar relationship of roof insulation to wall insulation was employed. Examples of this are the two housing schemes for North Sheffield Housing Association, described above. Both have a wall U value of 0.21 W/m²K; the Industry Road scheme has a roof U value of 0.13 W/m²K, while that of the Cresswell Road scheme is 0.08 W/m²K. The cost of increasing the thickness of insulation in walls and roof is really no more than the cost of the material – there is no additional labour requirement – so it seemed appropriate to have as much as possible in the autonomous house. It became more a question of setting an upper limit, and the thickness of 500 mm seemed appropriate. There is a point at which the increased thickness of insulation will take more energy to manufacture than it will save in use. Eurisol UK, a trade group representing mineral wool insulation manufacturers, have carried out an analysis, based on a 60-year building life, of the carbon dioxide emissions relating to the use of mineral-fibre insulation versus its manufacture. They have determined what they call the 'environmental thickness' of insulation, which is described as 'an optimum thickness which produces the minimum pollution level'. For walls this thickness is 700 mm, and for roofs it is 960 mm, assuming that mineral wool is being used as the insulation.[26] These thicknesses of mineral fibre would lead to U values of 0.051 W/m²K for walls and 0.038 W/m²K for roofs. The insulation used in the autonomous house roof is the Warmcel cellulose fibre made from recycled newspaper, which has a considerably lower manufacturing carbon dioxide emission than mineral fibre. This would mean that an even greater 'environmental thickness' would be appropriate for cellulose fibre. Excel Industries Ltd, the manufacturers of Warmcel, give the following manufacturing energy data.

Table 5.5: Energy in MJ for 'manufacturing equivalent quantities of common insulating materials'[27]

Warmcel cellulose fibre	2.5
rock-wool	25.0
polystyrene	35.0
glass fibre	47.0
polyurethane	98.0

A conventional roof with insulation between the rafters has a considerable amount of thermal bridging; with rafters at 500-mm centres, each metre width of roof will be 10% timber, assuming 50-mm wide rafters, and this will have an effect on the overall thermal performance of the roof. Timber is relatively a good insulator, but not compared to insulation materials; its thermal resistivity (1/K) is 7.7 m°C/W compared to 27.8 m°C/W for semi-rigid felted mineral fibre, for example.[28] In the autonomous house it was decided to make use of plywood spacers to create the space above the timber deck in which the insulating material would be placed. The plywood would be only 10 mm in thickness, which would minimize any thermal bridging effects. The result was the design of a

Fig. 26
The roof spacers in place

series of plywood 'rafters' in the form of I-beams, with 10-mm plywood webs and flanges of 50 × 50-mm softwood to give them rigidity, to which the decking below and the tiling battens above could be fixed. This technique was used before on the Birley Health Centre in Sheffield (architects Brenda and Robert Vale), although in that case the insulation thickness was 400 mm of mineral fibre, and the plywood beams were nailed through a vapour barrier and a decking of oriented strand board to the upper members of conventional gang-nailed trusses below the decking; this gave a U value of 0.09 W/m^{2}K.[29]

The plywood spacers on the autonomous house were made 500 mm deep, and were designed to have an upper layer of breather paper to reduce unwanted air movement through the insulation. On top of each rafter there was then a 50 × 100-mm batten in order to create an airspace above the insulation and carry the tiling battens, which were to be laid on a breather membrane. The Warmcel cellulose-fibre roof insulation, treated with a borax-based fire and rot retardant, has the merit of being made from material that would otherwise be waste, although it has been suggested that it might have carcinogenic properties. According to Greenberg, writing specifically about cellulose fibre, 'Studies of workers in industries where related materials are manufactured (wood, paper pulp) suggest a possible cancer hazard.'[30] To counter any possible problems, the cellulose insulation used in the autonomous house was blown into place slightly damp (which reduced the chance of dry fibres blowing about the site), and was installed from outside, (where the concentration of fibres would be unlikely to cause a problem, unlike the normal practice of installing insulation in confined attics). Once in place, the insulation is sealed from the building interior by the vapour barrier, and from the outside by the breather layer. Any possible problem due to loose fibres would occur at the time of demolition.

Discussion with the manufacturers of the chosen insulation suggested that the use of a breather paper on top of the plywood rafters would be inadequate to resist the pressure of the material being blown into place, so the specification was changed to a bitumenized fibreboard (Bitvent) with similar breathing properties but greater rigidity. The space between each parallel pair of rafters down the slope of the roof was divided up with plates of plywood running horizontally to form a series of separate chambers, each of which would be filled with insulation. This not only provided some horizontal bracing of the rafters, but also reduced the chance that the weight of the insulation would cause it to settle towards the eaves as a result of the steep (55°) roof pitch. The insulation was blown into the roof through holes cut in the fibreboard as necessary, and the U value of the finished roof was 0.065 W/m^{2}K.

The roof was finished with handmade clay pantiles from a factory at Barton-on-Humber, beneath the Humber bridge. The local Planning Officer suggested these tiles; the original intention was to use second-hand reclaimed pantiles, in order to minimize the tiles' embodied energy, but Council policy was that any of these that became available should be reserved for use in the repair of old buildings. The suggested alternative was a reasonable compromise between appearance (reflecting the houses opposite), and proximity to the site to reduce transport requirements (the distance was 101 km [63 miles]). The eaves and verges of the roof were formed entirely of facing brick and clay creasing tiles to eliminate any need for maintenance, or at least to put the roof maintenance schedule onto the same timescale as that for the brick walls.

The conservatory

The house was designed with a large conservatory facing 68° west of south, not the most auspicious orientation. However, the siting of the house was a response to significant contextual factors, as described in Chapter 3. The conservatory covers three of the four bays of the house, and is on two levels. The lower part is a continuation of the cellar of the house, and was intended to provide somewhere to grow tender plants; access to the main cellar without the need for a stair inside the house; and a space for the storage of bicycles, logs, garden tools and similar items. The upper level of the conservatory is at ground level and is formed of two timber decks spanning across the cellar below. The use of these decks, which occupy only part of the length of the conservatory, was to allow light into the lower part, and to permit the growing of large trees in the conservatory, which could be planted in tubs and allowed to grow up through the gaps between the decks. The total height of the conservatory, from cellar floor to the top of its roof is 6 m. The conservatory-floor area at cellar level is 28.1 m^2, and at deck level 20.1 m^2. The width of the conservatory at cellar level is only 2.7 m, but increases to 3 m at deck level, because the external wall above ground level is thinner than the wall used in the cellar part. The cellar wall in the conservatory is the same as that used for the rest of the house. At ground level this wall changes to a brick/insulation/brick wall that supports the glazed walls of the conservatory proper. This brick wall rises 600 mm above ground level, and incorporates 100-mm glass-fibre insulation batts, similar to those used in the main walls, but not so thick. The glazed wall is a timber frame, using ex 75 × 100-mm softwood, rebated to take the 20-mm thick glazing units. The glazed wall rises 2,100 mm above ground level, to allow the incorporation in it of a pair of doors to give access to the garden. The doors were purpose-made by the joiner and are of ex 75-mm-thick timber. The doors and the wall are glazed with 4-12-4 laminated-glass double-glazing units, with a low-emissivity coating on one pane. The roof uses similar glazing units, but whereas these are fixed with timber beads on the wall, on the roof a system of aluminium glazing bars is used, screwed down to the ex 75 × 175-mm rafters. The roof glazing is in two lengths, with a lap joint half-way down the slope of the roof. The spacings of the rafters and the vertical glazing bars in the walls vary to accommodate the module of the house and the bay construction. This caused no problems in construction, as each glazing unit for the conservatory walls and roof had to be purpose-made, as would be the case whether the dimensions were different or the same. The roof pitch was determined by the height needed for a door in the glazed wall, and by the gutter position on the main house. The conservatory roof comes in immediately below the gutter, at the base of the creasing-tile corbel that forms the maintenance-free eaves detail.

BUILDING ENCLOSURE

Thermal bridging

In relation to the thermal insulation of a building envelope, thermal bridging (or cold bridging, as it is often called) has been defined as follows:

> The thermal resistance through the thermal envelope of a building should, ideally, be approximately the same over the whole of the envelope. In practice the thermal resistance may be highly non-uniform. Those parts of the envelope where the thermal resistance is significantly lower are described as cold bridges. The large differences in conductivity between thermal insulants and other common construction materials mean that any discontinuity in a layer of thermal insulation will result in a cold bridge ... The effect of a cold bridge is to bypass thermal insulation, and to increase the heat flow through the thermal envelope. This leads to increased space heating requirements ..., low internal surface temperatures in winter, and the risk of surface condensation.[31]

Cold bridging can be responsible for a significant part of the heat loss of a well insulated building. Olivier says: '... in virtually all new buildings conforming to today's Swiss building codes, thermal bridges are significant; that is, their effect is tens of percent, or more. In very energy-efficient dwellings, thermal bridges raise the heat loss so much that they cannot be tolerated.'[32] The detailing for the autonomous house was intended to eliminate cold bridges wherever possible, and to minimize the effects of any that were unavoidable. The first part of the strategy was to ensure that the insulation was a continuous layer round the whole building, with no unheated voids; the second part was to ensure that where components were joined, the joints did not become a thermal bridge path. The construction details at each situation were then designed. A good example of the process is in the design of the window reveal details. A window or door opening in a conventional masonry cavity wall is formed by returning the inner leaf of the wall to meet the outer leaf, with a vertical damp-proof course to maintain the water barrier afforded by the cavity. When cavity walls were first used this was a reasonable thing to do, but more recently there has been a move to put insulation in the cavity. As the cavity is insulated, the relative thermal-performance difference in the heat path through the returned blockwork as opposed to through the insulated wall is increased, and the 'traditional' detail becomes a serious cold bridge. A serious cold bridge is defined by Lowe et al. as follows:

> As a rough guide, a cold bridge may be counted as serious when the thermal resistance through a given component is less than half of the nominal thermal resistance of that component or adjacent components. Thus for a wall with a total thermal resistance of 5.0 K m²/W (U value of 0.2 W/m²K), a path with a thermal resistance less than 2.5 K m²/W (U value of 0.4 W/m²K) would be counted as a serious cold bridge.[33]

The relative effect of cold bridges increases as the insulation value of a wall is raised. Table 5.6 shows the relative R values across varying widths of insulated masonry cavity walls compared with the R value of a conventional window reveal in the same wall (assuming a brick/insulation/aerated-concrete-block/plaster construction for the wall).

Table 5.6: Cavity walls and cold bridges at reveals

cavity width	U value (W/m²K)	wall R value (Km²/W)	reveal R value (Km²/W)	reveal as % of wall R value
uninsulated wall				
50 mm	0.88	1.136	1.269	112
insulated walls				
50 mm	0.42	2.346	1.269	54
75 mm	0.33	3.041	1.425	47
100 mm	0.27	3.736	1.581	42
150 mm	0.20	5.126	1.894	37
250 mm	0.13	7.906	2.519	32

According to the definition offered by Lowe et al., all the insulated walls can be regarded as having serious cold bridging problems, as even the wall with 50-mm-thick insulation is only marginally above the 50% level. The simple calculation of cold bridging based on the fractional area of the cold bridge is likely to underestimate its effect; Lowe et al. suggest that three-dimensional thermal modelling may be needed to give a reasonably accurate picture of the effects of cold bridges in practice.[34]

In an attempt to provide solutions to the cold-bridge problem, UK manufacturers have begun to offer insulated cavity closers, typically comprising an extrusion of PVC-U with a core of polyurethane foam. These were first used by Brenda and Robert Vale at the Heeley Green Surgery in Sheffield (designed 1986)[35] in an attempt to overcome the window reveal cold-bridge problem. The use of polyurethane and PVC-U was felt to be inappropriate to the autonomous house, a building that was attempting to have a minimal environmental impact.

Fig. 27
A window template
box in place

The extruded cavity closers also had the constructional problem that they were not made for a wide cavity; this meant that in the earlier buildings a partial return to the back of the closer, an awkward detail to construct, had been used, and the closers had to be attached to the back of the window frames, which were then built into the wall. The desire to use Swedish windows that had been glazed and painted in the factory for the autonomous house meant that a detail was needed that would allow the windows to be fitted at the end of the construction process, to prevent damage to them, and thus the extruded cavity closer was not appropriate. A detail was devised, which used a box of water- and boil-proof plywood (WBP) surrounded by a layer of damp-proof membrane and built in to the wall. This was first tried on the Industry Road houses for North Sheffield Housing Association.[36] The detail was originally made in 19-mm plywood, but was changed to 25-mm plywood for the Birley Health Centre[37] and subsequent projects. The plywood box is used as a permanent template to build the brickwork openings, with suitable reinforcement as necessary to keep it square. Instead of being thrown away after the brickwork is in place, as happens with the temporary profiles used by bricklayers when forming openings, the box remains as part of the building. It spans the cavity between the inner and outer leaves of the wall and is fixed to them with plugs and screws. The box is set back 75 mm from the outer face of the external wall to give some modelling to the elevation, and to provide a measure of rain protection to the window and the box.

On the earlier buildings the boxes were later encased in plasterboard finished with a skim coat of plaster, but in the autonomous house the intention was that the boxes would be left as plywood and finished with wax, as part of the desire to make the construction explicit. The windows can be fixed into the boxes at the very end of the work on site, which reduces the possibility of broken glass and damaged finishes. The exposed edge of the plywood on the outside is covered with a wooden bead which laps onto the face of the window. Internally, care has to be taken to seal the box to the inner leaf of the wall, as there is a possible air leakage path here from the cavity to the interior of the building; the boxes on earlier buildings were plaster lined for that reason. Because of the architects' desire to expose the plywood on the autonomous house, in order to provide the required air-tightness, the boxes were sealed to the inner leaf of the wall with silicone mastic.

The other constructional details were tackled in a similar way, always with the intention of reducing the possibility of cold bridges. Attention was paid to problem areas such as the inner leaf of the gable walls, which, if continued up to the same position as the outer leaf, would constitute a cold bridge through the roof from the underside of the tiles to the interior of the building. This was prevented by stopping the inner leaf at the underside of the roof decking and

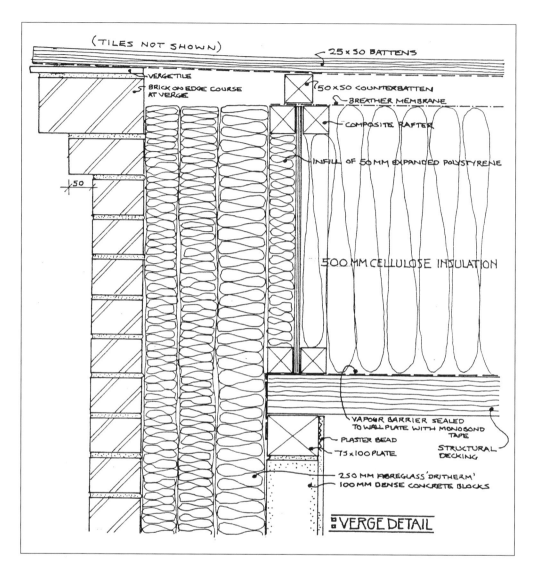

(TILES NOT SHOWN)

25 × 50 BATTENS

VERGE TILE

BRICK ON EDGE COURSE AT VERGE

50 × 50 COUNTERBATTEN

BREATHER MEMBRANE

COMPOSITE RAFTER

50

INFILL OF 50 MM EXPANDED POLYSTYRENE

500 MM CELLULOSE INSULATION

VAPOUR BARRIER SEALED TO WALL PLATE WITH MONOBOND TAPE

PLASTER BEAD

STRUCTURAL DECKING

75 × 100 PLATE

250 MM FIBREGLASS 'DRITHERM'
100 MM DENSE CONCRETE BLOCKS

VERGE DETAIL

Fig. 28
Anti-cold-bridge
verge detail

carrying the outer leaf only up as far as the underside of the roof tiles. At the junction of the house walls with the cellar walls, use was made of both Thermalite insulated-concrete blockwork and the continuation of the cavity insulation downwards into the first course of the cellar wall to try to reduce the cold bridge at this point. The aim throughout was to achieve an unbroken thickness of insulation round the whole building. This strategy breaks down to some extent at window and door openings, since these components are inherently cold bridges. A window with an overall U value of 1.1 W/m²K will represent a considerable weakness in a wall with a U value of 0.14 W/m²K.

Airtightness and ventilation

All authorities on low-energy housing stress the importance of airtight construction. Chapter 4 made clear why this should be the case – heat loss due to high levels of ventilation can be the largest element of heat loss in an otherwise well insulated building; it also showed that controlled ventilation with heat recovery offered a way of providing the necessary air ventilation without the related thermal penalty. It is clear that there is no point in using carefully designed mechanical ventilation systems if cold air is going to enter the building in uncontrolled ways.

The airtightness of construction is created by the details. Considerable care was taken with the detailing of the autonomous house, following the decision to use a masonry construction, to try to create an airtight shell. The use of precast concrete floor beams, for example, reduced the possibility of differential thermal movement that might occur with a timber floor joist built into a concrete-block

Fig. 29
The crosswall construction is seen clearly here, with the precast concrete floor beams of the north attic spanning onto the crosswall

wall, as well as the effect of possible shrinkage of the timber as it dried out. Both these factors could result in a crack at the point of entry of the joist into the wall, which would provide a path for cold air from the cavity to enter the house. Concrete beams and a concrete wall will tend to move as one. The block infill to the floor beams was screeded to tie the blocks together, but the screed also acted like the plaster on a wall to create an airtight barrier. Screeds were taken to the walls, which were then plastered down to the top of the screed. The electrical wiring was incorporated into the plaster, with all horizontal runs at skirting level. Normally the plasterers would leave off the plaster here, but in the autonomous house the plasterers were instructed to plaster over all the wiring at skirting level so that the wall plaster and the screed would form a continuous barrier to air movement. The soffits of the upper floors were plastered between the beams. This had several benefits; it allowed the visual display of the beam and block construction, with the regular lines of beams expressed and used as an ordering device for the ground-floor partitions; it increased the headroom in the rooms below by about 70 mm; and it meant that any subsequent cracking at the point where the beams entered the wall could be seen and filled, which would help to keep performance airtight. The exposed concrete beams also make a reference to medieval construction, and were seen as part of the timeless quality of the design, that was discussed in Chapter 3. The fact that the loadbearing walls of the house are the crosswalls serves to reduce the number of penetrations of external walls by beams, which also helps the airtightness to some extent. Beams enter the external walls only at the gables.

The roof construction was an obvious potential weak point in the airtight envelope, as the roof was made of wood rather than concrete. The structural decking that forms the roof was fixed to timber wallplates tied down to the crosswalls. The roof deck was overlaid with a reinforced polyethylene air/vapour barrier, which was sealed all round the house to the outer face of the dense-concrete-block inner leaf of the external wall. The blown-in-place method of installation of the slightly damp cellulose-fibre roof insulation offers excellent crack-filling properties, leading to better airtightness without the need for an air/vapour barrier. This is demonstrated in a project carried out by Gwalia Housing Society at Blaen-y-Maes, Swansea, where conventional timber-frame houses were compared with the same design insulated with cellulose fibre and no air/vapour barrier, to form a 'breathing wall':

> The raw results show that the breathing wall dwellings had, on average, an 18% lower specific heat loss rate than did the conventional timber frame dwellings (149 W/K breathing wall ... and 181 W/K timber frame ...) ... The average

*calculated fabric heat losses for the monitored dwellings were 106 W/K for the
breathing wall dwellings and 114 W/K for the conventional timber frame. While
this was considered good agreement with the monitored results it was noted
that the breathing wall dwellings were some 6% better than calculated while
the conventional timber frame performed about 15% worse than predicted ...
The fan pressurisation results indicated similar air leakage for the two
construction types, both being significantly lower than the national average with
the breathing wall dwellings having a lower air leakage than the conventional
timber frame (5.83 ach ... compared to 6.74 ach ... at 50 Pa).*[38]

In the autonomous house the decision was made to back up the cellulose fibre
with an air/vapour barrier, to ensure that the roof would be airtight, particularly
as the use of 500-mm-thick cellulose roof insulation represented a somewhat
unusual construction method.

Fig. 30
The airlock porch

The air sealing of the window openings was carried out in three stages. Windows and doors with in-built seals round the opening components were chosen; this was to ensure that there were no draughts when the windows and doors themselves were closed. These were then fitted into the plywood wall boxes, and a CFC-free expanding foam in an aerosol can was used to put a compressible airtight seal round the inner edge of each window or door frame between the frame and the plywood box. The boxes themselves were sealed to the inner face of the inner leaf of the wall with silicone mastic, prior to the plastering of the walls. The rooflights were fitted in a similar way, with a plywood box being constructed off the roof deck to fit the window. These boxes were then wrapped in the same air/vapour barrier material that was used to cover the roof decking; this material was then sealed to the main barrier with butyl tape. The rooflights were then fixed into the boxes in a similar way to that used for the windows and doors.

The use of a roof design with the insulation in the plane of the roof meant that there were few penetrations through the air/vapour barrier. Apart from the rooflights, the only others were the two flues, one serving the wood-burning stove, and one acting as a soil vent pipe to the sewage composter. These were sealed in the same way as the rooflights, with air/vapour barrier material and plenty of butyl tape. It was felt that the height of the chimney above the stove would minimize the risk of heat damage to the vapour barrier. The point at which the vapour barrier is fitted round the flue is 5.5 m above the top of the stove, and the flue pipe is an insulated construction with a ceramic liner in a stainless-steel outer jacket, so is unlikely to reach a high temperature, at least not at the point where the flue passes through the air/vapour barrier.

Other aspects of ventilation control were handled by design rather than detailing. Both the external doors, for example, were designed to open, not from the house interior direct to outside, but into a draught lobby that can act as an airlock. This is one of the 'twenty steps to energy efficiency in house design' recommended by the Building Research Establishment in 1988.[39] In the autonomous house there is a porch over the front door, and the back door opens into the large conservatory.

With a floor area of 7 m², the porch is large enough to allow entry into the porch and closing of the external door before the inner door to the house is opened. The porch is constructed with a timber frame, timber external board-and-batten cladding, and a timber internal lining to walls and ceiling; the roof is of recycled slates. The concrete floor slab has edge insulation of 50-mm-thick extruded polystyrene recovered from a demolished farm building, the remaining insulation is glass fibre, giving a U value for the walls and roof of 0.18 W/m²K. This is slightly lower than the value for the walls of the house, but significantly

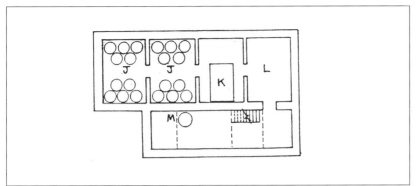

Fig. 31
Cellar plan:
J = rainwater tanks
K = sewage
  composter
L = workshop
M = sand filter

better than the walls of a conventional house, and means that the porch is part of the thermal envelope of the house, not an 'external' space like the conservatory. Cellulose-fibre insulation was specified for the porch, but the eventual construction sequence would have meant requiring the cellulose insulation contractor to come to the site again solely to insulate the porch, and this would have been expensive. The porch also incorporates a window of the same type as used elsewhere in the house, and a Swedish Ekstrands Ekodoor insulated front door. The letterbox in the front door has external and internal sprung flaps to reduce uncontrolled air movement through it. The conservatory, at the rear of the house, provides a covered route down to the cellar where the water tanks, sewage composter and photovoltaic inverter are located. If the house had used an internal stair to the cellar it would have been regarded as a three-storey house under the Building Regulations, which would have necessitated the design of a half-hour fire-protected enclosure round the stairs on all floors; in turn, this would have rendered impossible the open planning of the living accommodation on the first floor.

Following the creation of a relatively airtight envelope for the house, three ventilation techniques were introduced. The first relies on the opening of the windows: all rooms have openable windows which are used in summer as required. Secondly, during colder weather, use is made of adjustable trickle vents in the heads of the windows. Not all the windows have these, but each room has at least one trickle vent, with an area of 3,300 mm^2. Finally, the kitchen on the first floor and the two bathrooms on the ground floor have individual ADM Indux through-the-wall heat-recovery units. These E100 units are surface mounted and operated by a pull-cord switch on the unit itself. On the low setting each unit consumes 12 W and moves air at a rate of 43 m^3/h; on the 'boost' setting the figures are 32 W and 77 m^3/h. The heat-recovery efficiency is given as 70%.[40] The heat-recovery units are intended to be operated as necessary, not to run continuously.

SERVICES

Sewage

Sewage disposal in the autonomous house is discussed before water in this chapter, as it is central to both the water use strategy of the house and its internal planning. As was described above, the house is designed as a series of identical bays, which are then divided by non-loadbearing partitions to form smaller spaces as required. One of these bays, and one only, contains all the water-based services: this is to minimize the service runs for cost reasons. The bedroom accommodation of the house is on the ground floor, with the two bathrooms occupying the services bay along with the laundry area (containing the washing machine, the hot-water storage cylinder, and a shelf for storage of the laundry basket, the iron, ironing board and laundry detergents) and a spare bedroom. The laundry is a space won from the two bathrooms by making use of spare space beside the toilet seats. In the same bay, on the first floor above the bathrooms, is the kitchen/dining room, and above this on the attic level is the main water header tank which supplies the kitchen and bathrooms by gravity. There is no water pipework in any of the other bays of the house, and the visible vertical pipework in the bay is limited to a set of pipes in the kitchen that connect to and from the attic tank, and a descending waste pipe from the kitchen passing through the en-suite bathroom. Below the whole house is the cellar, which contains, directly beneath the bathrooms, the sewage composting unit, and the water storage tanks in the two northernmost bays.

The decision to opt for sewage composting was made largely in order to reduce the need for water for flushing the toilet. If water is to be collected from the roof there will be a limited supply, particularly on the eastern side of England, where rainfall is lower than on the west.[41] A waterborne sewage system would have required the collection of a third more water than otherwise needed for domestic purposes (– the relevant data are set out in Chapter 4). Waterborne sewage would also have needed a septic tank for treatment, with the accompanying seepage pipework, to allow the discharge of the waste water following treatment of the solids in the septic tank. The use of such systems is acceptable in a rural area, but would not be acceptable in the centre of a town, because of the proximity of other houses and the possibility of pollution spreading onto other property. This is the situation on Waiheke Island near Auckland, as described previously: the need to use septic tanks limits each house plot (or 'section') to a minimum of about 1,000 m^2, a quarter of an acre. The autonomous house plot is about 575 m^2 in area by comparison, suggesting that autonomous houses could be built at at least double the permitted density on Waiheke, about eight to the acre.

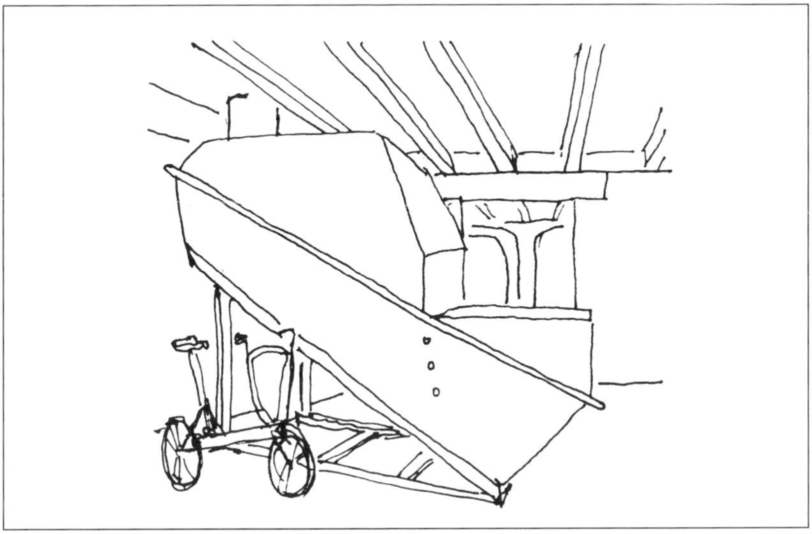

Fig. 32
The Clivus Multrum
unit in the cellar

The composting treatment of sewage allows the whole process to be contained within the dwelling, where spillage is unlikely, due to the nature of the process and the lack of added water. If spillage were to occur it would be a nuisance only to the occupants of the house involved. The other advantage of composting, as opposed to a septic tank, is that the final product from a composter is compost that can be used directly on the garden, whereas the sludge from a septic tank has to be sucked out by a road tanker and taken away for disposal. This both wastes the potential fertility, at least as far as the individual householder is concerned, and also involves a regular expense to pay for the services of the tanker. The composting system puts the whole process into the hands of the user, with no running costs to be considered, and allows the fertility in the sewage to be used for growing plants, rather than going to waste, thereby closing a cycle that the conventional system treats as an input-output situation, with sewage being regarded as a problem rather than as a resource. Even on Waiheke Island, where the septic tank is the accepted norm, the sludge that is removed from the tanks every three years[42] is spread on to 'a couple of farm paddocks', which are then not used for agriculture.[43]

A large tank type sewage composter was selected in place of a smaller unit that would fit in the bathroom, one model of which, the Swedal 'Lectrolav', has British Board of Agrément approval for use in the United Kingdom. This is mainly because the small unit has to use electricity to heat the sewage and evaporate the moisture rapidly, as the toilet unit, being small enough to fit in a conventional bathroom, cannot contain a large volume of waste. The necessary high electricity demand of 3 kWh/day[44] is significant, if it is intended to generate the electricity on site. A detailed study showed that the larger composter was cheaper, even if the cost of providing a cellar to contain it was included in the calculation.[45] Garden compost heaps work better in larger sizes; a slatted wooden box roughly 900 × 900 × 900 mm is given as a minimum size by the late director of the Henry Doubleday Research Association (an organic gardening organization).[46] This also suggests that the tank composter, with a volume of several cubic metres, will be a more robust system than a small electrically assisted unit, which could be overstressed by small variations in inputs.

The composting unit that was specified for the house is a Clivus Multrum Type M7 residential composter, supplied by the Eco-Clear division of Southern Water. The design of the Clivus Multrum originated in Sweden, where the first unit was installed in 1939,[47] but the system was developed in the United States, which is where the unit used in the autonomous house was manufactured. The Clivus Multrum sewage composting unit was chosen for a number of reasons, the first and most important of which was the fact that it was available. It was being marketed by an English water company (Southern Water), and it was hoped that this would make it more acceptable to the Local Authority compared with a unit from an overseas company. It would also provide a UK-based point of contact both for advice on the use of the unit, and for obtaining any necessary spare parts. Contact was made with the building inspectors at Newark and Sherwood District Council before the plans for the house were submitted for Building Regulations approval, in order to explain the proposed systems and to attempt to overcome possible objections. The initial reaction of the building inspectors at this first meeting was positive and supportive, and their attitude remained supportive throughout the whole design process and construction of the house.

A problem arose once the drawings were submitted to the Council, as the Council's Legal Department advised the Building Control Department that the 1984 Building Act required that any house within 100 m of a sewer should be connected to that sewer. The Council could not be seen to be allowing the construction of a house that was illegal, and they could see no way round this particular problem. The advice of the building inspectors was to install a single conventional toilet connected to the sewer, that need not be used, in addition to the Clivus, so that the letter of the law would be satisfied. The building inspectors agreed that it was not a very satisfactory suggestion, and from the point of view of the construction of the house, it would both add the expense of a sewer connection to the cost of the Clivus unit and require the creation of space to take the extra toilet.

At this point contact was made with the head of drainage at the Department of Environment in London, Mr Arthur Clarke. His response, on considering the problem, was to point out that the relevant part of the Building Act 1984 (Section 26) no longer applied, and had been replaced by the more flexible Part G1 of the Building Regulations. He conveyed this to the building inspectors, which allowed the Council to withdraw their objection on this score. The other problem connected with the Clivus was its lack of a British Board of Agrément certificate, or a European type approval (Eurocode). As the original design is Swedish, and the unit was being imported by Southern Water from Clivus Multrum in the United States, there were no relevant approval certificates. Southern Water had not yet set in train the expensive process of obtaining Agrément Board approval. Once again the Department of Environment assisted with the solution of this problem: it was agreed that a Clivus Multrum could be installed provided that it was accessible to the Building Research Establishment for the monitoring of its performance in use, and provided that it was agreed that it would be taken out and replaced by a conventional toilet linked to a sewer should it prove unsatisfactory in use, or create a nuisance.[48]

The Clivus Multrum system specified in the autonomous house is made in the United States of glass-reinforced plastic (GRP), with a wall thickness of 3–5 mm. This has recently been superseded by a newer version made of moulded recycled polyethylene.[49] Southern Water, through their associated company Eco-Clear, intended to manufacture the new version in the United Kingdom as soon as the market looked capable of supporting this, which would lead to reduced costs and lower transport energy use in shipping the units to sites in the United Kingdom.[50] However, the parent company closed down Eco-Clear in the mid-1990s. One possible advantage of the GRP Clivus over the newer version is that the more recent moulded version is available only in a dark grey colour, whereas the GRP version is gloss white, which makes the unit look more like a domestic appliance. This may help make the composting toilet more acceptable to users, since it looks clean.

The sewage system used in the autonomous house comprises two toilets and a composting tank. The toilets in the bathrooms are conventional in appearance, but made of white GRP and Acrylonitrile Butadene Styrene (ABS), and with no flushing cistern. Each has a seat and lid, with a gap between the seat and the bowl, as with a normal toilet. The top part of the toilet unit, under the seat, is conventional in appearance, but the lower part of the interior is made of dark grey plastic, and tapers only slightly from the diameter of the seat aperture at the top. The appearance is similar to the toilets used in airliners, except in the latter the dark grey bowl tapers to a diameter of about 50 mm. From each toilet unit a stainless-steel shaft 350 mm in diameter descends vertically to the composting unit in the cellar. The lower edge of the grey bowl fits over the top of this shaft, to ensure that there are no ledges to trap solids or collect urine. The connection between the stainless-steel shafts and the top of the composter is designed to be cut on site which allows a degree of adjustment of the toilet position relative to the compost container below, but the toilets need to be back-to-back (in this case separated only by a 70-mm thick timber partition) to enable two to be fitted on this particular model of composter.

The GRP compost container in the cellar is made in two sections bolted together on site using a wide flange moulded into the GRP, and a number of stainless-steel bolts, with a marine-grade silicone sealant between the two parts. All necessary bolts and sealant were supplied by the manufacturer. The upper part of the composter is fitted with an airtight access hatch of a type supplied for the decks of small yachts, which seals onto a compressible gasket; this allows access to the waste piles beneath the toilets. The hatch measures 300 × 450 mm and is probably large enough to permit entry of a person into the container, although this has not been attempted. The lower part of the composter has a flat sloping base that is supported on a wooden cradle made on site, imparting a 30° slope to the unit.

The base, which is something like an inclined bathtub, contains a GRP bulkhead about two thirds of the way along its length, dividing the compost container into an upper and lower section This bulkhead is sealed to the sides with bolts and silicone, but has a gap of 100 mm between its lower edge and the base of the container. A hinged access lid over the lower part of the container provides access to the finished compost, which appears through the gap under the bulkhead when it is ready to be removed for use in the garden. The lid also allows removal of liquid that collects at the base of the chamber, and a manual bilge pump, connected to a short length of hose, is fitted to the inner side of the tank to allow the liquid to be pumped out into a bucket as required. A stainless-steel clip holds the lid open when access is needed for compost or liquid removal. The liquid is described as a useful liquid fertilizer, needing only dilution with about ten parts by volume of water before use.[51]

A third connection to the top of the composter, apart from the two toilet inlets, is for a flexible ventilation pipe 150 mm in diameter. This comes up through the ground floor of the house, where it is fitted into a box of 20-mm plywood made by the builder and sealed to the tiled floor with silicone sealant to form an airtight joint. The box is 200 mm square, and on its top is fitted a 12-V 5-W electric fan, which delivers air at a rate of 44.8 l/sec.[52] To the top of the fan is bolted a circular flange, machined from 25-mm plywood (again made by the builder), that allows a further length of flexible ducting, also 150 mm in diameter, to be attached with a large hose clip. This duct joins to a vertical steel flue pipe that is 150 mm in diameter, which in turn connects to an insulated ceramic-lined stainless-steel vent stack that runs vertically through the kitchen and up through the roof. A steel flue pipe is used as its rigidity facilitates easier installation inside the laundry cupboard, while the length of flexible pipe at its base allows easy removal of the fan, since the flexible pipe can be moved up and down without needing to be disconnected. This combination of materials was designed to provide an uninterrupted vertical air path from the composter, with the insulated stack both retaining any heat in the air rising from the compost, and minimizing the cold-bridge effect of the stack's rising through the house and passing out through the superinsulated roof. The stack is a standard Selkirk flue, and is supported directly off the first floor. Because of the nature of the bay design of the house, the stack rises vertically through the centre of the kitchen, and the polished stainless-steel pipe is both attractive and robust enough not to need boxing in for protection. The 12-V fan works from a battery, so that a power cut would not mean a cut in the ventilation of the composter; it is also a way of minimizing the electricity used by the fan. The 12-V fan that was supplied by Eco-Clear for use with the Clivus is significantly lower in its energy demand than the 230-V version, using 5 W as opposed to 66 W.[53] It can be seen that daily electricity consumption of the 12-V fan is 120 Wh, and air flows at a rate of roughly 160 m^3/h. Air is drawn through a screened vent on the front of the composter, over the top of the compost and up through the vent pipe. The height of the pipe (9 m from the top of the composter to the 'chimney pot'), means that a good flow of air is likely to be created, helped by the heat-retaining nature of the pipe, and that the fan may not be necessary. It might be possible to operate the Clivus without the fan running, using the chimney effect to assure the airflow. This would be in keeping with the intention of building a largely passive house. The fan has been used to ensure that the airflow through the system is never likely to reverse, leading to possible smells from the composter entering the house. When an unconventional system of sewage treatment is proposed, it is important to take steps to ensure that it is likely to work better than a conventional system, as it will be subject to close, and potentially critical, scrutiny by users and visitors. The air that enters the composter is drawn from the conservatory via air bricks in the wall between the cellar and the bottom of the conservatory. This wall is insulated with 100-mm-thick glass-fibre batts built into the cavity between two walls of 250-mm-thick Thermalite aerated-concrete blocks. The aim of drawing the air through the conservatory is to take advantage of any solar preheat that may take place, particularly during daylight hours, so that the air flowing through the composter is warmer than external air, and can help to maintain the compost temperature at the suggested temperature of 32°C.[54]

Water supply
As part of the strategy of minimizing the environmental impact of the house, it was decided to make it independent of the conventional water supply system, so

that it would make use of such water as fell on the site for its servicing needs. The use of an independent water supply, provided that water demand could be managed so as to meet the supply available, would also show a cost saving in use compared to a conventional mains water connection, as there would be no charge for the water consumed. The water supply system was worked out once the house had been designed from an architectural and spatial point of view, since it seemed more appropriate to match the water demand to what was available, rather than to try to optimize the roof area in line with a predetermined water demand. Water demand is potentially far more flexible than the need for space, which predetermines the areas actually available for collecting water, by virtue of its importance in the plan area and hence roof area.

Rainfall at the site in Southwell, on the eastern side of England, is not high, at 576 mm/year.[55] Taking a figure of 500 mm to represent a non-typical year, and allowing for evaporation, it is possible to calculate the water available to the household over a typical year. The plan area of the main roof, covered in hand-made clay pantiles, is 102 m², and the plan area of the glass conservatory roof is 40 m², giving a total collection area of 142 m². With an annual rainfall of 500 mm, the water collection would be 71,000 l/year, or 194 l/day. This gives a target water consumption for the five occupants of the house of nearly 39 l/head/day.

Published water use figures, such as those given by Smith,[56] suggest that 39 l could not possibly meet one person's daily requirement for water, as the table below makes clear. Even if the water for flushing the toilet is eliminated, the water used for personal hygiene alone is greater than the quantity available. The decision was made to try to make a more accurate estimate of water demand

Table 5.7: Typical UK water demands in l/head/day

personal hygiene	45
laundry	15
dishes	15
drinking and cooking	5
garden and car	10
losses	20
(flushing toilet	50)

Note: data are taken from Smith.[57]

based on the habits of the intended occupants of the autonomous house, a family of two parents and three teenagers. The water uses were considered in the order they appear in the table above, with the exception of personal hygiene, which was calculated last, for reasons that will become clear.

Laundry was taken as three loads in the washing machine per week, with a figure of 70 l/wash used for water consumption. The water consumption was worked out as an average of the quoted figures for the range of washing machines on display in 1993 in the Nottingham branch of the John Lewis department store: the lowest water consumption quoted in John Lewis was 58 l, for a Bosch machine. No water consumption figures could be found for the washing machine in the autonomous house. The machine is a 1978 front-loading model, the AEG Lavamat 802T, and is probably not state-of-the-art. A further study of washing machines was made in New Zealand in 1995, to see both if the available technology had improved, and whether machines from other markets than Europe could offer better performance; for detailed results of this study, see Appendix 5.

Following the findings of this study, 70 l/wash still seemed a reasonable figure to use for the calculation of laundry demand, although the AEG Lavamat 802T used in the autonomous house probably has a water consumption nearer 110 l (assuming a comparison with the AEG Lavamat 502, a current model). Because of its age it will be replaced when it wears out (it has had one repair in 15 years), and the figure of 70 l/wash will be perfectly reasonable for a modern machine of similar quality. The laundry calculations, based on 70 l/wash, gave a weekly water demand of 210 l, or 6 l/head/day. Use of these figures was quite legitimate, since any discovery, once the house was in use, that the water supply was insufficient, could be remedied easily by replacing the washing machine with the latest model with the lowest water consumption. Since the water consumption of washing machines seems to be falling, perhaps because of water prices, any wait is likely to result in a better machine's being available. It also seemed inappropriate, in a house that attempts to make the best use of resources, to scrap a working washing machine unnecessarily.

The water consumption for washing up was measured in the house that was lived in while the autonomous house was being designed. The dishes were washed in a plastic bowl which held 5 l/wash, and the hot-water plumbing was such that the hot-water storage cylinder was sited close enough that no water needed to be run off to get hot water at the tap. A figure of two washes per day was used to calculate the demand, giving a figure of 10 l/day, or 2 l/head. If the water is at a temperature of 55°C and it is heated from a header tank temperature of 18°C, it will take 0.43 kWh, giving an energy demand of 0.86 kWh/day, or

314 kWh/year. This can be compared with the quoted lowest demand for a dishwasher of 17 l and 1.3 kWh (475 kWh/year if the machine is used once a day) for a standard load of 12 place settings.[58] A dishwasher is probably no less efficient than washing up by hand, given that a single bowl of washing up probably does not cover 12 place settings, but the idea of using a dishwasher was excluded largely on the grounds that the detergents used by such machines appear, from the warnings provided on the packets, to be relatively toxic. Vallely et al. say that dishwasher powder can be made at home by mixing one part of borax with one part of bicarbonate of soda,[59] but even borax is a toxic material, used as a wood preservative.

The figure for drinking and cooking was taken as being the same as the published data at 5 l/head/day, and that for garden and car washing was ignored, as was that for losses. Garden watering would be done with waste water, after the water had been used for other purposes, and car washing was carried out at intervals of several months, so was deemed to be insignificant. The final result was the following table of values.

Table 5.8: Water demands in l/head/day for the autonomous house (excluding personal hygiene)

laundry	6
dishes	2
drinking and cooking	5
total	**13 l/head/day**

The total figure could then be subtracted from the available 39 l/head/day to give a daily personal hygiene allowance of 26 l. Based on a flow rate of 6 l/minute as being the minimum flow rate that could be achieved from a conventional shower head fitted with a controlled flow restrictor,[60] this would allow one four-minute shower per person per day. Four minutes is a reasonable length for a shower, as shown by an Australian shower timer, designed 'in an effort to outwit three teenagers who were in the habit of using all the hot water taking long showers'.[61] The timer senses the sound of water, and beeps loudly after four minutes of showering. The final figures for the calculated water consumption of the autonomous house are shown in Table 5.9.

The next step in the design was to provide adequate storage of water to meet the demand. Two bays of the cellar were allocated to water storage, and the original intention, once a local manufacturer of storage tanks had been located via the *Yellow Pages*, was to have some tanks fabricated from steel and installed

Table 5.9: *Water demands in l/head/day for the autonomous house (including personal hygiene)*

laundry	6
dishes	2
drinking and cooking	5
personal hygiene	26
total	**39 l/head/day**
total house demand	**195 l/day**

before the cellar was closed in. There was some concern that this would be expensive, and that the tanks would not be able to be removed or maintained at a later date. This was considered important, as the fabric of the house was designed to have a long life, and the tanks could quite conceivably corrode well before the house came to the end of its design life, even if they were correctly coated with appropriate paints. If this happened, the tanks could not be removed without cutting them up *in situ*, and similarly, new tanks would need to be welded out of parts that could be carried into the house. The tank fabricator (Pevco of Nottingham) then offered some second-hand Israeli bulk orange juice containers as an alternative, and these seemed preferable to the fabricated steel tanks.

The juice comes from Israel in large cylindrical plastic tanks with screw lids on the top. The empty tanks are not returned to Israel, so become available as a relatively cheap source of liquid storage. The capacity of each tank (written on

Fig. 33
The water tanks before installation

the side) is 1,520 l, with a height overall of 1,700 mm and a diameter of 1,050 mm. It proved possible to accommodate twenty tanks conveniently in the two cellar bays, with access possible to all tanks individually. This gave a total capacity of approximately 30,000 l of water, which, at a daily consumption rate of 200 l/day, would allow a period of 150 days without rainfall. The only disadvantages of this system are the fact that the tanks, being cylindrical, do not pack very neatly into the space, although this does allow access all round, and the need for a large number of connections between the tanks. At least if a tank fails, it can be removed and replaced, as all doorways from the exterior to the tank bays are 1,200 mm in width, and the tanks are light enough to be carried easily by two people.

The water calculations were based on a slightly reduced annual rainfall figure (500 mm instead of 576 mm, a reduction of 13% of the average), but it was important to test the water system design against a possible drought situation. Lyall[62] gives a table (Table 5.10) of rainfall measurements for the worst recorded drought period in Newark, from May 1975 to August 1976.

It can be seen from the table that the rainfall needed to meet a month's water demand (assuming a month of 31 days) is 44.3 mm. In a typical year only March, April and October do not have enough rainfall (although, strictly speaking, the demand in April is only 6000 l because the month is only 30 days in length, and the necessary rainfall is therefore 42.9 mm), but the preceding and succeeding months are easily able to make up the shortfall. It can also be seen that the storage capacity of 30,000 l provided by the water tanks, representing roughly 150 days of usage at the standard calculated rate, would almost have coped with the worst recorded drought without any need for water saving measures on the part of the household. Only in August 1976 does the cumulative shortfall of water exceed the 150-day tank capacity, and the overrun is only four days. It would have been relatively easy to reduce water use slightly to compensate for this as the drought progressed. The simulation is, of necessity, crude, as the rainfall data are available only as monthly rather than daily figures, and the calculation assumes that the tanks are full at the beginning of the drought. The ultimate fall-back position in the case of a very extended drought would be to buy water by the tanker-load from the local water company.

The rainwater collected from the roof is treated before being used in the house. The first part of this treatment is concerned with minimizing the pollutants that enter the water before it is used in the house. To reduce any problems, the main roof of the house, covered with clay pantiles, has no lead flashings. This has resulted in a very simple roof form, a double pitch without projections or dormers. The local Planning Officer, when consulted about the design before the plans were submitted, asked if some dormers or other visual

Table 5.10: Rainfall in the drought year 1975–76, compared to water demand

month	rainfall	%	average	yield	days	demand	shortfall (cumulative)
May	39.88	84	47.75	5583	31	6200	617 (3 days)
June	9.65	20	49.02	1351	30	6000	5266 (26 days)
July	48.51	84	57.40	6791	31	6200	4675 (23 days)
Aug.	33.53	55	60.96	4694	31	6200	6181 (31 days)
Sept.	49.02	100	49.02	6863	30	6000	5318 (27 days)
Oct.	16.00	38	42.67	2240	31	6200	9278 (46 days)
Nov.	37.34	66	56.90	5228	30	6000	10050 (50 days)
Dec.	44.20	86	51.05	6188	31	6200	10062 (50 days)
Jan.	44.96	91	49.28	6294	31	6200	9968 (50 days)
Feb.	12.95	28	45.47	1813	29	5800	13955 (70 days)
March	17.53	42	41.40	2454	31	6200	17701 (89 days)
April	12.19	30	40.89	1707	30	6000	21994 (110 days)
May	47.75	100	47.75	6685	31	6200	21509 (108 days)
June	7.37	15	49.02	1032	30	6000	26477 (132 days)
July	48.51	84	57.40	6791	31	6200	25886 (129 days)
Aug.	8.89	15	60.96	1245	31	6200	30841 (154 days)

Note: rainfall data have been converted to mm. Demand is based on 200 l/day, supply on a roof plan area of 140 m²; both figures are slightly conservative compared to the figures quoted earlier. The third column compares the percentage of rainfall actually received to the amount expected in an average year; the fourth column shows the number of mm of rainfall in a normal year; during the 16-month period the rainfall was normal for only two months. The final column is a running total of the number of days of shortfall of supply compared to the demand.

'variety' could be introduced, but was prepared to withdraw this suggestion when the problem of flashings was explained. There are some penetrations of the roof slope on the western half of the roof, caused by two chimneys (one is the Clivus vent), and a pair of Velux roof windows. The flashings for the chimneys were made by the builder from sheet copper, and the standard lead flashings of the Velux windows were cut off and replaced with copper sheet rivetted in place. Copper was used as the least toxic alternative to lead,[63] but the use of copper caused slight problems in conjunction with a pantile roof, as the less ductile copper could not easily be dressed over the tile profile to give a close fit. Eventually, the copper was dressed over the tiles to some extent, and a cement mortar fillet was laid between the copper and the tiles to make up any gaps. This has proved satisfactory to date in both appearance and performance. The rainwater gutters and downpipes were also made of copper, using the German Klöber system, which is available off-the-shelf in Britain. The gutters are half round, 110 mm in diameter, and the downpipes are 75 mm in diameter.

There are two downpipes at the northern end of the house, and one at the same end of the conservatory. The downpipes discharge to Hepworth clayware garage gulleys, chosen for the fact that each contains a perforated galvanized-steel bucket, which acts as a primary strainer to exclude from the incoming rainwater leaves and any other large items. The pipes connect to the gulleys through large copper shrouds, in the form of elongated pyramids, which were made up by the builder to act as a dirt excluder above each gulley. Each pyramid is circular at the top to fit round the downpipe, and is a close fit over the square top of the gulley. The discharge pipes from the gulleys come through the cellar walls horizontally, with waterstops cast into the reinforced-concrete core at the centre of the wall, and discharge the rainwater into two tanks at the corners of the north end of the cellar. The north end of the cellar is occupied by a total of four tanks, which are connected with purpose-made stainless-steel pipes 100 mm in diameter to form an overflow and equalizing pipe. The rainwater discharges into the outer two tanks in the row. The tank on the west side of the cellar has, in addition to the rainwater input and the connection to the other three tanks in the row, an overflow pipe leading from it. This pipe is again purpose-made in stainless steel, and connects to a standard Hepworth drain 100 mm in diameter passing through the cellar wall. The inner end of the pipe, at the tank, is capped with a perforated stainless-steel plate, 6 mm thick, to obviate the possibility of rats coming up the overflow pipe and entering the water tanks. The purpose of connecting the four tanks together was to ensure that any excess of rainfall would be able to overflow to waste without flooding the cellar. The rainwater pipe from the west-facing conservatory roof is connected round to the gulley on the west side of the house through an additional hole in the back of the copper pyramid.

The tanks themselves are interconnected with copper pipe 25 mm in diameter, fitted about 50 mm above the base of the tanks to allow sediment to settle out of the water without blocking the pipes. Tanks on the east and west sides of the cellar are connected together in two banks, which are then joined at the southern end. The intention was to ensure that the water level in all tanks went down together when the water was drawn off, so that there would be no stagnation, such as might occur if a sequential draw-off pattern was employed. A sight gauge, comprising a transparent tube for a domestic-heating oil tank, was fitted to show the level of water in the tanks. Each tank has a screw lid, and in each lid a screened air vent was fitted to allow water to be added or removed without creating changes of pressure, and preventing the ingress of insects.

The two banks of tanks are joined to a manifold pipe from which the water is pumped to the primary filter in the conservatory. The pump is a 12-V Shurflo pump (Model 2088-403-144) with a pressure-operated switch that turns on the pump when it senses a drop in pressure caused by the demand for water. The pump (in the situation here, where it is pumping against little or no head of pressure) has a flow rate of 10.2 l/minute, and an electricity demand of 3.5 amps at 12 V.[64] A 12-V system is used for the water pumps so that there is no interruption of the water supply in the event of a mains power cut. The same battery as supplies power to the Clivus fan is used, a 12-V 100-AH gel electrolyte lead-acid battery; the gel electrolyte minimizes the possibility of hydrogen's being emitted by the battery during charging, which could carry an explosion risk. Battery charging is by means of a mains-operated charger specially made for this type of battery.

The pump takes the raw rainwater to the primary filter which is sited in the cellar part of the conservatory, where it is exposed to light. The filter itself is another orange juice tank with the whole top cut off to form an open cylindrical container. There is a draw-off pipe at the bottom, and the tank is filled with layers of pebbles, then gravel, then washed sand, with each layer separated from the next by a layer of geotextile to reduce the chances of blockage by the fine sand, and to allow the sand layer to be changed as necessary. A float valve controls the inlet of water to the top of the tank. The rainwater enters the tank and splashes over a clay tile laid on top of the sand in an attempt to aerate the incoming water. Further aeration is provided by a 230-V 5-W aquarium fountain that circulates the water that lies over the top of the sand.

To avoid difficulties in the matching of flow rates through the various parts of the system, and to provide a buffer storage in the event of repairs or breakdowns, the water from the filter passes by gravity to a further secondary storage tank in the cellar, one of the total of 20, which holds 1,500 l of sand-filtered water. Water for the house supply is taken from this secondary tank, but the presence of this large volume means that the rate at which water is drawn off does not have to match the rate at which water passes through the sand filter. A second Shurflo pump, of the same type as the first, takes the water from the secondary tank to supply the house. The water is pumped up 7.5 m to a 250-l header tank in the attic, which supplies the house by gravity, and forms a further back-up storage and buffer in the water supply. When water is used in the house, the pump from the secondary storage to the header tank does not have to supply water at the rate at which it is withdrawn from the header tank, just as the water can pass through the sand filter at a variable rate which is not the same as that at which it is withdrawn from the secondary storage. Having buffers in the system in the form of storage tanks makes the design of the system considerably simpler.

All taps in the bathrooms and kitchen are fed by gravity, with the exception of the kitchen sink, which is supplied with cold water from the 'rising main' (i.e., directly from the pump). The reason for this is that the kitchen sink has two cold taps; one, a mixer, supplies sand-filtered water used for washing up and general cleaning; the other is a separate drinking-water tap and is connected to a ceramic-filter cartridge with activated carbon core, contained in a stainless-steel housing under the sink. The system is made by Atriflo, and uses a Doulton ceramic-filter element. The pump provides a satisfactory flow through the filter, whereas by gravity alone the pressure would not force the water through the fine pores of this particular type of filter. The filter is designed to remove both bacterial contamination (via the ceramic component) and chemicals (via the carbon core). The manufacturers claim that the 'Supercarb' filter element 'reduces to safe levels' bacteria, cysts, chlorine, rust and sediment, taste and odour, and organic chemicals.[65] The children's bathroom is also fitted with a similar filter, connected to a third tap in the wash basin, to allow the cleaning of teeth with drinking water. In the parents' bathroom a jug of drinking water is used for teeth cleaning, and this is refilled from the kitchen tap as necessary. A cold-water feed of sand-filtered water is also provided for the washing machine, which is sited in the laundry area between the two bathrooms. The washing machine has no hot-water supply, and all washing is done in cold water, with the heating system of the machine turned off. Ecover clothes washing liquid is used: this detergent is made by a small Belgian company which received the United Nations Global 500 Award for Environmental Achievement in 1993.

Hot-water supply is entirely conventional, using a copper hot-water cylinder of overall dimensions 550 × 1,000 mm, with a factory-fitted Economy 7 insulating jacket of foam with zero-ozone-depleting potential. The thickness of the foam is approximately 60 mm and the cylinder capacity is 120 l. The manufacturers, IMI, quote a standing heat loss from the cylinder of 2.7 kWh/day for a water temperature of 60°C, a rate of 112.5 W.[66] At the base of the cylinder is a 3-kW electric immersion heater. The cylinder is gravity fed from the header tank in the attic. The original design for the house included two banks of evacuated-tube solar water-heating units, plus a 1,000-l insulated hot-water storage tank in the cellar, but at an estimated cost of £6,000, this was considered too expensive.

Hot-water demand was calculated as shown in the following table.

Table 5.11: Hot-water demand in l/head/day

dishes	2
personal hygiene	26 (of which 23 are assumed to be hot, and 2 cold)
total	25 l/head/day
total for whole house	125 l/day

This gives an annual hot-water demand of 45,625 l. The specific heat of water is 4.2 kJ/kgK or 1.16 Wh/kgK. If the water comes in at a temperature of 18°C, having been stored in the attic header tank (which will be at the same temperature as the house), and is heated to 55°C, this amount of water will need 1,958 kWh, an energy consumption rate of 5.4 kWh/day, to which must be added the standing loss from the hot-water cylinder, producing a total of 8.1 kWh/day.

All waste water (or 'grey' water) is handled conventionally. The baths, kitchen sink and children's wash basin have conventionally sized traps and wastes. The wash basin in the en-suite bathroom is not plumbed to any waste; here a traditional canal boat wash bowl is used, which is filled from the telephone type shower mixer on the bath, and tipped into the bath to empty. The traps are all plastic, but wastes are in copper pipe of the appropriate sizes, as this was felt to be more recyclable in the long run. All waste pipes run internally, and exit through the cellar wall in the conservatory to join a horizontal drain 50 mm in diameter that runs out at the north end of the conservatory. The drain is joined to a clayware Hepworth drain 100 mm in diameter where it passes through the wall, with a waterproofing sleeve built into the wall to maintain the watertight integrity of the cellar wall. This drain connects to a Hepworth clayware grease trap, intended to remove any grease that may have entered the waste water from the kitchen sink. From the grease trap the drain joins with the overflow from the rainwater storage tanks and passes to the soakaway, which handles all the grey water from the house.

Permission to discharge waste water to a soakaway was granted by the Nottingham office of the Pollution Inspectorate of the National Rivers Authority, which referred to the discharge as 'sullage'. The permission was sought on the grounds that, because all the water used in the house was rainwater collected from the roof, no more water would pass into the soil than had been entering the soil before the house was constructed. It was also explained that the water would contain only soap and Ecover detergents. The soakaway was constructed at a depth of about 1.5 m. The site rises slightly from the back of the house, and the key determinant of the depth of the drain entering the soakaway was the grease trap, which tended to leave the drain deeper than would have been preferred. The soakaway was constructed with a 150-mm-thick concrete base, which measured 1.5 × 1.5 m. On this were built walls of 225-mm-thick perforated brickwork, 900 mm in height, which carry a further reinforced-concrete slab that forms the top of the chamber. From one corner of this chamber rises an access shaft formed with concrete manhole sections, with step irons to allow access. The total capacity of the soakaway is 1,350 l, and this is increased by a backfilling of broken brick rubble round the outside of the chamber excavation. The capacity is therefore about 7 days of water use from the house. The soil of the site is clay, but relatively free-draining. The soakaway was fitted with a hand-operated bilge pump that could be used by removing the manhole cover, so that waste water could be pumped up for watering the garden, and excess water could be pumped away in times of heavy rainfall.

Space heating

The insulation installed when the house was built was intended to allow space heating to be provided by the body heat of the occupants, heat losses from the electric lights and appliances, and the effect of solar gain through the windows and conservatory. The wall insulation is 250-mm-thick resin-bonded glass fibre in a brick and concrete-block cavity wall; the roof insulation is 500-mm-thick cellulose fibre made from recycled newspaper; the windows are triple-glazed with two low-emissivity coatings and krypton gas filling between the panes. These insulation levels made it unnecessary to install a central-heating system in the conventional sense, but a source of heat was provided in the form of a wood-burning stove. This is a Danish Morsø 'Squirrel' rated at 4 kW.[67] The stove was obtained from a boat chandler's (Sawley Marina, near Long Eaton, Nottinghamshire) and is commonly used for heating on canal narrowboats. The stove is placed in the hall, at the foot of the stair, and is connected to a ceramic flue 150 mm in diameter with a mineral-fibre insulating jacket and stainless-steel casing, similar to that used to vent the sewage composter. The flashing for the flue where it passes through the roof was purpose-made in sheet copper, and there is a copper plate on the inside of the ceiling to allow the pipe to be separated from the wooden roof structure for fire protection.

Electricity

The loads to be supplied by electricity include:
domestic hot water
cooking

heat-recovery ventilation

lighting

appliances (refrigerator, washing machine, vacuum cleaner, kettle, toaster, blender etc.)

television, video, stereo, computers

power tools

water pumps and sewage ventilation fan

garden compost shredder

Appliances include a Gram LER 200 ultra-low-energy refrigerator, a washing machine operating with cold-water detergent, and electronic compact fluorescent light bulbs, all intended to reduce the electricity demand.

The most important decision that was made with regard to electricity for the autonomous house was to use a grid-linked system rather than batteries, for the reasons set out in Chapter 4. This had advantages that have been described there, but also meant that the electricity generation system could be installed after the house was occupied. The benefits of this strategy were twofold: firstly, the electricity demand could be measured in use, so that the system could be sized according to actual consumption rather than a theoretical estimate; secondly, it brought a financial advantage – the electrical system could be bought once the house that was being lived in during the construction of the autonomous house had been sold. This would reduce the amount of money that had to be borrowed to finance the construction of the new house. The other main decision was to use photovoltaics as the source of electricity. Although more expensive than a wind turbine in terms of expected electricity output per pound of capital cost, the photovoltaics have the twin advantages of having no moving parts (so no need for regular maintenance) and being far less visually intrusive – important in a town centre site.

The decision was taken at the initial design stage to separate out the main solar collecting photovoltaic system from the house fabric and mount it on a pergola in the garden. This was for a number of reasons: it would free the orientation of the building; it would give a better, less obstructed orientation to the south for the photovoltaic panels; it would allow the photovoltaic panels to operate with air cooling, raising their efficiency; it would give easy access for maintenance; it would allow simple expansion of the system; and it provided a model that could be applied easily to existing buildings.

The question of cooling of the photovoltaic panels is important: the current from all modules (as photovoltaic panels are also known) fades somewhat at higher temperatures. This is not an important consideration until ambient temperatures climb above 27°C (80°F), which is not uncommon in the sun. The backs of modules should be as well ventilated as possible. In very hot installations where surplus water is available, sprinklers are sometimes employed to cool the modules.[68]

Built into a roof, the panels would be likely to reach high temperatures as there would be little chance of efficient ventilation. The detailed design of the electricity system will be covered in Chapter 6, as the system was installed after the house had been occupied and its electrical consumption become known.

Fig. 34
The autonomous house from the garden

CONCLUSIONS

This description of the design decisions made for the autonomous house makes clear some of the compromises that were reached in the design process. In the end, the building is a home as well as a set of systems for achieving autonomy. Some of the decisions made were more to do with purely architectural considerations, such as the orientation of the house on its site. In constructional terms, the roof of structural softwood decking was a way of making a superinsulated roof with an exposed internal ceiling, but it is neither the only, nor the cheapest way of creating a roof with high insulation. Some decisions, such as the initial use of an electric immersion heater for hot water, were made on cost grounds, as there was not enough money for more sophisticated systems.

In many ways the house at Southwell was designed not as a prototype, but as an assembly of possibilities. It is *an* autonomous house, not *the* autonomous house. There are many other ways that the goal of autonomy could have been achieved, just as there are many ways that any building can be designed. It is hoped that this chapter has clarified the decisions that were made in arriving at the solution for this particular case.

6 | *Performance in Use*

THE PERFORMANCE OF THE FABRIC

The autonomous house was first occupied in mid-November 1993, although the conservatory was not completed until 24 December of that year. The areas of the completed house are given in Table 6.1.

Table 6.1: The areas of the autonomous house in m²

porch	7.0
ground floor	73.7
first floor	73.7
attic	21.6
area inside insulated envelope	176.0 m²
main cellar under house	66.0
cellar under conservatory	28.1
conservatory decks	20.1
total conservatory area	**48.2 m²**
total built floorspace area	**290.2 m²**
volume of main house	415.3 m³
volume of porch	15.4 m³
total volume of insulated envelope	**430.7 m³**

The fabric U values and heat losses from the house are given in Table 6.2.

Table 6.2: Fabric U values and heat losses for the autonomous house

element	U value (W/m²K)	area (m²)	heat loss (W/K)
walls	0.140	138.6	19.40
roof	0.065	125.4	8.15
ground floor (actual)	0.630	73.7	
cellar	0.190	142.6	
ground floor (apparent)*	0.200	73.7	14.74
glazing: north	1.100	3.2	3.52
glazing: south	1.100	7.9	8.69
glazing: east	1.100	9.9	10.89
glazing: west	1.100	10.1	11.11
rooflights	1.800	2.9	5.22
total glazing loss			**39.43 W/K**
total fabric loss			**79.74 W/K**
ventilation	0.2 ac/h	430.7 m³	28.43
total heat loss from house			**110.15 W/K** **0.63 W/m²K of insulated space** **0.26 W/m³K of insulated space**

Note: The value/m² of heated space includes the ground floor, first floor and attic, but excludes cellar and conservatory. U values for the building elements are calculated with the manufacturers' data for purchased components such as windows.

The value for the volumetric specific-heat loss of the autonomous house, 0.26 W/m³K of insulated space, can be compared with Table 6.3, which shows values quoted by Olivier.[1] It can be seen that the overall value for the autonomous house, at 0.26 W/m³K, is slightly greater than that achieved in the zero-energy houses in Germany and Switzerland, which are situated in colder

[To Table 6.2]
*The ground floor, unlike the ground floor of a conventional house, loses heat not to the ground but to a cellar. Cellar walls and floor lose heat to the ground. The calculated U value for the cellar (walls and floor, 0.19 W/m²K) is based on area-weighted data used for the ground floor slabs of conventional houses, and gives a U value which is intended to be used at the same temperature difference (Δt) as the other elements of the house. The calculation was made by considering the area of the floor and walls as if laid out flat, which approximates to a slab 20 × 10 m; the U value of such a slab would be 0.48 W/m²K. The walls are 500-mm-thick aerated concrete, which has a U value of 0.32 W/m²K. Adding the reciprocals of these two values gives a composite R value for the walls which makes allowance for the fact that the walls are not losing heat to the outside air, but to the ground (in other words the walls are behaving like a slab with 500-mm aerated-concrete insulation). The reciprocal gives the U value of 0.19 W/m²K. This is used for walls and floor because the cellar floor is so far below the ground that its heat loss will be much lower than that of a slab on ground, since the heat flow path to the outside air is not directly from the edge of the slab, but through about 2.5 m of soil.

The heat flow from the house to the cellar through the ground floor must be equal to the heat flow out of the cellar to the surrounding soil. This can be used to derive an apparent U value for the ground floor that sets aside the fact that the ground floor loses heat to a cellar whose temperature is governed by the average temperature of the ground, rather than external air temperature. In turn, this U value can then be used in conventional heat loss calculations as if it were the U value of the ground floor of a conventional house. If the cellar temperature is assumed to be at the temperature given by Page for a depth of 3.05 m below ground, an annual average of 10°C,² heat loss from the cellar to the outside, assuming an external temperature of 0°C will be:

142.6 m² (area of cellar walls and floor under the house, minus conservatory)
× 0.19 W/m²K (cellar overall U value)
× 10°C (Δt)
= 270.94 W

Heat loss through the ground floor will be given by:

floor area
× floor U value
× Δt,

and this should be equal to the loss from the cellar. Therefore, if the house is at 18°C, the apparent U value of the ground floor can be calculated as follows:

heat loss from cellar divided by (floor area × Δt)
= 270.94 divided by (73.7 × 18)
= 0.20 W/m²K.

climates. The performance in use of any house will be affected not only by its fabric insulation, ventilation levels, and the effects of its occupants, but also by the climate in which the house is situated. The site of the autonomous house, in Southwell, Nottinghamshire, is located at latitude 53° 4' N and longitude 0° 57' W. Page gives climate details for a number of sites in the United Kingdom,

Table 6.3:
Volumetric specific heat loss in W/m³/K of houses built to various insulation standards

UK 1990 Building Regulations	0.90
Netherlands	0.75
Germany	0.75
Switzerland	0.60
Sweden SBN-80	0.55
German low-energy	0.40
Dutch low-energy	0.35
German/Swiss 'zero-energy'	0.20
autonomous house	**0.26 W/m³/K**

Table 6.4:
Climatic data for Birmingham

month	monthly average dry-bulb air temperature (°C)*	monthly average sunshine (hours)**	daily incident radiation received by a vertical solar south-facing surface (kWh/day)***	maximum solar altitude****
Jan.	3.3	1.38	0.98	16.8°
Feb.	3.5	2.03	1.50	24.7°
Mar.	5.7	3.14	2.23	35.7°
April	8.5	4.55	2.53	47.3°
May	11.4	5.47	2.76	56.4°
June	14.5	6.15	2.82	60.6°
July	16.0	5.29	2.59	58.7°
Aug.	15.7	4.86	2.60	51.2°
Sep.	13.0	3.92	2.44	40.4°
Oct.	10.7	2.81	1.97	28.8°
Nov.	6.5	1.61	1.20	19.2°
Dec.	4.5	1.35	1.01	14.6°
Annual average: 9.5°C (monthly average); 3.55 h/day (= 1,296 h/year).				

*data from 1941–70;[4] **data from 1941–70;[5] ***data from 1949–70[6]

of which the closest to Southwell is Manchester (53° 30' N, 2° 15' W). However, the study of maps of seasonal duration of solar radiation in Fullard and Darby[3] suggests that the more appropriate climate comparison for Southwell, at least in respect of sunshine hours, would be Birmingham (52° 30' N, 1° 55' W). Page gives the data in Table 6.4 for Birmingham.

VENTILATION

Carpenter made a study for the Centre for Analysis and Dissemination of Demonstrated Energy Technolgies (CADDET) and the International Energy Agency of the world's advanced houses.[7] The autonomous house in Southwell is the only house in the United Kingdom considered sufficiently advanced to be included in the study. The average ventilation rate under pressure testing of the 16 advanced houses for which data are given by Carpenter (out of 25 houses studied by him) is 1.5 ac/h at 50 Pascals. Lowe et al. suggest that background ventilation rates under normal conditions can be determined by dividing the air change rate at 50 Pa by 20.[8] This calculation is confirmed in the *Draft Revision* of BS 5925: 1980, the Code of Practice for ventilation,[9] and would give a background ventilation rate for the advanced houses of 0.075 ac/h. Assuming that the autonomous house is typical of the other advanced houses of the world, in terms of its airtightness (although described in his study, it is one of the nine houses for which Carpenter does not have pressure test data), it could be assumed to have a similar background ventilation rate. Carpenter also lists the actual ventilation rates used in 20 of the 25 advanced houses, which vary from 0.18 to 0.72 ac/h;[10] the average is 0.41 ac/h. In the autonomous house, with its internal volume of 430.7 m³, this average rate would give ventilation of 176.6 m³/h, or 49.1 l/sec. The air supply rate recommended by the Chartered Institution of Building Services (CIBS, now the Chartered Institution of Building Services Engineers [CIBSE], but see Chapter 4) was 5 l/sec/person, which would give 25 l/sec for a five-person household. This would be a rate of 90 m³/h, or roughly 0.21 ac/h in the autonomous house. It can be seen that the average ventilation rate used in the advanced houses would be equivalent, in the autonomous house, to roughly 10 l/sec/person.

The use of heat-recovery ventilation allows a proportion of the heat in the air that leaves the house to be transferred into the air that comes in. For the ADM Indux heat-recovery ventilation units used in the autonomous house the manufacturer gives a heat-recovery efficiency of 70% (see Chapter 5). This alters the apparent rate of air change, at least in terms of the effect of the ventilation heat loss on the total heat loss of the house: 1 ac/h (actual) becomes, at 70%

heat exchange efficiency, 0.3 ac/h (thermal). At the average rate of ventilation for the advanced houses (0.41 ac/h), the air change rate (thermal) with full heat-recovery ventilation would be 0.12 ac/h; at the CIBS rate for the autonomous house volume it would be 0.06 ac/h. The rate of 0.2 ac/h that is used in Table 6.2 above is intended to represent a reasonable value for the house in the absence of detailed pressure test measurements.

The autonomous house makes use of heat-recovery ventilation, but this is operated only when required (i.e., when showering in winter, to remove condensation from the bathroom, or when carrying out elaborate or smelly cooking operations in the kitchen). For most of the time the ventilation in the house is provided by natural air leakage, and by use, as required, of the trickle vents above the windows. Semenenko[11] measured an air velocity of 0.8 m/sec in the extract duct of a passive stack ventilation system, when the inlet duct was closed, at a temperature difference (inside/outside) of 10K. This situation (one side opened, one side closed) is analogous to an open trickle vent in the window of a bedroom in the autonomous house, where considerable efforts have been made to reduce uncontrolled ventilation (similar to having the inlet duct closed). The area of the trickle vent is 3,300 mm^2, and in the main bedroom it serves a room with a floor area of 17.85 m^2 and a volume of 41.06 m^3. If air flows through the open trickle vent at a velocity of 0.8 m/sec, it will provide air at a rate of 2.64 l/sec or 9.5 m^3/h; this is a ventilation rate of 0.23 ac/h in the room. If there are four trickle vents in use, one in each bedroom, the total air supply rate to the house will be 38 m^3/h, or a rate for the whole house of 0.09 ac/h. The total number of trickle vents fitted in the house is 16, eight on the ground floor, six on the first floor and two in the attic. If all were open, the ventilation rate would increase to 0.37 ac/h, but this situation never occurs in winter, when all the vents are kept closed. In Table 6.2 a ventilation rate of 0.2 ac/h is used as an indication of the likely heat loss; it is reasonable to assume from the above calculations that this rate is not an underestimate. The rate was chosen as it is comparable to the lower range of ventilation rates reported by Carpenter for the advanced houses.

SPACE HEATING

In Chapter 4 use was made of a 'hypothetical room' that was similar to one of the bays of the autonomous house as built. The main bedroom of the finished house is one whole bay, and can be used as the basis of a simple heating calculation. Table 6.5 below shows the heat losses from the room.

As this room is occupied regularly by two people, it can be shown that the external air temperature has to fall to 3.5°C before the body heat of two people

Table 6.5: Heat losses from main bedroom with trickle vent open

element	area (m²)	U value (W/m²K)	heat loss (W/K)
external walls	22.50	0.14	3.15
floor	17.85	0.20	3.57
window	3.43	1.10	3.77
door	1.90	1.10	2.09
ventilation	41.06 m³	0.23 ac/h	3.12
total heat loss from room			15.70 W/K

(taken as 115 W each, as used in earlier calculations) is insufficient to heat the room to 18°C (15.7 W/K × 14.5K Δt = 228 W). However, if the people are asleep, the heat output is reduced, and it will also be reduced if the people are a man and a woman, as women tend to have a lower heat output than men. Table 6.6 below shows the heat output for men, women and children over a number of activity ranges.[12] It should be noted that these data (from the *European Passive Solar Handbook*) assume a skin surface area for an adult man of 1.8 m², whereas the CIBSE data used in Chapter 4 are based on a man with a surface area of 2 m².

Table 6.6: Heat emissions in W from people

	sleeping	sitting	light activity	medium activity
men	72	99	140	198
women	64	88	125	176
children	40	55	78	110

Note: the assumed skin surface areas are 1.8m² (for men), 1.6 m² (for women), and 1 m² (for children).

If the bedroom contains a man and a woman, their combined heat output, when asleep, will be 136 W. This will be sufficient to heat the bedroom to 18°C until the exterior temperature falls to 9.3°C. In a study of sleeping, Achard and Gicquel comment: 'The bedclothes also reduce conductive, radiative or convective heat loss, so that temperature levels in the room can be below the daily average standard.'[13] Brundrett gives an optimum operative temperature range for sleeping, which will result in only 10% of occupants experiencing discomfort, of 18°C, ± 3°C.[14] This would suggest that the bedroom temperature could be allowed to fall to 15°C, which would mean that the exterior temperature could fall to 6.3°C before discomfort was reached. This assumption omits any effects from both solar gains and thermal mass. A bedroom temperature lower than 15°C need not be assumed to be unacceptable; Höppe reported the result of experiments in which subjects slept for several nights in a climate chamber: '... the difference between the sleep quality at air temperatures of $T_a = 12°C$ and $T_a = 18°C$ is rather small.'[15] If Höppe's lower temperature limit is acceptable, the outside temperature could fall to 3.3°C before discomfort was experienced and, as shown in Table 6.4, this is the lowest monthly average dry-bulb air temperature, experienced in January.

There may be seen to be a potential problem related to the trickle vent, in that the CIBS recommendation for air supply is 5 l/sec/person (see above), but the trickle vent provides only 2.64 l/sec. However, the CIBS figure is not the amount of air required to sustain life. Billington and Roberts reported that in the 19th century, Péclet found that one person required only 0.1 l/sec of fresh air for respiration.[16] Péclet also recommended a rate of 2.3 l/sec to prevent body odours from being detected in ordinary rooms. The trickle vent in theory is certainly providing an adequate air supply for both the maintenance of life, and to ensure that the room is not smelly.

These calculations and comments have been borne out in practice, where the effects of thermal mass and solar gains come into play. The bedroom is perfectly comfortable in use. On winter nights when the external temperature falls, the trickle vent may be closed, and it is left closed during the day to allow the temperature to rise due to any solar gain. If the background ventilation rate of the room with the vent closed is the same as that reported for the other advanced houses (0.075 ac/h), the airflow into the bedroom will be 0.86 l/sec with the vent closed, more than enough, according to Péclet, to sustain life. The fact that both occupants have remained alive after nights with the vent closed confirms this theory. Heat gains from the occupants during the night are supplemented by passive solar energy received during the day through the large south-facing window and stored in the floor slab and the mass of the walls. When the exterior temperature falls close to freezing, minor condensation sometimes occurs on the window glass close to the lower edge of the window frame; this is wiped up as required. There has been no evidence of mould growth in the room, except when the house was first occupied and was drying out; the occurrence of condensation was expected at this time, due to the high-mass masonry construction and wet plaster. The lowest recorded temperature in the bedroom in the winter of 1994–95 was 15°C, in February. By 22 October 1995, the lowest temperature recorded for the bedroom for the forthcoming winter was 20°C. The only problem in the bedroom is that the tiled floor (for maximum exposure of mass) feels cold to bare feet in the winter. This is alleviated by wearing slippers, and by the use of rugs either side of the bed.

The bedroom has also performed satisfactorily in extremes of heat. In the hot summer of 1995, the bedroom was ventilated by means of the trickle vent. The windows were left closed as the bedrooms are on the ground floor, and it was felt that open windows might be a security problem. The opening of windows at night had also caused problems previously with the unexpected arrival of cats in the night; cats on the bed tended to cause respiratory distress. Additional secure night ventilation in summer was achieved by opening the door into the conservatory at night, with the conservatory vents and rooflights also open, and the cat flaps locked shut to keep the cats out in the garden – there are two lockable cat flaps at either end of a plywood tunnel through the brickwork of the conservatory wall, forming a cats' air lock. The conservatory vents are a series of airbricks with adjustable sliding covers, so having them open does not mean that the security of the space is reduced. In spite of daytime external temperatures in excess of 30°C on occasion during the summer of 1995, the bedroom temperature never rose above 23°C.

With a single occupant in the room it was noticeably colder in the bedroom in the winter; this was reported by Brenda Vale, who remained in the house while Robert Vale was on sabbatical in New Zealand from 12 February 1995 for five months. During the first part of this period she made use of a hot water bottle to offset the missing heat output. A hot water bottle holds 1 l of water; to operate the hot water bottle, it is filled with water that has been boiled, and then allowed to cool to 95°C. The bottle then loses heat overnight, ending at a temperature of 20°C in the bed. At a specific heat of 1.16 Wh/kgK the water will have given off 87 Wh over the night, which is equivalent to little more than one hour of a person in the same bed. However, the maximum heat loss occurs at the highest temperature difference, so the bottle will be emitting heat at an average rate of perhaps 70 W during the first hour of its use; during this time the occupant of the bed is awake and then falling asleep, so gains the maximum benefit from the additional heat input from the hot water bottle. The main bedroom and the children's bedrooms (which are half the floor area of the main bedroom, but each of which contains only one person as opposed to two) are, in practice, heated adequately by their occupants.

The definition of what might constitute an 'adequate' or even 'comfortable' temperature is extremely imprecise. Assuming that the temperatures at which people keep their houses represent the temperatures at which they wish to live, it is clear that preferred temperatures are rising in parallel with the increasing use of central heating, which grew from 13% of UK households in 1964 to 66% in 1984.[17] Lowe et al. give the following data for average internal winter temperatures for houses in a number of post-war field trials.[18]

Table 6.7: Whole house average internal winter temperatures

year of study	range of average temperature (average)	no. of houses
1948–49	12.2–16.3°C (14.3°C)	36
1949–50	12.0–17.5°C (14.8°C)	36
1949–50	(13.2°C)	259
1969–73	17.0–19.5°C (18.3°C)	60
1971	18.0–19.0°C (18.5°C)	10
1977	16.3–16.7°C (16.5°C)	11
1977	(14.6°C)	12
1978	(15.6°C)	24
1981–82	(17.8°C)	37
1981–82	(18.4°C)	18
1981–82	(19.1°C)	17
1982–83	(18.6°C)	6

The rise in average temperatures is not steady, but it is apparent. The reasons that rising temperatures in housing present a potential problem are twofold. The first is that increasing temperatures must mean increasing energy consumption, as Lowe et al. explain: 'In the sort of houses being studied here a 1°C increase in the mean internal temperature will cause a 10–15% change in space heating energy, 1,000–2,000 kWh/year of useful energy, or 1,500–3,000 kWh/year of gas. In other words a 1°C temperature rise is about equivalent to the maximum estimate of the benefit from the passive solar design.'[19]

More recent measurements than those in the table above suggest that the trend for temperatures to rise is continuing. Monitoring by Pilkingtons of the Cresswell Road houses in Sheffield designed by Brenda and Robert Vale in 1992 showed whole-house average temperatures of 21.2°C and 21.6°C.[20] Calculations of the effect of these high internal temperatures on the overall energy consumption of the houses are given in detail in Appendix 6. These calculations show that the houses would have used, overall, 125 kWh/m^2, had they been heated to normal internal design temperatures, rather than the measured 134 kWh/m^2. The overheating causes an increase in overall energy consumption of only 7%.

The results from the Cresswell Road monitoring show three important points: that superinsulation makes space heating relatively unimportant as a determinant of whole-house energy consumption; that the biggest scope for energy saving in a superinsulated house is in hot water, which is the largest energy consumer; and that a superinsulated house needs to have highly energy-efficient lights and appliances if it is to show significant energy savings.

In conclusion, it should be pointed out that the Cresswell Road houses appear overall to have a reduced energy consumption, of about 50% of the UK national average. Rising temperatures do not, therefore, seem to necessitate great increases in the overall energy consumption of superinsulated conventional houses, provided that such houses have efficient space-heating systems, such as the gas-fired condensing boiler and thermostatically controlled radiators used at Cresswell Road.

The main problem of rising internal temperatures for the designer of an autonomous house is that the higher the required temperature, the more difficult it will be to operate the house on renewable energy sources. This suggests that it is important to consider what temperatures it might be reasonable to provide in the house. A conventionally serviced house can draw on its energy supply in the form of electricity, gas or other non-renewable fuels to achieve any temperature that the occupants desire or can afford. The effect of higher temperatures in a highly insulated house has little overall effect on its consumption of fuel, because space heating is such a small part of the total energy requirement. In the Cresswell Road houses, the increase in measured space-heating energy consumption over the predicted consumption was 37%, but the total space-heating demand was so small that this increase represented only 763 kWh/year.

The problem of the autonomous house is different; it is similar to that faced by the Ice Age inhabitants of Europe.

Although clothes had been made from skins for hundreds of thousands of years, life in Europe, at the height of the last glaciation, required major improvements in survival techniques. Hoods, gloves and foot mittens were produced and by 20,000 years ago, eyed needles and fine thread (a product of fur trapping) were being used. Good insulation from the cold provided by warm clothing meant that the level of calorie intake necessary for survival in the harsh conditions was kept low enough to be extractable from the environment.[21]

Fig. 35
*The Cresswell Road
houses, Sheffield*

The occupants of an autonomous house face a similar task of extracting sufficient calorie intake (for heating) from the environment. The lower the temperature that they need in order to feel comfortable, the less difficulty they face in attempting to achieve this temperature by using ambient energy sources, as they do not have access to non-renewable energy sources to allow them to select any required level of space heating.

Table 6.7 above makes clear that modern houses tend to be kept at higher temperatures than they were in the late 1940s, and the results from the Cresswell Road houses show that, all other things being equal, people will attempt to maintain quite high temperatures in houses. However, temperatures vary considerably, and perceptions of comfort vary also. Goulding et al. sum up the situation as follows:

> *The research in thermal comfort in passive solar buildings ... has been backed up by additional field trials to investigate people's experiences of indoor climates, both transient and steady-state, in buildings they use in real life. The study has been carried out in houses, schools, offices and hospitals in Germany, France and the United Kingdom. Some are conventional buildings, others contain passive solar features. The results show that generally the temperatures required for thermal comfort are significantly lower in all building types than those predicted from models established through laboratory-based research. They gave, for example, the following operative temperatures for optimal conditions:*

21°C for office workers in Germany and France; 19°C for schoolteachers in France; 19°C for hospital occupants in the United Kingdom: and still lower temperatures for houses in the United Kingdom and France. These figures compare with predicted operative temperatures for thermal neutrality in the range 23–25°C.[22]

Humphreys[23] has produced a graph which relates indoor comfort temperature to outdoor temperature, on the premise that the body accepts differing temperatures depending on the temperatures to which it is exposed. In a similar vein, Bainbridge remarks: 'The comfort range will be tempered by climate as experience has shown that the desert heating season begins when indoor temperature drops below 75°F [24°C], while in Alaska it may be shirtsleeve weather in the 50s [10–15°C].'[24] He adds: '... with proper radiant temperature it can be quite comfortable with [internal] air temperature as low as 60°F [15.6°C].'[25]

Referring to Humphreys' work, Evans makes a similar point about the relationship between thermal comfort and external temperature: 'The study ... indicates that the comfort range within which people feel comfortable extends to a band width of about 4K, and that the centre of the comfort zone varies linearly from about 16°C to 31.5°C as the *average temperature* experienced during the month varies from 16°C to 35°C.'[26] Average temperature is defined in this instance as follows: 'This is not average *external* temperature but the average of the internal *and* external temperatures to which the individual is exposed.'[27] This would imply a comfort zone that had a lower end band width from 14°C to 18°C, but Evans also comments:

> *The range of dry bulb temperatures within which comfortable conditions may be established is approximately between 16°C to 28°C: below 16°C excessive clothing or high activity rates are required, and even this temperature is cool if activity rates are low ... The maximum clothing which could be worn in the house without restricting movement for normal household activities is just over 1 clo unit.*[28]

It is appropriate here to define the 'clo' unit, mentioned by Evans. It is the unit that expresses the insulation value of clothing, first proposed by Gagge et al. in 1941.[29] One clo is defined as a 'typical business suit'; nudity is 0 clo, and a suit with waistcoat and overcoat will give a value between 1.5 and 2.0 clo.[30] The detailed (US) table of clo values (Table 6.8 overleaf) allows the calculation of the clo value of a given clothing ensemble by the formula $I_{cl} = 0.82 \times \sum I_{cli}$, where I_{cl} is the total insulation value of the whole outfit in clo units, and I_{cli} is the value in clo of each individual garment.

Table 6.8: Clo values for individual garments

garment		clo
pantyhose		0.01
socks	light	0.03
	heavy	0.04
underwear	bra and panties	0.05
	half slip	0.13
	full slip	0.19
	briefs	0.05
	undershirt	0.05
shirts	t shirt	0.09
	light: short sleeved	0.20
	light: long sleeved	0.28
	heavy: short sleeved	0.25
skirt	warm	0.22
dress	light	0.17
	heavy	0.63
sweater	light: short sleeved	0.17
	heavy: long sleeved	0.37
jacket	heavy	0.49
trousers	heavy	0.26
	medium	0.32
	heavy	0.44
shoes	light	0.04

Note: the table, garment nomenclature and formula for adding clo values are taken from Ruck.[31]

Using Ruck's formula and the values in Table 6.8 (although the garments given do not seem to form an exhaustive list) suggests that the clothing levels normally worn in the autonomous house in the middle of winter offer a clo value of between 1.0 and 1.1 clo. Experience of this would suggest that the comment made by Evans is true; it would be difficult to wear clothing with a much higher insulation value, although thermal underwear (long johns and a long-sleeved vest) might be a possibility. Thermal underwear was not needed in the 1994–95 winter; it seemed important to experience the house and its temperatures in a range of more-or-less normal clothing.

The variation of indoor comfort temperature with outdoor temperature is also reported by Auliciems.[32] In addition, writing a handbook on climate change for the Royal Australian Institute of Architects, Szokolay states:

> It is generally accepted and axiomatic that the design of a building must suit the climate. Climatic design must start with the setting of appropriate design indoor conditions. A progressive school of thought recognises that the temperature perceived as comfortable varies with the climate and with the season. The theoretical 'neutrality temperature', the mid-point of the comfort zone, can be found as:

$$T_n = 17.6 + 0.31 \times T_{av}$$

> where T_{av} = mean outdoor temperature of the month; provided that the result is between 18.5°C and 28.5°C (some authors suggest 17°C and 30°C as the limits).
> The width of the comfort zone can then be taken as 4 degrees, i.e., from T_n – 2 to T_n + 2. Setting the indoor design temperatures in this way would already lead to energy conservation.[33]

The figures given here would suggest a possible lower limit for the comfort zone of between 15°C and 16.5°C. Szokolay's formula can be used to calculate a set of monthly comfort temperatures for the autonomous house during the winter heating season, using the temperature data from Table 6.4; these temperatures are given in Table 6.9. It can be seen that the house temperature did not fall below the lower limits of Szokolay's comfort criteria during the winter of 1995–96.

Some work has been carried out on counteracting lower indoor temperatures by the use of warmer clothing in houses, notably in a book by the Director of the Office of Energy Conservation in Boulder, Colorado, which proposes the idea of insulating the occupants as opposed to heating the space:

*... we are simply adjusting to a drop of the thermostat to 65 or 55 degrees
Fahrenheit [18.3°C/12.8°C] ... Tightly woven cotton trousers can be replaced
with lightweight wool ones, loose enough to permit the addition of long
underwear if needed. This combination of wool trousers and long underwear
allows a four degree [2.2°C] drop in air temperature without a loss of comfort ...
Adding a light sweater permits the thermostat to be lowered an additional two
degrees [1.1°C] ... A heavy sweater permits a drop of four degrees.*[34]

The total suggested reduction in temperature here, assuming wool trousers, long
underwear and a heavy sweater, is 8 deg F, or 4.4K. This would give, if applied to
Szokolay's range of neutrality temperatures, a lowest mid-point temperature (T_n
rather than $T_n - 2$) of 14.2°C in January. Interestingly, this temperature is the
average winter temperature reported by Schipper et al. for Japanese houses.[35]
They found that in winter, households with similar annual incomes in countries
with similar energy prices kept their houses at very different average
temperatures. These ranged from about 14°C in Japan to 17°C in Norway and
21°C in Sweden. Clearly, temperature in houses is determined by culture as much
as by external climate.

The temperature in the living room of the autonomous house was measured
initially during the winter of 1994–95. It declined steadily from 22°C in mid-
September 1994, to a low point of 16°C in mid-January, with daily variation of no
more than half a degree. (As the house is of high-mass masonry construction, it
may well not have been fully dried out by September 1994, which was less than a
year after initial occupation; in mid-October 1995, the living room temperature
was still 23°C.) At the beginning of March 1995 the temperature began to rise and
reached a high point of 27°C in the very hot August of that year. The lowest
recorded temperature occurred on two occasions in February 1995, in the
evening, and was 15.5°C. The readings were taken from a thermometer issued by
Newark and Sherwood District Council to its housing tenants. This is a simple
dial thermometer with a white band within which tenants are advised to keep
their heating for maximum comfort and economy, and to avoid condensation.
The band covers the range from 16–21°C. Tenants are advised: 'Temperature just
right – stay in the white.' Readings were made also with a liquid crystal
thermometer. Both thermometers were checked by spot readings against a
British Gas ESMI electronic thermometer made by Portec of Ampthill, Bedford,
and were found to give accurate readings.

The temperatures achieved in the autonomous house, with a January and
February average in the living room of 16°C, are not what is generally considered
to be comfortable, although the examples given above suggest that such
temperatures might be acceptable. There is a reasonable match between the

Table 6.9: Monthly winter 'neutrality temperatures' for the autonomous house, where $T_n - 2$ represents the lower limit of the comfort zone

month	T_{av} (°C)	T_n (°C)	$T_n - 2$ (°C)	average living room temperature 1995–96 (°C)
Oct.	10.7	20.9	18.9	22.4 (1995)
Nov.	6.5	19.6	17.6	18.3 (1995)
Dec.	4.5	19.0	17.0	18.0 (1995)
Jan.	3.3	18.6	16.6	17.7 (1996)
Feb.	3.5	18.7	16.7	17.7 (1996)
Mar.	5.7	19.4	17.4	17.5 (1996)

1995–96 winter temperatures in the living room and Szokolay's $T_n - 2$ values as shown in Table 6.9, but these figures are for a year later than the values discussed above. During this time the house dried out further, losing construction moisture from its plastered masonry walls and concrete floors, and was therefore able to maintain higher temperatures.

From October 1996 the autonomous house was rented out by the Nottingham Community Housing Association, a provider of social housing. The tenants have measured the living room temperature, and have commented: 'from the first lighting of the Squirrel [the wood-burning stove] on the 21st November [1997] to the last fire of the winter (5th Feb) [1998] the range was between 17°C and 15.5°C.'[36] Apart from the similarity of the figures to those given in Table 6.9, the other interesting point in these comments is the shortness of the heating season. The standard heating season for houses in the United Kingdom runs from the beginning of October to the end of April, a total of 212 days. The heating season experienced by the tenants of the autonomous house is only 76 days. During this period, only 278 kg of wood were burned.[37]

Also of interest, as an occupant of the house, is the feel of the temperatures achieved in it. Under apparently similar conditions, at similar times of day, and at similar temperatures, comfort appeared to be determined largely by mental state. If one occupant was depressed or anxious, they would feel cold while another was quite comfortable in identical conditions. The problem of the house was that it was not possible to turn up the heat if one did feel depressed or 'cold'. This sense of 'psychological coldness' was compensated for to some extent by the Morsø 'Squirrel' wood-burning stove in the hall, which was designed for this purpose to provide some visual cheer during long periods of overcast weather. During the 1994–95 winter, the stove was used on numerous occasions, particularly at weekends, and consumed a total of 315 kg of wood; Appendix 7 shows the details of the wood usage over that winter. The wood was all waste found on the site in the form of old hen houses and sheds, and trees felled by the previous owners of the land. All branches with a diameter less than about 20 mm were shredded for compost, and all other wood was sawn up for fuel. The wood was stored in the conservatory, for six months. The moisture content of a range of samples was measured at 9–14%, using a Protimeter TimberMini moisture meter. The Timber Research and Development Association (TRADA) gives a minimum value for air-dried timber of 17%.[38] The effect of the conservatory has been comparable to kiln drying. Various authorities give differing values for the calorific content of wood as a fuel. Page suggests 16.5 MJ/kg for wood at 20% moisture content,[39] while Sunley gives 16.0 MJ/kg for wood at 25% moisture content, and 20 MJ/kg for dry wood.[40] Helbro gives a value of 5.2 kWh/kg (18.7 MJ/kg) for totally dry wood, and 4.5 kWh/kg (16.2 MJ/kg) for wood at 20% moisture content. He adds that it is 'not realistic' to count on a higher energy content than this.[41] Taking an average of these values (excluding those for totally dry timber) gives a figure of 16.2 MJ/kg, or 4.5 kWh/kg, which will be used here. This suggests that the space-heating energy consumption of the autonomous house for the 1994–95 winter was 1,418 kWh, or 8.1 kWh/m² (based on a heated floor area of 176 m²); this is the delivered-energy consumption. If the stove is 65% efficient, the useful heat gain to the house will have been 922 kWh.

Whether or not this energy input to the house is significant depends on how the matter is viewed. As wood is a biological fuel, it could be assumed to be comparable to the use of solar energy or other renewable energy sources. As Helbro says:

> Wood is completely decomposed in a proper combustion. It must be said to be our most environmentally compatible fuel (except hydrogen), as the only pollutants are NO_x [oxides of nitrogen] which appear from every combustion where atmospheric air is used. If the combustion, on the other hand, is incomplete then some harmful and malodorous substances appear, which can be of great inconvenience in the local environment. However, they are not comparable to the substances that occur from combustion of oil and coal which may do irreparable harm to the global environment.[42]

The use of the wood-burning stove was not connected to the need for heat, and had as much to do with mood and a sense of well-being as with straightforward thermal considerations. Perhaps the best analogy lies in a comparison of wood with food. Both are an external source of solar-derived biomass energy input to the building and its occupants. In the winter in the autonomous house it is noticeable, if not surprising, that the intake of food rises, and the type of food changes to hot dishes with high carbohydrate content. This use of food to compensate for low external temperatures can be seen clearly in most Victorian novels, where the characters seem to consume huge quantities of food compared to the late 20th century.

It is instructive to compare the intake of food by the inhabitants of the autonomous house with the energy used by the wood-burning stove.

occupant	sex	age	daily intake (kcal)	MJ/day	kWh/day
Robert	m	47	3,200	13.40	3.73
Brenda	f	46	2,300	9.63	2.68
(William	m	20	3,200	13.40	3.73)
Ellen	f	17	2,400	10.05	2.79
Richard	m	15	3,100	12.98	3.61

Table 6.10: Theoretical food consumption in the autonomous house

total daily recommended food energy consumption	46.06 MJ, 12.81 kWh
annual net food energy consumption	4,676 kWh
annual net food energy consumption/m²	27.7 kWh/m²/year
annual primary food energy consumption	23,380 kWh
annual primary food energy consumption/m²	132.8 kWh/m²/year*
annual delivered wood fuel consumption	1,418 kWh
annual delivered wood fuel consumption m²	8.1 kWh/m²/year
annual net wood fuel consumption at 65% efficiency	922 kWh
annual net wood fuel consumption/m²	5.2 kWh/m²

Note: these values for daily food intake are the recommended daily calorie allowances given by the Food and Agriculture Organisation of the United Nations for the ages and sexes of the people listed.[43] The ages of the occupants are those at the beginning of October 1995. It should be noted that the eldest son was not at home during much of the period under study, so his food consumption is excluded from the total. If there had been five people living full-time in the house, the annual net food energy consumption would have been 6,033 kWh, or 35.7 kWh/m²/year.
*figure obtained using the 'energy ratio for food production' for 'all food supply, UK, 1968' calculated by Leach, 1975.[44]

The figures for the food energy for the autonomous house, and therefore for any house, since these figures assume a standard diet, can be compared with the overall energy consumption of a typical house, and that of the Cresswell Road houses in Sheffield. The energy consumption figures in Appendix 6 are calculated from data in Shorrock et al.[45] and Bell et al.[46]

Table 6.11: Annual food and energy consumption in various households

use of energy	delivered energy consumption (kWh/m²)
Typical UK house	
space heating (gas)	146
hot water (gas)	65
lights and appliances (electricity)	28
cooking (gas)	18
total for house	257 kWh/m²
food	53 kWh/m² (21% of the total)
Cresswell Road houses	
space heating (gas)	32
hot water (gas)	59
lights and appliances (electricity)	26
cooking (gas)	17
total for house	**134 kWh/m²**
food	53 kWh/m² (40% of the total)

Note: it is assumed that the floor area of the typical UK house is 88.2 m², as the Cresswell Road houses.

It is clear from these figures that the importance of food as an energy input to houses rises as the houses' energy consumption falls. If Leach's energy ratio of 0.2 is brought into the calculation to give the primary energy content of the food, the situation looks much worse. The food primary energy becomes 265 kWh/m², comparable with the total delivered-energy consumption of the typical house, while for the Cresswell Road houses the food energy input is twice the house's total

Table 6.12: Thermal mass in the autonomous house

element	volume (m³)	mass (kg)	thermal storage (kWh/K)
ground-floor screed	3.685	7,739	2.167
first-floor screed	3.335	7,004	1.960
attic screed	0.998	2,096	0.587
ground-floor tiles	0.884	2,044	0.470
first-floor tiles	0.800	1,850	0.425
floor beams	4.698	11,134	3.118
floor blocks	12.922	18,608	5.210
plaster soffits	0.807	1,049	0.294
(total for floors	28.129 m³	51,522 kg	14.231 kWh/K)
roof decking	8.469	5,496	4.232
exterior walls	14.549	33,463	9.370
exterior-wall plaster	1.746	2,270	0.635
crosswalls	11.535	26,531	7.427
crosswall plaster	1.846	2,399	0.672
internal walls	1.937	4,455	1.247
internal plaster	0.465	604	0.169
partitions	0.727	472	0.363
(total for walls	32.805 m³	70,194 kg	19.883 kWh/K
total for house	69.403 m³	127,213 kg	38.346 kWh/K

volume of mass/m² of floor area: 0.39 m³

mass/m² of floor area: 723 kg/m²

thermal storage/m² of floor area: 0.22 kWh/K/m² (0.78 MJ/K/m²)

delivered-energy consumption. Leach's calculation relates to 1968. The increase in processed foods in the last 30 years may well have made the ratio even less advantageous. It is clear that significant savings in the fossil-fuel consumption of the domestic sector may be achieved by encouraging the use of home-grown food, produced using methods that avoid oil-based fertilizers and insecticides.

Any discussion of space heating should also consider the thermal mass of the house. Table 6.12 itemizes the various mass elements used in the house, and shows their relative contributions to the total mass. The thermal mass of the autonomous house can be compared with the mass proposed by Lund (see Chapter 4) which had a volume of over 1 m^3 for each square metre of floor area, and would give a storage capacity of 1.96 $MJ/K/m^2$, two and a half times that achieved in the autonomous house. It is interesting to compare the autonomous house with the Hockerton earth-sheltered houses, a group of five autonomous houses designed by Brenda and Robert Vale and built about 5 km (3 miles) north of Southwell. The Hockerton houses have been designed to give a much higher thermal mass than that of the autonomous house.[47] The autonomous house is designed to be as massive as is possible without increasing the dimensions of components beyond what is needed for structural and constructional purposes. In the case of the Hockerton houses, additional mass has been incorporated giving a total of 2,278 kg/m^2, which has a thermal-storage capacity of 2.3 $MJ/K/m^2$, in excess of Lund's requirement.

Table 6.2 showed that the specific-heat loss from the autonomous house was 0.63 W/m^2K. During January, the coldest month of the year, with an average temperature of 3.3°C, the heat loss (using the data in Table 6.4) will be 9.26 W/m^2, assuming a house temperature of 18°C. The mass, with its thermal capacity of 0.22 $kWh/m^2/K$, will store enough heat to meet this heating demand for roughly 24 hours for each degree Kelvin that the temperature of the mass is reduced. Over the heating season as a whole, from October to April inclusive, the average external temperature will be 6.1°C, giving a heating demand of 7.5 W/m^2. The mass will store enough heat to meet this demand for 29 hours for every degree drop in the temperature of the mass.

WASTE AND WATER

When the autonomous house was first occupied in the middle of November 1993, the plumber had half-filled the rainwater storage tanks with water from a bowser to check the joints for leaks and the operation of the pumps. The Clivus Multrum had been charged with a mixture of softwood shavings and activated sewage sludge supplied by Southern Water.

The Clivus Multrum

The Clivus Multrum composter was one of the principal determinants of the design of the house. Finding space for it determined to some extent the bay size, and the need for a cellar; the decision to put the bathrooms on the ground floor was also partly related to the desire to minimize the drop from the toilet seat to the compost chamber. The Clivus Multrum was also the key factor in the ability to reduce water consumption to a level where the water supply could be collected from the roof. Finally, it was one of the most important symbolic elements of the design; the majority of the house systems were more-or-less conventional, but the use of a composting toilet was a potentially different approach to sewage treatment, which might prove unacceptable in use.

In fact, the Clivus has proven to be quite simple and trouble-free in operation. The large diameter (350 mm) of the shafts that connect the toilets to the compost tank means that very little waste touches the sides of the toilet chute, which is formed in dark grey plastic. The end result is that there is seldom any need to clean the toilets, unlike with a conventional water-flushed toilet. The positive ventilation provided by the 5-W fan eliminates any smell in the bathrooms, as air is always drawn from the room into the toilet, rather than the reverse, which happens with a conventional toilet and wall-mounted extractor fan.

At intervals of four to six weeks the liquid that collects in the base of the composter is pumped into a bucket. This liquid is very dark brown in colour, slightly frothy, and has a faint smell similar to that of seaweed liquid fertilizer from a garden centre. The liquid has been used in three ways: in the summer of 1994 it was diluted with water and used to water the tomato, pepper and melon plants in the conservatory; in the winter, when little growth was taking place in the conservatory, the liquid was poured round the base of apple trees and hedges in the garden; and finally, it was used as an activator on the compost heap. No other fertilizer was used on the plants in the conservatory, and they grew well. It was very satisfying to see a supposed waste product turned into a resource that eliminated the need to buy in garden fertilizers and compost activators. Except when liquid is being pumped up at weekly intervals for the conservatory, the other maintenance tasks for the Clivus are performed at the same time as the liquid removal. The first task is to clean the toilet and wipe round the inside of its shaft with toilet paper, which can then be dropped down into the compost container. The second job involves opening the sealed access hatch on the composter and using a rake (supplied with the unit) to level off the waste piles which have built up in a cone shape under each of the toilets.

Initially, this was the only part of the whole maintenance procedure that was in any way unpleasant, as the tines of the rake had to be wiped clean when it was withdrawn through the hatch. This problem has been solved by shortening the

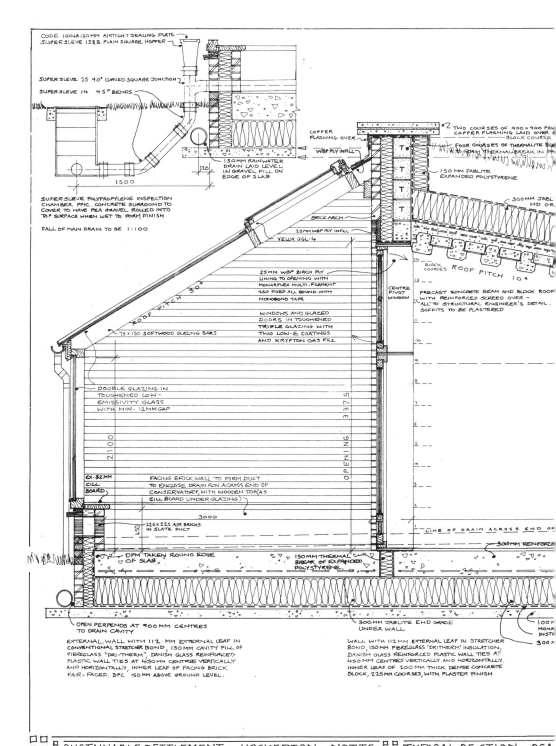

CODE 100 & 150 MM AIRTIGHT SEALING PLATE
SUPER SLEVE 158 B PLAIN SQUARE HOPPER

SUPER SLEVE 25 90° CURVED SQUARE JUNCTION

SUPER SLEVE 14   45° BENDS

SUPER SLEVE POLYPROPYLENE INSPECTION
CHAMBER PPIC, CONCRETE SURROUND TO
COVER TO HAVE PEA GRAVEL ROLLED INTO
TOP SURFACE WHEN WET TO FORM FINISH

FALL OF MAIN DRAIN TO BE 1:100

150MM RAINWATER
DRAIN LAID LEVEL
IN GRAVEL FILL ON
EDGE OF SLAB

COPPER
FLASHING OVER
WBP PLY INFILL

TWO COURSES OF 900 × 900 PAV
COPPER FLASHING LAID OVER
BLOCK COURSE
FOUR COURSES OF THERMALITE BL
WITH FOAM THERMAL BREAK IN PA

150 MM JABLITE
EXPANDED POLYSTYRENE

300MM JABL
HD GR

BRICK ARCH
25MM WBP PLY INFILL

VELUX GGL·4

BLOCK
COURSES ROOF PITCH 10°

25MM WBP BIRCH PLY
LINING TO OPENING WITH
MONARFLEX MULTI-FILAMENT
150 FIXED ALL ROUND WITH
MONOBOND TAPE

CENTRE
PIVOT
WINDOW

PRECAST CONCRETE BEAM AND BLOCK ROOF
WITH REINFORCED SCREED OVER -
ALL TO STRUCTURAL ENGINEER'S DETAIL.
SOFFITS TO BE PLASTERED

ROOF PITCH 30°

WINDOWS AND GLAZED
DOORS IN TOUGHENED
TRIPLE GLAZING WITH
TWO LOW-E COATINGS
AND KRYPTON GAS FILL

75 × 150 SOFTWOOD GLAZING BARS

DOUBLE GLAZING IN
TOUGHENED LOW-
EMISSIVITY GLASS
WITH MIN. 12MM GAP

3375 OPENING

2000

FACING BRICK WALL TO FORM DUCT
TO ENCLOSE DRAIN RUN ACROSS END OF
CONSERVATORY, WITH WOODEN TOP (AS
CILL BOARD UNDER GLAZING)

EX. 32MM
CILL
BOARD

3000

225 × 225 AIR BRICKS
IN SLATE DUCT

450

DPM TAKEN ROUND EDGE
OF SLAB

150MM THERMAL
BREAK OF EXPANDED
POLYSTYRENE

LINE OF DRAIN ACROSS END OF

300MM REINFORCE

OPEN PERPENDS AT 900MM CENTRES
TO DRAIN CAVITY

300MM JABLITE EHD GRADE
UNDER WALL

100 M
MONA
INSTA

300 M

EXTERNAL WALL WITH 112 MM EXTERNAL LEAF IN
CONVENTIONAL STRETCHER BOND, 150MM CAVITY FILL OF
FIBREGLASS "DRI-THERM", DANISH GLASS REINFORCED
PLASTIC WALL TIES AT 450MM CENTRES VERTICALLY
AND HORIZONTALLY, INNER LEAF OF FACING BRICK
FAIR-FACED. DPC 150MM ABOVE GROUND LEVEL.

WALL WITH 112 MM EXTERNAL LEAF IN STRETCHER
BOND, 150MM FIBREGLASS 'DRITHERM' INSULATION,
DANISH GLASS REINFORCED PLASTIC WALL TIES AT
450MM CENTRES VERTICALLY AND HORIZONTALLY,
INNER LEAF OF 200 MM THICK DENSE CONCRETE
BLOCK, 225MM COURSES, WITH PLASTER FINISH

SUSTAINABLE SETTLEMENT AT HOCKERTON · NOTTS · TYPICAL SECTION · SCA

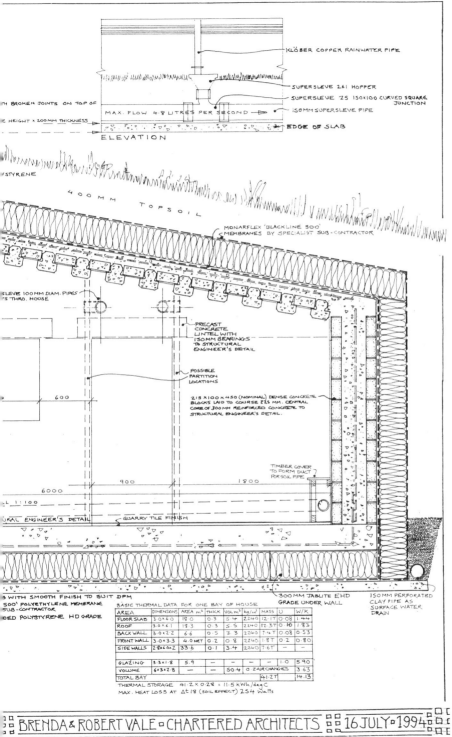

Fig. 36
The Hockerton
houses in section

wooden handle of the rake so that it can be left inside the tank, with the handle hung from a loop of cord just inside the hatch. When not in use the rake is left on the centre line of the tank and it is not struck by additional waste entering through the toilet shafts. The only other maintenance task is to pour about 5 l of untreated softwood shavings down each toilet to provide material to aerate the wastes.

In total, the full maintenance cycle takes 30 minutes every six weeks, but as the regular cleaning associated with a conventional toilet is eliminated, this seems to be very little trouble. When the system was first installed there was occasionally some smell in the bathrooms associated with the stirring of the waste, but this disappeared after about half an hour. After the first year of operation this was no longer apparent at any time, and is probably a function of the volume of waste in the compost container, and the need for the composting process to become established. The smell was not one of sewage or manure, it was more of a 'tarry' nature, something like a newly made compost heap. Compost was first removed from the unit after about three years of use. The compost slides down in the tank and appears when ready in the access area at the base of the tank. Inspection of the contents through the hatch suggested that the wastes were breaking down slowly into a crumbly, open-textured material resembling garden compost. The removed compost still contained some visible faeces, but the material appeared to be quite dry, and had no smell. The removed compost, about 30 l in volume, was added to the garden compost heap. There is a manure heap smell if one's head is put right into the Clivus compost container through the access hatch, but it is not strong; there is no odour when the access lid is lifted to gain access to the area at the base of the container from which the liquid fertilizer is removed.

The only problem with the Clivus to date has been an outbreak of fruit flies inside the tank. These then made their way into the house through the toilet seats, which are not designed to be airtight. On inspection, it was found that the screening on the air vent through which ventilation air is drawn by the fan into the compost container was a mesh, the interstices of which were bigger than a fruit fly. The mesh was replaced, and the inside of the tank was sprayed with a domestic fly spray based on permethrin to attempt to kill off the flies already inside. Further sprayings were made to catch flies as they hatched. The use of a chemical fly spray was rather contrary to the spirit of the system, but it was felt that the flies could pose a health hazard, or at least a nuisance, if they were in the building. By January 1995 the fly problem seemed to have been solved. In the summer of 1995 there was another outbreak of fruit flies, which was controlled in the same way. Discussion with the manufacturers confirmed that there was no possibility of harming the composting process by the use of domestic fly spray.[48]

Locally, during the summer of 1995, there were reports of large numbers of flies of various types; the hot weather presumably favoured the growth of flies generally. An attempt has been made to control the flies in the Clivus by catching spiders and dropping them down the toilet chutes in order to introduce a predator to the system, but it is not possible to say if this has been effective. Although the number of fruit flies was small in absolute terms, on occasion the insects become a definite nuisance; at most there were about 30 flies in each bathroom at the height of the outbreaks.

A proposed modification to the system was to put some worms in the composter to assist with the aeration of the wastes and their breakdown. The presence of the worms may also help to create an ecosystem in the tank which might reduce the chance of the fruit flies' taking up residence again. The appropriate species is the brandling or tiger worm, *Eisenia fetida*,[49] and these were obtained from the garden compost heap and added to the Clivus Multrum on 29 September 1995. A decision was taken at the start of using the Clivus to put no conventional compost materials (fruit peelings, vegetable wastes, etc.) into the tank in an attempt to reduce the chance of a fruit fly outbreak, but this strategy has not proved to be entirely successful. The only materials that go into the tank, other than human wastes, are occasional cardboard (torn up toilet-paper rolls), the toilet paper itself, sanitary towels, the woodshavings added at maintenance, household dust and sweepings and cold wood ashes from the stove when this is in use. In October 1995, the ventilation fan was disconnected for cleaning. One of the side-effects of the fruit-fly infestation is that the flies go through the fan and gradually build up a deposit of dead flies which blocks the blades as they revolve in their shaped metal duct. This leads to an increase in the noise of the fan, and additional irregular noise caused by the flies hitting the fan as it turns. When the fan was disconnected for cleaning, the opportunity was taken to use the flyspray on the unventilated compost chamber. This has eliminated the fly problem, and is the strategy that would be used immediately if a fly outbreak occurred again. The spray is not very effective while the fan is in use, as the spray vapour is drawn efficiently out of the chamber by the fan.

Water supply
The principal difference between the systems as designed and the house in use is that the water consumption in use is less than that calculated. The reason for this is that the amount of water used for personal hygiene is reduced. Showering has proved to be at the rate of three showers per day on average, regardless of whether there are four people in the house or five. The use of water for showers was measured by collecting all the water in the bath instead of allowing it to run to waste, and then baling it out with a measuring jug. This revealed that an adult

shower used an average of 15.7 l, including the water that was run off before the shower water became hot. The value used in the table below assumes four showers per day at 20 l per shower, to allow both for use by the teenagers, who tend to be slightly longer in the shower than the adults, and for the amount of water taken for hair washing. Table 6.13 below shows a revised estimate of daily water use.

Table 6.13: Water consumption in use for five-person autonomous household in l/head/day

laundry	6 (3 washes/week)
dishes	2 (2 washes/day)
drinking and cooking	5 (as conventional house)
personal hygiene (washing)	5 (assumes occasional use of washbasin)
personal hygiene (showers)	16 (4 showers of 20 l/head/day)
total	**34 l/head/day**
total for house	**170 l/day**

This water consumption can be compared with that for the Brampton Advanced House in Canada, built as part of the International Energy Agency's Task XIII, which used 428 l/day (143 l/head/day) compared with a typical Canadian household's water consumption of 683 l/day.[50] The average water consumption per household in the United Kingdom is given by Smith as 160 l/head/day,[51] of which 50 l is used for flushing the toilet. The consumption of a typical household without a flushing toilet would be 110 l/head/day, so the autonomous house is showing a reduction of 69% compared to the normal house. The data given by Smith are broken down into categories as shown in Table 6.14, which also shows the corresponding figure for the autonomous house.

It might be more appropriate to compare only those categories in which the autonomous house was intended to improve on the performance of the conventional house. As it has no losses from the system, and as no provision is made for the 'garden and car' category (except for water which is pumped up from the grey-water soakaway), it is perhaps unreasonable to include these in the water consumption comparison. Therefore, taking only the first four categories, the conventional house uses 80 l/head/day and the autonomous house uses 34 l/head/day, a reduction of 58%.

It can be seen that the 30,000-l storage capacity for water will give a supply (based on the amount of water used in practice) of 176 days, rather than the 150

Table 6.14: Water consumption comparisons

category	UK house (l/head/day)	autonomous house (l/head/day)	% reduction
personal hygiene	45	21	53%
laundry	15	6	60%
dishes	15	2	87%
drinking and cooking	5	5	0%
garden and car	10	0	100%
losses	20	0	100%
flushing toilet	50	0	100%
total	160 l/head/day	34 l/head/day	79%
five-person household	800 l/day	170 l/day	

days of the design calculation; as a result, there is ample capacity for extended periods of drought. This was well tested in the drought of the summer of 1995. At the end of the drought, which was at the beginning of September as far as the site in Southwell was concerned, the remaining water in the tanks was two thirds of the total capacity, or 20,000 l. As mentioned above, the Chairman of Yorkshire Water and his wife were reported at the time as having not had a bath or shower for three months.[52] The story subsequently achieved such notoriety that it was the subject of an editorial in *The Times*.[53] During the period of the drought, the occupants of the autonomous house made no attempt to conserve water any more than normal.

The lower water consumption in the autonomous house was not achieved by rigorous attempts to make the occupants of the house more water-conscious than usual; there is no sense of deprivation, compared with when the occupants lived in a conventional house with mains water supply. However, it should be admitted that the household had been conscious of water as a limited resource for many years, and had managed their water demand accordingly. Olivier and Willoughby report: 'In most aspects, it appears that the standard of living [in the autonomous house] has been on a par with normal UK households. There are differences, in particular the plumbing, but they do not seem to have made the house less convenient to live in.'[54] This comment is significant, in that it sums up the essence of the autonomous house: it is different to, but not worse than, a conventional house.

There were problems with the water supply caused by the filtering and pumping system rather than by the availability of water. After about six months of use, the water coming out of the kitchen tap (direct from the pumped supply, rather than from the header tank in the attic) began to acquire a sulphurous smell. This was not removed by the drinking water filter, but would disappear if the water was allowed to stand for 10 minutes. Eventually, following discussions with David Leigh of David Leigh Landscapes, who was involved in the design of a reed bed and water supply system for the Hockerton Housing Project,[55] the sand filter was taken apart and reconstructed. It was suggested that the water in the filter was lacking in oxygen and minerals, so the 230-V 5-W aquarium fountain was installed in the top of the sand filter to aerate the layer of water over the top of the sand. It was also proposed to hang bags of limestone chippings in some of the tanks to mineralize the raw water. To date, the limestone chippings have not yet been installed.

The problem of odorous water was solved fairly simply, but it also demonstrated the basic simplicity and robustness of the system. While the sand filter was out of action, water was routed direct to the house from the bulk rainwater storage, relying on settlement in the tanks for the primary treatment process, as used on Waiheke Island in New Zealand. This re-routing was achieved very easily by disconnecting the flexible pipe from one pump and connecting it to the other. The only measurable result in the house was that the drinking-water filter needed to be cleaned at intervals of two days rather than about two weeks, as it was treating the raw water that had not had the benefit of sand filtration.

A second, minor, filter problem arose in relation to the drinking-water filter in the children's/guest bathroom. This has a head of 4.5 m from the tank in the attic, but supplied only a trickle of water. Study of available filter elements[56] suggested that this problem could be cured by changing to a filter element designed for gravity feed, and this was done, resulting in an increase in the water supply rate.

Some problems were experienced with the pumps that supply water to the sand filter and to the house. The first one is that the pump supplying the house suffers from water hammer in the pipes. This is only a problem if someone uses the bathroom after other members of the family have gone to bed, a common situation in a family with three teenagers. No serious attempt has been made to cure the noise, as it is felt that it probably acts as an audible reminder that the water being supplied, particularly to the shower, is coming from limited resources, and that energy is being used to pump it. Two switches have been installed in the laundry area, outside the main bedroom, so that the pumps can be switched off at night if wanted. Water will then be supplied to the shower and the bathroom taps by gravity from the header tank in the attic, and the pump will refill the tank the next morning when it is switched on.

The second problem was related to the fact that the pump that supplies the house is connected to a considerable length of pipework, but the one that feeds the sand filter has only about a metre of pipe between it and the float-operated valve at the top of the filter. As water is drawn off from the filtered-water supply, the level drops slowly in the sand filter, and the Torbeck float-operated valve opens and turns on the pump to refill the sand filter. The effect of this is that the pump 'hunts' on and off as the water drains slowly through the filter and the float valve calls for water to top it up. The 'hunting' is probably a combination of the minimal water capacity of the pipework in the pump system, plus the very slow rate of passage of water through the filter, which means that the pump is being called on to deliver tiny quantities of water at frequent intervals. This has resulted in the failure of the pressure switch on this pump several times. As with the filter, this is not a serious problem; the switch can be changed in five minutes without removing the pump – it is a matter of two screws only. Shurflo, the pump manufacturers, suggested the fitting of a standard pressure accumulator in the pipework, to allow small changes in the water level in the filter without the pump's being actuated. It is hoped that this might extend the switch life, but so far the accumulator has not been installed. The most recent technique for the solution of this problem has been to turn the pump on only for an hour in the morning and an hour in the evening, to top up the sand filter. It is then left off the rest of the time. An alternative suggestion would be to fit a float switch to the pump rather than a pressure switch, and control it by turning its power supply on and off.

The only other problem to have occurred with the water supply system was that the filter pump once developed a leak in its casing which resulted in its pumping water over the cellar floor all night; the problem was cured by tightening the screws that hold it together. It was heard running during the night, but no notice was taken, with the result that the cellar floor had to be mopped up in the morning. The floor dried out in a day once the standing water, about 10 l, had been removed. This may be a good reason for turning off the pumps at night.

Perhaps the aspect of the water supply that has proved most satisfactory in use is its simplicity and ability to be repaired by the user without any specialized tools or knowledge. The pumps and pipes are very basic pieces of equipment that can be repaired and replaced, probably because they are designed for use for water supply on boats and recreational vehicles. If there is a problem with the water supply, there is no need to telephone the water company and wait powerless for repairs to be carried out – the user can do what is needed. As there is always a 1,500-l tank of sand-filtered water (about 10 days' supply) waiting to be pumped to the house, it is possible to replace a pump, or even wait to obtain a new one, without interrupting the supply, and the pumps can be swapped if necessary. The Shurflo pumps are easily available at boat chandlers and caravan suppliers, meaning that there is no difficulty in obtaining spares. During the design stage many attempts were made to devise a system that used only one pump, but the use of two pumps has proved convenient in practice, allowing a failed pump to be bypassed by a simple alteration of the hose connections on the relevant pump.

Hot water

It was assumed, when the house was being designed, that the hot-water use would be 125 l/day (see Table 5:11), giving an energy demand for heating it of 8.1 kWh/day. The water usage that resulted from using the house was lower than calculated, and this meant that the hot-water usage was also lower. The hot-water demand in use is as shown in Table 6.15, based on the values from Table 6.14.

Table 6.15: Hot-water demand in use

category	total consumption (l/head/day)	cold water (l/head/day)	hot water (l/head/day)
laundry	6	6	0
dishes	2	0	2
drinking and cooking	5	5	0
personal hygiene (washing)	5	0	5
personal hygiene (showers)	16	10	6
total	34 l/head/day	21 l/head/day	13 l/head/day
total for house	170 l/day	105 l/day	65 l/day

Note: this table assumes a five-person household; figures have been rounded off to the nearest whole numbers

The hot-water demand for most of the categories is straightforward, but that used for showers needs some explanation. A typical shower was measured as using roughly 20 l (see above). The temperature of the water when showering is

35°C. The hot-water cylinder is maintained at a set temperature of 60°C, and the cold water, supplied from the header tank in the attic, is assumed to be at a temperature of 18°C; it will be the same as the house temperature, since the attic is an integral part of the heated volume of the house. This differs from the situation in a normal house, where any water tanks are usually placed in unheated attic spaces. The shower water has been heated through a temperature difference of 17K, which, given that the specific heat of water is 1.16 Wh/kgK, represents 394.4 Wh per shower. This is a mixture of hot and cold water, so it is possible to calculate that the same energy consumption would result from the heating of 8.1 l of water to a temperature of 60°C. Thus the four showers each day, which use 80 l/day in total, are using a total of 32.4 l of hot water and 47.6 l of cold.

These figures give an annual hot-water demand of 23,725 l. To heat this from 18°C to 60°C will use will use 1,156 kWh/year, an energy consumption rate of 3.2 kWh/day, to which standing losses from the hot-water cylinder must be added. Standing losses must be checked against the manufacturer's figure of 2.7 kWh/day, which is quoted for all sizes of cylinder.[57] Since the 120-l hot-water cylinder used in the autonomous house is the smallest in the manufacturer's range, its standing loss is likely to be lower than other cylinders. A more accurate figure can be calculated by using the surface area of the hot-water cylinder, calculated as a cylinder 450 mm in diameter and 675 mm high, with a circular base and hemispherical top, both 450 mm in diameter. This gives a surface area of 1.27 m² for the insulated top and sides, and 0.16 m² for the uninsulated base. The insulation is urethane foam (with a blowing agent of zero-ozone-depleting potential) and the thickness and k value of the insulation (60 mm and 0.03 W/mK) give a U value for the insulation of 0.5 W/m²K. There is no insulation on the base, which is assumed to lose heat at a rate of 6.0 W/m²K (comparable with the U value of single glazing). These figures give a rate of heat loss from the cylinder of 1.6 W/K, 0.64 W from the insulated part, and 0.96 W from the uninsulated base, or 67 W at a temperature difference of 42K (house temperature of 18°C, water temperature at 60°C). Over 24 hours this gives a heat loss rate of 1,608 Wh, or 587 kWh/year. The hot-water cylinder has a number of areas where the insulation is thinner or missing, such as the upper and lower pipe connections and the immersion heater boss, so the figure should be increased to perhaps 2 kWh/day, or 730 kWh/year. If this figure is added to the water-heating load, the total electricity demand for water heating is 1,886 kWh: this is the demand using a direct acting immersion heater, and represents about 5.2 kWh/day. These figures (65 l/day of hot water, requiring 5.2 kWh/day) can be compared with the original estimate for hot-water demand, which was 125 l/day with an energy demand of 8.1 kWh/day.

In order to reduce the energy needed for heating water, it is intended to replace the immersion heater with a heat pump that is being developed by EA Technology at Capenhurst. This is designed to take the heat from ventilation air in order to heat domestic hot water, and is reported to have a coefficient of performance in the range 3–3.5.[58] The heat pump will use the air that is drawn through the Clivus Multrum by its 5-W fan, the duct from which rises through the house immediately adjacent to the hot-water cylinder. The fan provides an airflow rate of 160 m³/h. At a density of 1.2 kg/m³ and a specific heat of 0.28 Wh/kgK,[59] this amount of air will have a heat content of 54 Wh/K, so could provide 540 Wh if its temperature were lowered through 10K. To meet the average daily hot-water demand, including standing loss, of 5.2 kWh, the heat pump would need to operate for about 10 hours a day. The heat pump has been chosen as a cheaper alternative (by a factor of ten) to active solar heating, although this cost comparison is relevant only in respect of a solar heating system designed to provide long-term hot water storage for the winter. The replacement of the existing immersion heater with a heat pump, assuming a coefficient of performance of 3, would reduce the electricity demand for water heating (excluding standing losses) from 1,156 kWh/year to about 385 kWh/year. However, the standing loss from the cylinder, calculated above at 730 kWh/year, has to be made up by the heat pump, adding a further 243 kWh, giving a total of 628 kWh/year.

The figure for energy needed for hot-water heating could be reduced further by improving the insulation of the hot-water cylinder. Insulation of the base of the cylinder to the standard of the rest of it, and improved insulation to the remainder, equivalent to a 100-mm-thick jacket of mineral fibre, could reduce the standing loss from the cylinder to 544 Wh/day, or about 199 kWh/year. The heat required for the heating of the water, 1,156 kWh/year, added to this standing loss, would give a total demand of 1,355 kWh/year. Using the heat pump, this would be reduced to 452 kWh/year.

Waste water

The operation of the soakaway has been relatively straightforward. Problems did arise from the combination of two factors: the relatively non-porous nature of the clay soil, and the lower than calculated water use. The water does not soak away as quickly as had been hoped. Because the tanks remain nearly full most of the time (due to the low rate of water use in the house), when it does rain, the rain does not fill the tanks (subsequently to be discharged as waste water at a regular daily rate), but overflows in bulk and fills the soakaway. This means that the soakaway needs to be checked regularly and pumped out, using the bilge pump, usually at the weekend. It takes about 10 to 15 minutes of pumping to reduce the level to a satisfactory height. The pump, a Whale Urchin, moves water at the rate of about 30 l/minute (depending on the speed of pumping), so 10 minutes corresponds to 300 l. Pumping ceased after March 1995, and was not necessary up to 22 October 1995.

In the summer of 1994 the problem of the soakaway not soaking away was reduced considerably because water was pumped up daily into a watering can to water the plants growing in pots in the conservatory. The use of soapy water seemed to cause no problems to the plants, but the water had a sulphurous smell which lingered in the conservatory. Later in the year, the water was pumped from the conservatory onto the garden, and allowed to soak into the soil away from the soakaway. This seemed unsatisfactory, again because of the smell of the water, so the pipe from the bilge pump was eventually led underground to discharge into the large volume of brick rubble that had been was used to fill the excavation round the cellar walls, creating a large *ad hoc* soakaway. The potential of this soakaway was not used at the outset, as it seemed likely to compromise the watertightness of the cellar; however, it did seem acceptable to use it as an overflow soakaway. The use of the backfill in this way has given no apparent problems. In mid-1996 the system of using the bilge pump to pump water into the rubble round the cellar was replaced by an overflow drain 100 mm in diameter, so that manual pumping would no longer be needed. It has been suggested that the smell of the grey water in the conservatory would be eliminated by the use of a simple aquarium aerating pump to bubble air through the soakaway in order to oxygenate the water.[60] This could be powered directly by a small wind turbine or a photovoltaic panel, so that it would operate whenever energy was available.

Electricity
Electricity is the only connected mains service in the autonomous house, apart from the telephone. Electricity provides the loads in the completed house listed in Table 6.16 overleaf.

Much of the electrical equipment in the house is quite old: the cooker is 15 years old, as is the washing machine; the stereo system is 14 years old, the video recorder 13 and the television 12 years old. These devices could be replaced by newer, more energy-efficient models, and this might achieve significant reductions (in terms of this house, where each kilowatt hour is counted), were this needed.

Daily measurements of electricity consumption made from 1 February 1994 to 28 July 1994, before the installation of the photovoltaic generator, showed that the house consumed a total of 1489.5 kWh of electricity over 177 days (or 8.42 kWh/day) for water heating, cooking, lights, appliances, etc. This gives an

Table 6.16: Electricity uses in the autonomous house

water heating (3-kW immersion heater in 120-l copper cylinder)
cooking (Husqvarna Culinar electric cooker)
microwave oven
washing machine (AEG Lavamat 802T used only without heating element, with Ecover liquid detergent)
iron
refrigerator (Danish Gram LER 200 ultra-low-energy refrigerator)
electric kettle
toaster
television
stereo
computers
compact fluorescent lights
12-V halogen lights
battery chargers for Walkman batteries, etc.
gel battery charger for 12-V battery (pumps and fan)

annual predicted demand for electricity for all purposes of 3,073 kWh, of which 1,886 kWh is for hot-water heating (see calculations above); 1,187 kWh therefore covers all other uses.

It is useful to look at the electricity demand related to the floor area of the house. The basic house has a floor area of 176 m²; the cellar and conservatory are additional to this, making a total built floor area of 290.2 m², but these areas are excluded from the electricity calculation, as they do not form part of what would be considered in a conventional house to be the serviced, habitable floor area. Using the basic house as the area for calculation, the electricity consumption as measured, before installation of the photovoltaic system, is 17.46 kWh/m²/year, or a rate of slightly under 2 W/m². When the heat pump is installed, with the increased insulation of the hot-water cylinder, it is hoped that the total electricity consumption will drop to 9.31 kWh/m²/year, or 1,639 kWh/year. It should be

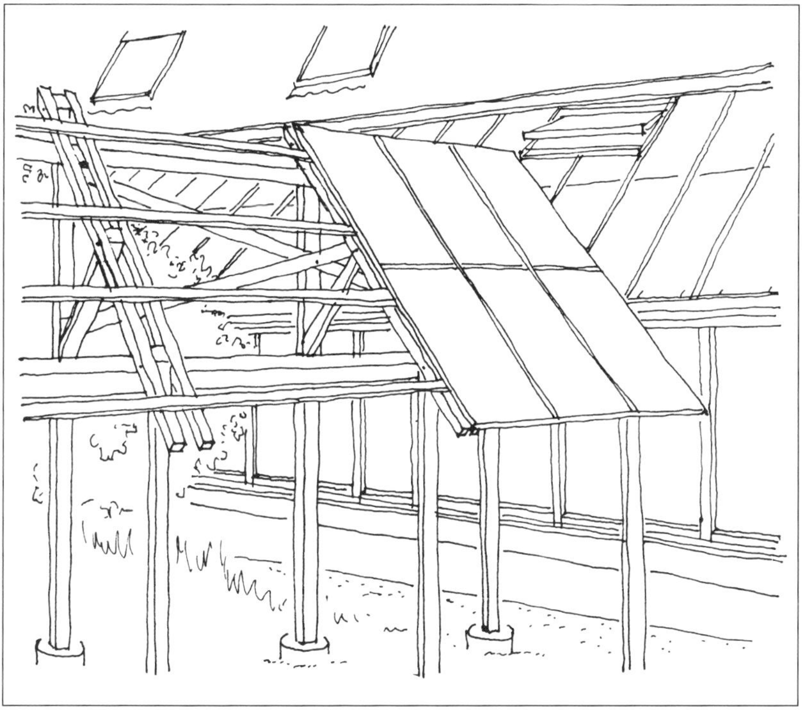

Fig. 37
The photovoltaic array

noted that this is roughly the amount of electricity intended to be supplied annually by the 2.2-kW grid-linked photovoltaic generating system that was completed on 28 July 1994. The photovoltaic system comprises 36 Solarex MSX-60 polycrystalline panels of a total nominal rating of 2.16 kW. These panels were selected on the grounds that the manufacturer offered a 20-year guarantee (see Appendix 8). The Solarex panels are connected to the electricity grid through a German SMA 1800 1.8-kW grid-linked import-export inverter. The whole system was supplied and installed by Steve Wade of Wind and Sun of Oxford, and set in operation at 5.00 pm on 28 July 1994. Using the supplied pv-data (photovoltaic data) program to download the data-logger built into the inverter, the electricity production in the first 12 months from 28 July 1994 to 28 July 1995, was measured. The production of electricity was 748 kWh per kilowatt of installed photovoltaic capacity, giving a total output of 1,616 kWh for the year.

The photovoltaic panels are connected to the inverter in strings of six, giving a nominal output of 72 V. The inverter can handle a further 12 panels, making a total of 48 in all, and the supporting structure for these was installed when the system was set up. The additional panels were intended to allow the purchase of additional appliances (such as a freezer perhaps, or an electric car) as required. If the 48-panel system were in operation, it would have a nominal installed capacity of 2.88 kW, and would be expected to generate 2,154 kWh/year, based on the performance of the existing system in its first year.

The photovoltaic system operated without problems for its first year, but it produced very little output for two weeks in May 1995, as the inverter kept shutting down. This was reported by the data-logger, which has a fault-tracing system, as 'grid-overvoltage'. The local electricity company carried out checks and found that a transformer had failed locally, allowing the grid voltage to rise beyond the in-built limits of the inverter (grid specified voltage: ±10%), causing it to shut down. In fact, the grid was operating beyond its legal parameters, at 258 V.

In spite of the variations in grid voltage, which resulted in considerably reduced solar output for two weeks during a period of bright sun, the following results were measured for the first year of operation of the photovoltaic system.

Table 6.17: Electricity consumption and generation for one year from 28 July 1994

imported from grid	2475.8 kWh
exported to grid	975.8 kWh
net electricity demand	1,500.0 kWh
total domestic electricity consumption	3,116.0 kWh
solar generation in total	1,616.0 kWh
% of solar generation exported	60.4% (975.8 kWh)
% of solar generation used directly	39.6% (640.2 kWh)
solar generation as % of total consumption	51.9%

The loss of meaningful output for two weeks in May 1995 was compensated for by the excellent weather in the summer of that year, suggesting that the electricity output in the first year may be representative of future results, although there may be a loss of output over time as the panels age.

COST

The autonomous house was built in the normal way, following submission of tenders by a number of contractors. The successful tender was made by Nick Martin of NSM, based in the neighbouring village of Hockerton. The total cost of building the house, including all the servicing systems and the photovoltaic array, was £145,000, but this does not include either architects' fees or the cost of labour provided by the clients, who did the internal decorating. The site for the house cost £69,000. Funding was provided through savings, plus a conventional mortgage from Lloyds Bank.

The cost of the house per square metre can be considered in two ways. If the usable floor area of the 'heated' space is used as a measure, that is, the space which is occupied and furnished as part of a normal dwelling, (the ground floor, first floor, attic and porch), the cost of the house is £823.86/m². However, this price brings with it a two-level, double-glazed conservatory and a cellar. If the total built floor area is costed, the cost is £499.66/m², but not all this space is finished to the same standard as the main part of the house, or maintained at the same temperatures. The Cresswell Road low-energy houses in Sheffield, described in Chapter 4, cost £515.31/m², so the overall cost per square metre of the autonomous house complete with its servicing systems is comparable to the cost of state-funded social housing.

CONCLUSIONS

The autonomous house has the performance data in use listed in Table 6.18.

Table 6.18: Energy inputs and outputs in the autonomous house 1994–95

net food energy input	4,676 kWh/year	27.7 kWh/m²/year
net space heating energy (wood)	922 kWh/year	5.2 kWh/m²/year
delivered space heating energy (wood)	1,418 kWh/year	8.1 kWh/m²/year
electricity (total)	3,116 kWh/year	17.7 kWh/m²/year
(electricity for hot water	1,886 kWh/year	10.7 kWh/m²/year)
(electricity for lights and appliances	1,230 kWh/year	7.0 kWh/m²/year)
photovoltaic generation	1,616 kWh/year	9.2 kWh/m²/year
electricity from non-renewable sources*	1,500 kWh/year	8.5 kWh/m²/year

Note: this is the only non-renewable energy input to the house. It can be compared to the current average UK domestic electricity consumption for 'lights and appliances' of 3,000 kWh/year quoted by Boardman et al.[61]

Table 6.19 overleaf shows the expected situation once the heat pump has been installed, along with increased insulation of the hot-water cylinder.

Table 6.19: Expected electricity consumption with hot-water heat pump

electricity for hot water	452 kWh/year	2.6 kWh/m²/year
electricity for lights and appliances	1,230 kWh/year	7.0 kWh/m²/year
total electricity demand	1,682 kWh/year	9.6 kWh/m²/year
photovoltaic generation (measured)	1,616 kWh/year	9.2 kWh/m²/year

Since the photovoltaic generator had two weeks of running at reduced output in May 1995 owing to problems with the grid, it is possible that the output in a normal year will be sufficient to meet the demand of the house. At this point, the house will be using, on an annual basis, no non-renewable energy. This is a slightly simplistic argument, since the use of a grid-linked photovoltaic system means that grid electricity produced by non-renewable energy is used at the times when the solar power system is not generating. The use of biomass for space heating may be seen also to be an additional input to the system that might be avoided in a purer version of the house. However, the arguments for the use of these systems have been presented earlier. It should also be noted that a simple option for expansion of the photovoltaic output is in place, and requires only the installation of the extra 12 panels. This would take half a day, and would boost the solar output (based purely on the 1994–95 measured data) to 2,154 kWh/year, or 12.2 kWh/m²/year. There is therefore a convenient fall-back position if the energy consumption of the house increases, or if the annual yield of the photovoltaic system falls off over time.

The autonomous house has been occupied continuously since the end of 1993, for three years by the original designers, and then by tenants, and it is possible to draw some conclusions about it. The first is that it has been as satisfactory as many conventional houses in terms of overall levels of service provision and comfort. The second is that it is clearly different from a conventional house, in that it operates on a different premise. In a conventional house, the availability of any service is limited by the users' ability to pay for that service, which in turn bears no relation to the environmental impact of the use of that service. The autonomous house provides services based on what it can collect from its immediate surroundings, and the users do not have to pay for the use of the services. However, the services are limited in their availability. If the occupants use their services at an excessive rate, they will run out, but by doing this they affect only themselves, whereas the consumption of water, for example, by conventional systems may have an effect on the availability of water to other users. Similarly, in the autonomous house, the users could throw chemicals or solvents down the toilet and put the composting process out of operation, but the disadvantage of this would affect only themselves. With a conventional sewage treatment system, members of the public have no responsibility for what they put down the drains, they can assume that the water company will solve any problems. The electrical system in the autonomous house does not have an in-built safeguard against excessive use. This is one of the possible advantages of a battery system over the grid-linked system that was used; the grid-linked system can never run out.

The lessons of the autonomous house are threefold. It confers on the occupants responsibility for their actions, and for the effects of their actions on themselves, their fellow citizens and on the environment. At the same time it puts the occupants in control, turning them from passive consumers of services over whose provision they have little choice, into active resource managers. Finally, it gives the users control of the on-going cost of services, since these have been paid for as part of the capital cost of the house, rather than as part of its running costs.

FURTHER RESEARCH

The design and construction of the autonomous house was funded entirely by Brenda and Robert Vale, and this meant that there was no money to spare for monitoring equipment. Funding for monitoring was sought from UK-government academic research-funding bodies, but all applications were rejected. Staff at the Engineering and Science Research Council said that nothing could be learned from the study of a single house; however, staff at the Fraunhofer Institute beg to differ. If equipment or funding were to become available, the following aspects of the house would benefit from more detailed study:

1. external weather data – solar radiation, wind speed and direction, temperatures, rainfall, all recorded at 15-minute intervals;
2. internal temperatures recorded at 15-minute intervals (to see the diurnal variations in temperature in a number of areas including the conservatory, cellar, living room, main bedroom, kitchen, studio, a child's bedroom);
3. detailed analysis of the thermal aspects of the house with thermal imaging and pressure testing;
4. detailed measurement of water consumption by metering of supplies (kitchen sink, drinking-water tap, washing machine, parents' shower, children's shower, outlet from hot-water cylinder) to give an accurate breakdown of total consumption and hot- and cold-water use;

5. analysis of water for health aspects, looking at incoming water, water in main tanks, post-sand-filter water, post-drinking-water-filter water;
6. detailed measurement of electricity consumption of appliances, particularly refrigerator, cooker, hot water immersion heater – ideally, all socket outlets would be monitored.

As well as the monitoring, the installation of the heat pump and the additional insulation of the hot-water cylinder are actions that could be carried out relatively easily if funding were available. Since the house was constructed, heat pumps for domestic hot-water supply have become commercially available, and have been used in the five earth-sheltered Hockerton houses. Not all further work is dependent on the availability of funding. It is intended that an analysis of the house's embodied energy be carried out using the detailed records of the materials bought and their places of origin, to see if the construction phase of a zero-energy house involves significantly greater energy than that of a conventional house. In addition, a detailed breakdown of the costs of the house will be made, with comparisons with conventional and low-energy houses for which costs are available.

The ideas behind the autonomous house are already being applied elsewhere. The five earth-sheltered Hockerton houses were occupied in 1998. They use different design and servicing strategies to the Southwell house, highlighting the point that the original house is only one possible way of achieving the goal of autonomous servicing; they were also cheaper to build. In 1997, Newark and Sherwood District Council and the BRE commissioned some studies of the application of autonomous servicing techniques to conventional UK house types. This is in part an attempt to see if the techniques can be applied to social housing: tenants on low incomes could benefit from houses with no running costs. It is also important to see if the techniques are applicable to housing with a conventional floor area, as the Southwell house is larger than the UK norm.

7 | *Conclusions*

At the time of writing, the autonomous house at Southwell has been occupied for five years. In this time it has dried out, and the occupants have become familiar both with its operation and with its strengths and weaknesses. It should be reiterated that the Southwell house is a specific architectural response to a specific site, and to the requirements and expectations of a specific family (see Chapter 5). The house has also met the requirements of a family for whom it was not designed, the tenants who took it on in October 1996. Two families do not constitute a statistically significant sample, so it is very hard to draw general conclusions from their experiences with the house. Nevertheless, it is possible to make some judgments about the systems contained within the house, their interactions and their applicability to housing in the future.

The first two chapters of this book discussed the idea of building a house that was autonomous in terms of sustainability and alternative technology, which was seen as an approach to technology that gave control to its users. As far as alternative technology is concerned, the autonomous house has met all expectations. As described in Chapter 6, the users have been able to deal with a number of operational problems without the need to call for expert assistance. The simple technologies used, for sewage treatment, water supply and waste water disposal for example, have been easy to manage, and easy to adjust and modify as necessary. The servicing systems employed in the house are generally much simpler than the technology involved in a conventional gas central-heating boiler as used in the majority of British homes.

The servicing systems of the house interact with one another: the electricity-generating system has to provide energy to operate the pumps of the water system for example, but the pumps can be considered, to some extent, as separate entities as far as assessment of their performance and their possible application to more general housing design is concerned. The rainwater collection system has certainly been a success, as was shown by the way the system coped with the drought of summer 1995 (see Chapter 6). However, the Southwell house is large compared with a normal house, having a roof area for water collection of 140 m², compared with one of perhaps 70 m² for a 90-m² house on two floors with a conservatory. A house of conventional size, at least on the eastern side of the United Kingdom, where rainfall is lower, would need to make use of additional roof areas such as carports and porches, to collect enough rainfall (although the fact the autonomous house used only one third of its stored water supply through the drought suggests that the roof area and storage volume may be oversized). However, to reduce the water-collection area and storage capacity would run the risk of reducing the ability of the water system to cope with differences between households and their individual demands. The Southwell water consumption of 170 l/day for the whole house represents a figure for a five-person household that is unlikely to be reduced without the use of some sort of recycling system; another household might find that its consumption was greater than this.

The water storage tanks of the autonomous house hold a total of 30,000 l. This volume of water, in 20 cylindrical tanks, occupies half of the area of the cellar, or 33 m². In a normal sized house of 90-m² floor area, the cellar area (if a cellar were used for water storage) would be 45 m², the same area as the ground floor, so there would be ample space for the same number of water tanks as used in the Southwell house. The cellar would have also enough space for the Clivus Multrum composter, which makes the use of rainwater for general purposes practicable by eliminating the need for a flushing toilet. Perhaps the least satisfactory part of the water system in the autonomous house has been the waste-water soakaway, but the redesign of this in a future scheme with a greater volume and a better provision for overflow during periods of high rainfall should not prove difficult. The effective operation of the soakaway is not helped by the clay soil, despite the fact that it was relatively free-draining.

The experience of using the composting toilet has been entirely satisfactory; it is convenient and odourless, but this is obviously an area in which the acceptability of the technology to the wider public is an unknown. However, the fact that many people seem able to cope with changing babies' nappies and with clearing up after their dogs suggests that operating an odourless sewage composter might not be too great a problem. Perhaps if the technology became widespread, some of the savings in water and sewerage charges for an individual household could be paid as a type of 'service charge' to employ a community janitor who would deal with the water and waste systems of those who did not wish to do it themselves. There is no doubt that the use of the rainwater collection system and the Clivus Multrum provides a considerable increase in the overall sustainability of the household, in minimizing environmental impact, in providing efficient use of local resources, and in returning what is often deemed a waste product to the soil to grow crops.

In terms of space heating, the autonomous house performs satisfactorily, if austerely (see Chapter 6). The winter thermal comfort levels are adequate but not luxurious. This is another area where the whole question of acceptability is raised. In a house of conventional size, the need for heat would be lower due to the reduced surface area, and the heat output of a household would represent a greater proportion of the necessary input. The Southwell house probably suffers thermally by virtue of its open planned living areas with large open roof spaces above; a conventional house, with flat ceilings and a door to the living room, would concentrate the heat output of a family watching television into a smaller volume, with a corresponding increase in the room temperature. The construction methods and detailing used at Southwell could be applied easily to a smaller house – indeed, many of them are developments of the techniques devised for the Cresswell Road houses (see Appendix 6).

The Southwell house, for reasons of context, is not optimally orientated to take advantage of the sun (see Chapter 3), but this aspect of the design could be remedied in another situation. The thermal-mass provision of the Southwell house could be increased in line with the recommendation made by Lund (see Chapter 4), but to increase the mass further would mean enlarging elements beyond the dimensions that they need for constructional and structural reasons. In a smaller house the provision of increased mass would become more difficult, unless the design were totally different, as in the unconventional earth-sheltered Hockerton project (see Chapter 6).

With regard to back-up heating, the wood-burning stove constitutes a simple and direct means of providing additional heat input from biomass, in keeping with the spirit of alternative technology, but it is not a heating system that works particularly well for a household of people who are out all day. A larger stove, able to burn unattended for a longer period, would remedy this, but would tend to require more wood, which would raise the back-up heat input. The fact that it is not worth lighting the stove for the evening acts as a brake on excessive wood consumption in the house, but also means that temperatures are sometimes slightly lower than might be desired. The temperatures in the Southwell house are acceptable to the occupants, not only because they are adequate for them in terms of comfort, but because they are the temperatures that can be achieved by exploitation of the available heat gains. In a house where the occupants were not the designers, or where they had less interest in their environmental impact, this might not be the case.

In a smaller house, there might well be a need for greater control of ventilation, because of the smaller volume (207 m^3 for a 90-m^2 house, as opposed to 431 m³ for the autonomous house). If this resulted in the use of a whole-house mechanical ventilation heat-recovery system, there would be scope for linking this to a heat pump to provide back-up heating as required, by using the waste heat from the outgoing air as the heat input. A space-heating demand of 1,500 kWh/year, slightly less than that calculated for the Cresswell Road houses (see Appendix 6) together with a heat-pump coefficient of performance of 3 would require 500 kWh of electricity annually, which could be provided by less than 1 kW of photovoltaic modules (see Chapter 6). It would be essential that such a system employed very-high-efficiency fans to minimize the electricity needed for air movement. The use of this technology would allow simple back-up heating from the point of view of the user. Heat-pump technology is arguably less complex than a central-heating boiler, but more complex than a wood-burning stove. In fact it is proposed to install a heat pump for domestic hot-water provision in the Southwell house, as described in Chapter 6. Using a photovoltaic-powered heat pump for back-up space heating suggests that the technology of the zero carbon dioxide house could be applied to a dwelling that might seem relatively conventional to its occupants, and possibly therefore, more acceptable.

The idea of generating electricity for back-up heating from photovoltaics would mean using a larger photovoltaic array area than that used for the Southwell house. This is another aspect of the whole field of acceptability of the idea of the autonomous house to possible users. The Southwell autonomous house is operated on a small electrical input because some appliances are deemed to be either unnecessary (a dishwasher, a tumble dryer, a freezer), or are operated differently from normal (for example, the use of unheated water in the washing machine). These omissions and differences did not cause any sense of deprivation to the original occupants of the autonomous house, because they made their own choices as designers of the building. Were these aspects of appliance provision and use to be made mandatory for the occupants of hypothetical future autonomous housing, there might be a degree of dissatisfaction. This could be investigated by interviews with a range of future users or possible tenants. It might be that some occupants would be prepared to exchange a limited choice of appliances for the possibility of no-cost servicing.

A feasible alternative technical route towards allaying this dissatisfaction in autonomous housing would be to provide a larger photovoltaic-array area, perhaps 40 m² as opposed to the 20 m² used in the Southwell house, giving an output of about 4 kW, or 3,000 kWh/year (see Chapter 6). This would provide sufficient electricity for back-up heating as described above, as well as for the use of a wider range of appliances, provided that these appliances were chosen to be as efficient as possible. There is clearly scope for further work in the improvement of appliance efficiency in a wide range of areas. One interesting aspect of an increased photovoltaic area, especially if it were mounted separately from the building, would be its potential as a water collection surface to compensate for the smaller roof area of a house of conventional size. However, the greater cost of the larger area of photovoltaics would be a greater proportion of the overall cost of a smaller house.

The question of electricity demand raises the most difficult aspect of the autonomous house and its further application. In the domestic sector, the trend of the 20th century has been towards greater domestic appliance ownership and increased indoor air temperatures. Current calls for sustainable development may be seen as acting counter to the pressures that demand more. The question that must be asked is: what level of service provision is acceptable, and what level might be considered unsustainable? The autonomous house in Southwell is designed to offer a range of compromises to its users, in an attempt to provide a standard of living that is sufficiently comfortable and sufficiently sustainable. The discussion above suggests that the techniques used in the Southwell house could be applied to a dwelling of more conventional size, but the question of acceptability would remain pertinent. Some of the techniques that might be used in an autonomous house are probably neutral in terms of acceptability (such as high-efficiency refrigerators), some are probably quite acceptable in some cultures (such as the growing of vegetables in the garden), and some may be perceived as less acceptable than the norm, such as lower indoor temperatures, or the elimination of certain appliances.

Perhaps one way to improve acceptability would be to provide performance incentives. One simple measure would be net billing of electricity, so that electricity exported to the grid from the photovoltaic array would be used to offset electricity supplied to the house from the grid on a kWh for kWh basis, equivalent to running the meter in two directions. Unlike a system based on batteries, the technology of grid-linked photovoltaic generation has no inherent limits on consumption. Some sort of simple read-out could be used to allow the occupants to see the state of their electricity balance at any particular time, providing the necessary information to achieve an annual electricity bill of zero, apart from the infrastructure charge. This would provide the incentive to reduce demand, but would also give the provision, through the purchase of additional energy from the grid, to meet emergency or temporary situations (the need to provide additional heating to a sickroom or nursery, for example) if required. A similar read-out could be provided for the water storage. Emergency water demands beyond the supply capability of the storage tanks in the house could be met by the purchase of a tanker load of water to refill the storage tanks. The use of displays of energy and water consumption might enable users to make more informed decisions about the operation of their house, and might give them a greater interest in its performance.

It was shown in Chapter 1 that the Cambridge University 'autonomous' (self-governing) house project became the 'autarkic' (self-sufficient) house project. In the end, even with the addition of the hot-water heat pump, which will give zero annual non-renewable energy demand, the Southwell house is not autarkic. To increase its autarky would require the elimination of the electricity grid connection and the installation of a large set of batteries, similar to the RAPS systems used in the outback of Australia (see Chapter 4). Ironically, this increase in autarky and the resultant increased resource consumption would result in a decrease in sustainability. In the United Kingdom, with its dense population and its national electricity grid, it would make no sense to abandon the resources that have been put into creating the grid, and replace them with new resources in the form of batteries in order to achieve a symbolic self-sufficiency. The house at Southwell is not therefore an autarkic house, but it can be described as an autonomous alternative-technology house, in that it is self-governing to a far greater extent than a conventional house. It gives its users control of their collection, management and use of their share of the Earth's resources to provide their servicing needs.

Appendices

Appendix 1: Agenda 21

Agenda 21 is the major outcome of the United Nations Conference on Environment and Development (UNCED) which was held in Rio de Janeiro in June 1992. It provides a common framework of action for all countries to achieve sustainable development. Although Agenda 21 is not a legally binding document, the commitment of 180 countries helps to give it a moral standing at an international level as well as at a national one ... Agenda 21 is a complex document of some 500 pages. The process of negotiation by consensus, and the need to reflect the hopes and aspirations of 180 diverse nations, has resulted in a document which is repetitive and contains difficult language. Some of the repetition is a result of the holistic nature of sustainable development, and the interlinkages between different environment and development issues.

UNCED is about making connections: between humans and their environment, between people from the diverse nations of the earth, and between our generation and the generations of the past and the future. Agenda 21 helps us to make these connections by suggesting ways to tackle environmental and developmental problems in a holistic manner. It also sets out ways to make decisions that ensure all sectors of society are involved.

The 'Rio Declaration' recognises *the integral and interdependent nature of the Earth, our home'*. This view acknowledges that humans are part of global ecosystems and that nature is not simply a resource to be exploited by humans.

Recognition of this interdependence is an essential first step in dealing with environmental and developmental issues. The acknowledgement of the organic nature of human society has profound implications for the way we deal with the world around us. It means that we cannot just conserve the environment without worrying about social and economic development. At the same time, we cannot have sustainable development without protecting the environment.

The compartmentalised ways of dealing with environmental and developmental issues which have been used in the past have caused many of the social, economic and environmental problems facing humanity.

Ministry for the Environment, Making Connections: an Overview of Agenda 21 (Wellington, New Zealand: Ministry for the Environment, Manatu mo te Taiao, undated), pp. 3–4.

Appendix 2: Robin Clarke's list of criteria for a 'soft-technology' community

	Hard Technology Society	Soft Technology Community
*1.	ecologically unsound	ecologically sound
*2.	large energy input	small energy input
*3.	high pollution rate	low or no pollution rate
*4.	'one-way' use of materials and energy sources	reversible materials and renewable energy sources only
*5.	functional for limited times only	functional for all times
*6.	mass production	craft industry
*7.	high specialisation	low specialisation
8.	nuclear family	communal units
*9.	city emphasis	village emphasis
*10.	alienation from nature	integration with nature
11.	consensus politics	democratic politics
*12.	technical boundaries set by wealth	technical boundaries set by nature
*13.	world-wide trade	local bartering
*14.	destructive of local culture	compatible with local culture
*15.	technology liable to misuse	safeguards against misuse
*16.	highly destructive to other species	dependent on well-being of other species
*17.	innovation regulated by profit and war	innovation regulated by need
*18.	growth-oriented economy	steady-state economy
*19.	capital intensive	labour intensive
*20.	alienates young and old	integrates young and old
*21.	centralist	decentralist
*22.	general efficiency increases with size	general efficiency increases with smallness
*23.	operating modes too complicated for general comprehension	operating modes understandable by all
*24.	technological accidents frequent and serious	technological accidents few and unimportant
*25.	singular solutions to technical and social problems	diverse solutions to technical and social problems
26.	agricultural emphasis on monoculture	agricultural emphasis on diversity
*27.	quantity criteria highly valued	quality criteria highly valued
28.	food production specialized	food production shared by all industry
29.	work undertaken primarily for income	work undertaken primarily for satisfaction
*30.	small units totally dependent on others	small units self-sufficient
*31.	science and technology alienated from culture	science and technology integrated with culture
*32.	science and technology performed by specialist elites	science and technology performed by all
*33.	science and technology divorced from other forms of knowledge	science and technology integrated with other forms of knowledge
34.	strong work/leisure distinction	weak or non-existent work/leisure distinction
35.	high unemployment	(concept not valid)
*36.	technical goals valid for only a small proportion of the globe for a finite time	technical goals valid 'for all men for all time'

Note: the asterisks set against 29 out of the 36 items on this list indicate those categories that can be assumed to relate to the technology of the society being described, rather than to its social or agricultural aspects.

R. Clarke, 'Soft Technology: Blueprint for a Research Community' Undercurrents 2 (May 1972), unpaginated. (Undercurrents, the 'Journal of Radical Science and People's Technology', was formerly supplied as a series of loose-leaf items in a biodegradable cellophane bag.)

Appendix 3: Graeme Robertson's 'required changes to produce a sustainable future'

Old paradigm	New paradigm
'Design' of ultimate importance	Understand the limitations of 'design'
Ignorance of the 'wider' world	An integral part of the 'total' environment
Isolation from surrounding environment	Strong connections with surroundings
Arrogant denial of nature	Recognise the interdependence of nature
Narrow materialistic approach	Respect material/spiritual connections
Ignorance of consequences of actions	Acceptance of responsibility for actions
Depersonalizing	Humanizing
Design dominated by visual aesthetics	Design balancing all sensory needs
Imposed on the natural world	Organic, from the local ecosystem
Dominated by short-term consumerism	Objects and systems of long-term value
Unlimited use of resources	Elimination of the concept of waste
Polluting high CO_2 emissions systems	Responsible low CO_2 emittance system
High-energy materials and systems	Low renewable-energy approaches
Isolated concepts and approaches	Holistic considerations throughout
Closed competitive processes	Knowledge sharing/open communication
Damaging to personal health	Healthy caring environments
Speculative developments	Community or self-built projects
Satisfying multi-national needs	Responsive to local social needs
'International' style	Vernacular
Large-scale design solutions	Human-scale design solutions
Male-dominated design approach	Male/female design approaches
Uniform, predictable, conventional	Unpredictable and perhaps surprising
Ignoring of importance of 'craft'	Respect for the notion of 'craft'

G. Robertson, 'New Paradigms for Ecobalance' Paper given at invitation of New Zealand Planning Institute Proceedings of New Zealand Planning Institute Conference 1993 (Auckland, New Zealand: The University of Auckland, Centre for Continuing Education, 1993), p. 26.

Appendix 4: Recommendations for a battery room

The following list is the State Electricity Commission of Victoria's recommendations for a battery room for a remote area power supply system.

Battery bank/room layout

Battery banks can be very hazardous. Batteries store a great deal of energy in a small space and during charging dangerous quantities of explosive hydrogen may be liberated. The danger of explosion or fire is very real.

The battery bank should be installed on its own in a well ventilated shed, remote from living areas. All work in the area should only be done using tools with insulated handles to avoid the possibility of accidental short circuits and creating a spark. It is also good practice to remove metal bracelets, watch bands etc. when working in the area.

All battery rooms/stores should have the following features:

1. Heavy duty level wooden planking for shelves. Shelves should be spaced to allow easy reading of electrolyte specific gravity and allow checking and topping up of electrolyte.
2. Cartridge type fuses for short circuit protection
3. Rubber gloves for battery maintenance. Keep in good condition. **Do NOT** use cloth gloves because sulphuric acid can attack them.
4. Goggles should be worn at **all** times while maintaining batteries to protect eyes from corrosive sulphuric acid which may be splashed.
5. Bottle of eye wash in case of inadvertent acid spills or splashes.
6. Hydrometer in good working order (always handle with gloves and goggles).
7. 8. Full bottle and reserve supply of distilled or de-ionised water.
9. Portable voltmeter to check cells and batteries.
10. Covered bucket always filled with wash-down water in case of acid spills.
11. Adequate ventilation to prevent build-up of explosive gas (hydrogen is produced by batteries).
12. Sodium bi-carbonate (bicarbonate of soda) for neutralising acid spills.
13. Safety and warning signs – 'No Smoking', 'No Sparks', 'No Flames', 'Hazchem', 'Electrolyte burns', see current Australian Standards AS2676.
14. Petroleum jelly to provide a corrosion coating over terminals.
15. Secure the area with a lock and key.
16. First aid instructions, plus Poison Information Line phone number.
17. Cleaning rag for keeping batteries in clean condition.

The State Electricity Commission of Victoria and Energy Victoria Remote Area Power Supplies (Melbourne, Australia: The State Electricity Commission of Victoria and Energy Victoria, 1993), pp. 58–9.

Appendix 5: Washing machine water consumptions

made in	type	make and model	load size (kg)	water use (l)	l/kg
USA	top	Maytag LAT9304	7.0*	151	21.6
USA	top	Westinghouse LD850SA	7.0	130	18.6
USA	top	Westinghouse LE555S	5.0	91	18.2
USA	front	Philco WMN1063	5.0	70	14.0
USA	front	Philco WDN1053**	5.0	70	14.0
Australia	front	Hoover Electra 545***	4.0	115	28.8
Australia	top	Hoover 1500	6.0	170	28.3
Australia	top	Hoover 1000	5.0	140	28.0
New Zealand	top	Simpson Aquarius 711	7.0	130	18.6
New Zealand	top	Simpson Aquapulse 513	5.0	70	14.0
Germany	front	AEG Lavamat 645	5.0	68	13.6
Germany	front	AEG Lavamat 850	5.0	88	17.6
Germany	front	AEG Lavamat 620	5.0	78	15.6
Germany	front	AEG Lavamat 538	5.0	98	19.6
Germany	front	AEG Lavamat 502	5.0	110	22.0
Germany	front	Bosch WFM 3030	5.0	79.6	15.9
Germany	front	Bosch WFB 2000	5.0	80.6	16.1
Sweden	front	Asko 20004****	4.5	63	14.0
Sweden	top	Asko 112	3.5	47	13.4

Note: Where a manufacturer's range includes a number of machines with the same water consumption, differing only in price and features, only one machine is shown in the table. All machines were on sale in Auckland, New Zealand, in March 1995.

*The load size is not given in the manufacturer's leaflet and is assumed to be 7 kg, as this is the maximum load capacity of any of the machines studied. The leaflet speaks of 'a washing capacity big enough for the largest family'. (Maytag, 1994)

**This is a combined washing-drying machine.

***The manufacturer's catalogue says of the Electra 545: 'This economical machine actually uses 22% less water than an equivalent sized conventional washing machine. (Over one year, this works out to be a saving of about 14,000 precious litres) ... Further, in an independent study ('Life cycle analysis' 10/92 – Deni Greene Consulting Services) to determine the environmental impact of washing machines, the Hoover Electra was compared with one of Europe's popular front loading washing machines and an Australian conventional washing machine. The study found that the conventional washing machine was the most polluting, generating twice as much air pollution and three times as much polluted water. Of the two front loaders tested, the Hoover Electra was more environmentally friendly than its considerably more expensive imported counterpart.' (Hoover, undated). Note that in Australia, New Zealand, the United States of America and Canada, the 'conventional' washing machine is top-loading.

****The Asko catalogue, which gave the most technical detail of all the literature studied, states that the water consumption of all the machines (with the exception of the top-loading Model 112) is 63 l with five rinses. If a cycle with only three rinses is chosen, the machines will all use only 49 l for a full load, giving a figure of 10.9 l/kg. However, research at the University of Helsinki suggests that the water demand of washing machines has decreased by 50% in the last six years, and this is tending to lead to increasing chemical residues from laundry detergents remaining in clothing, leading to possible skin irritation effects. The residues are reduced by increasing the number of rinses.'

The main difference between the models in the Asko range is that the more expensive machines have faster spinning times, with the top model, the microprocessor-controlled 20004, having a maximum spin speed of 1500 rpm: 'The more water you can extract from your wash, the shorter the drying time in the tumble dryer, and, therefore, the more electricity you will save. 1kg of wet cotton contains 2 l of water. The maximum that can be removed by spinning is 1.6 l. In other words, even the maximum possible water extraction will always leave 0.4 l of residual moisture. The Asko 20004, spinning at a speed of 1500 rpm, leaves a residual moisture of only 0.49 l – 94% of the maximum possible water extraction.' (Asko, undated).

The tumble dryer data in the Asko catalogue quotes the electricity consumption for drying a 5-kg wash load after both an 800 rpm spin and a 1500 rpm spin. For the Asko 7704 condenser dryer, the 800 rpm figure is 3.8 kWh, but the 1500 rpm figure is 2.7 kWh, a saving per load of 1.1 kWh (Asko, undated).

It is interesting to see that there is a very wide range of water consumptions in washing machines, with the worst using twice as much water as the best, but there is little difference between the best top loaders and the best front loaders. There is also no way of differentiating on price, since the Simpson, the best of the top-loaders, is a relatively low cost model, while the Asko is a high-price machine. It is ironic that such claims of environmental friendliness should be made by Hoover of Australia for their Electra 545, which has the highest water consumption of all the models studied. Given the number of households in the more remote parts of Australia which rely on roof collected water for all their needs, it seems surprising that an Australian machine should perform so poorly.

Appendix 6: Performance analysis of the Cresswell Road houses, Sheffield

Olivier and Willoughby[2] report that the monitored gas consumption for the Cresswell Road houses in Sheffield, designed by Brenda and Robert Vale, is 108 kWh/m²/year, and the electricity consumption is 26 kWh/m²/year. Shorrock et al.[3] give the following breakdown for UK domestic delivered-energy use, and say that the proportions have remained relatively stable in the last 30 years.

Bell et al.[4] give the total delivered-energy demand per household for space heating as 43–50 GJ per dwelling, so it is possible to construct a table of the energy consumption under the headings provided by Shorrock et al.

Table A6.1: Proportional delivered-energy use in the domestic sector

space heating	57%
hot water	25%
lights and appliances	11%
cooking	7%

Table A6.2: Delivered-energy consumption per dwelling in the United Kingdom

category		consumption (GJ)	consumption (kWh)	average (kWh)
space heating	57%	43–50	12,000–13,900	12,900
hot water	25%	18.9–21.9	5,200–6,100	5,700
lights/appliances	11%	8.3–9.6	2,300–2,700	2,500
cooking	7%	5.3–6.1	1,500–1,700	1,600
total		75.5–87.6 GJ	21,000–24,400 kWh	22,700 kWh

The Cresswell Road houses have a measured electricity consumption of 26 kWh/m²/year (see above), which is 2,293 kWh for the whole house of 88.2 m² floor area. The figure for 'lights and appliances' in the Cresswell Road houses (the only category in Table A6.2 for which electricity is used in the Cresswell Road homes) is almost identical with the lower consumption figure in Table A6.2. Substitution of the lower values from Table A 6.2 for cooking and hot water (both provided by gas at Cresswell Road), and calculating the space-heating load by subtracting the hot-water and cooking averages from the measured total gas consumption (108 kWh/m²/year, or 9,526 kWh/year for the whole house) gives the following results.

Table A6.3: Energy consumption in kWh in the Cresswell Road houses

	whole house	per m² (kWh)	% of total	normal %
space heating	2,826	32	24	57
hot water	5,200	59	44	25
lights and appliances	2,293	26	19	11
cooking	1,500	17	13	7
total	11,819 kWh	134 kWh/m²		
(electricity	2,293 kWh	26 kWh/m²)		
(gas	9,526 kWh	108 kWh/m²)		

The calculated space-heating load for the houses in terms of useful energy is 20 kWh/m²/year, which is 1,764 kWh. At an overall space-heating efficiency of 85.5%[5] the delivered energy for space heating would be 2,063 kWh, or 23.4 kWh/m². The additional space-heating delivered-energy demand, 763 kWh/year, is attributable to the fact that the houses are maintained at a very high temperature. Monitoring by Pilkingtons found mean daily air temperatures in the two houses to be 21.2°C and 21.6°C.[6] This can be compared with the highest average whole house temperature reported for the Pennyland houses in Milton Keynes during the 1981–82 monitoring period of 19.1°C. The Cresswell Road houses are being operated at an average temperature that is, in the case of one of the houses, 2.5°C higher than the Pennyland average. Had the Cresswell Road houses been operated at the design temperature given in the Building Research Establishment Domestic Energy Model (BREDEM) analysis process, which predicted a space-heating useful energy demand of 20 kWh/m², leading to a gas consumption for space heating of 23.4 kWh/m², the houses would have used 125 kWh/m² overall, rather than the measured 134 kWh/m². The overheating causes an increase in overall energy consumption of only 7%.

Appendix 7: Wood fuel consumption in the autonomous house over the winter of 1994–95

date	wood burned (kg)	date	wood burned (kg)
Saturday 22 October	10.5	Sunday 1 January	7
Saturday 29 October	10.5	Monday 2 January	5
Sunday 30 October	14	Wednesday 4 January	9
Saturday 12 November	14	Saturday 7 January	14
Sunday 13 November	7	Tuesday 10 January	7
Saturday 26 November	7	Saturday 14 January	7
Friday 2 December	13	Sunday 15 January	14
Saturday 10 December	8	Saturday 21 January	20
Sunday 11 December	14	Sunday 22 January	8
Thursday 15 December	7	Thursday 26 January	14
Saturday 17 December	7	Friday 27 January	14
Wednesday 21 December	8	Tuesday 31 January	14
Thursday 22 December	11	Friday 10 February	14
Friday 23 December	8	Sunday 19 February	14
Monday 26 December	8	Saturday 25 February	7
Note: the stove was lit only on the days indicated.		total	315 kg

Appendix 8: The Solarex guarantee

'For twenty years from the sale of the product to the original consumer purchaser, Solarex will replace the lost power of any modules that fail to produce at least eighty percent of the minimum power output specified by Solarex at the time of delivery.

For ten years from the sale of the product to the original consumer purchaser, Solarex will replace the lost power of any modules that fail to produce at least ninety percent of the minimum power output specified by Solarex at the time of delivery.

Power output shall be measured by Solarex using standard Solarex test conditions. Solarex will replace such lost power, up to the minimum output originally specified, either by providing the purchaser with additional modules to make up the total wattage lost, or by repairing or replacing the module, at Solarex's option. This warranty shall only apply while the original consumer purchaser owns the product.'[7]

Notes

Chapter 1

1. Friends of the Earth, *The Stockholm Conference: Only One Earth* (London: Earth Island, 1972).
2. A. Pike, *The Autonomous House Research Programme* SRC/DOE Autonomous Housing Study (Cambridge: University of Cambridge, Department of Architecture, Technical Research Division, October 1974), p. 1.
3. Ibid., p. 1.
4. Ibid., p. 8.
5. K. Lapthorne, *Integration of Autonomous and Industrialized Building Systems* Working Paper 7 (Cambridge: University of Cambridge, Department of Architecture, Technical Research Division, March 1973), p. 4.
6. B. Vale and R. Vale, *The Autonomous House: Design and Planning for Self-sufficiency* (London: Thames and Hudson, 1975), p. 7.
7. Pike, *The Autonomous House Research Programme*, p. 8.
8. A. Pike, 'Autarkic Housing Research', *Forma* 4,4 (1976), pp. 193–7.
9. C. Onions (ed.), *The Shorter Oxford English Dictionary* (Oxford: Clarendon Press, 1973), Volume 1, pp. 134–5.
10. E. White, 'SESCI Sponsors Second Annual Autonomous House Award', *Sol: the Voice of Renewable Energy in Canada* (November–December 1992), p. 3. (*Sol* is published by the Solar Energy Society of Canada Inc.)
11. L. Imre, 'Autonomous Energy School for Hungary' *Sun at Work in Europe* 6,2 (1991), p. 16.
12. M. Parnell and G. Cole, *Australian Solar Houses* (Leura, New South Wales: Second Back Row Press/Solar Scope, 1983), p. 216.
13. Ibid., pp. 142–3.
14. World Commission on Environment and Development, *Our Common Future* (Oxford: Oxford University Press, 1987).
15. J. Oliver, *Climate and Man's Environment: an Introduction to Applied Climatology* (New York: John Wiley and Sons Inc., 1973), p. 389.
16. S. Manabe and R. Wetherald, 'Thermal Equilibrium of the Atmosphere with a Given Distribution of Relative Humidity' *Journal of Atmospheric Science* 24 (1967), pp. 241–59.
17. A.D. Brown, 'Guidelines for the Future' *Soil and Health: The Official Journal of the Soil Association of New Zealand* (1971), p. 11.
18. P. Cox and C. Miro, 'Ozone Depletion Theory Marks 20th Anniversary' *ASHRAE Journal* (December 1994), p. 16.
19. World Commission on Environment and Development, *Our Common Future*, p. 43.
20. Ministry for the Environment, *Making Connections: an Overview of Agenda 21* (Wellington, New Zealand: Ministry for the Environment, Manatu mo te Taiao, undated), p. 3 ... p. 4.
21. Ministry for the Environment, *Living for the Future: a Guide to Agenda 21* (Wellington, New Zealand: Ministry for the Environment, Manatu mo te Taiao, 1993), p. 1.
22. Ministry for the Environment, *Living for the Future*, pp. 20–22.
23. British Wind Energy Association, *Wind Energy: the Facts* (London: British Wind Energy Association, 1995), p. 6.
24. J. Leggett (ed.), *Global Warming* (Oxford: Oxford University Press, 1990), p. 480.
25. Intergovernmental Panel on Climate Change, *Report to IPCC from Working Group 1: Policymakers' Summary of the Scientific Assessment of Climate Change* (June 1990), p. 6.
26. J. Leggett, 'The Nature of the Greenhouse Threat' in Leggett (ed.), *Global Warming*, pp. 25–6.
27. Ibid., p. 26.
28. J. Bookout, 'Two Centuries of Fossil Fuel Energy' *Episodes: Journal of the International Union of Geological Sciences* (December 1989), pp. 257–62.
29. Leggett 'The Nature of the Greenhouse Effect', pp. 27–8. Leggett's data are taken from R. Houghton and G. Woodwell, 'Global Climatic Change', *Scientific American* (April 1989), pp. 36–44.
30. G. Rattray Taylor, *The Doomsday Book* (London: Thames and Hudson, 1970).
31. Friends of the Earth, *The Stockholm Conference*.
32. D.H. Meadows, D.L. Meadows, J. Randers and W. Behrens, *The Limits to Growth: a Report for the Club of Rome's Project on the Predicament of Mankind* (New York: Universe Books and London, Earth Island Ltd, 1972).
33. Rattray Taylor, *The Doomsday Book*, p. 59.
34. Ibid., p. 207.
35. J. Holdren, 'Global Thermal Pollution' in J. Holdren and P. Ehrlich (eds), *Global Ecology* (New York: Harcourt Brace Jovanovich, 1971), p. 85, quoted in Meadows et al., *The Limits to Growth*, pp. 73–4.
36. J. Sinclair, 'Outlook: Changeable' *New Zealand Listener* (25 February – 3 March 1995), pp. 19–23.
37. Ibid., p. 19.
38. N. Nuttall, 'Climate Experts Predict 100-Year Drought in Africa' *The Times* (Wednesday, 18 October 1995), p. 12.
39. Data taken from Department of Trade and Industry, *Energy Related Carbon Emissions in Possible Future Scenarios for the United Kingdom* Energy Paper 59 (London: Department of Trade and Industry, HMSO, 1992), quoted in M. Bell, R. Lowe, P. Roberts and D. Johnston, *Energy Efficiency in Housing: a Literature Review for the Joseph Rowntree Foundation* (Leeds: Leeds School of the Environment, Leeds Metropolitan University, 1994), p. 17.
40. British Wind Energy Association, *Wind Energy: the Facts*, p. 6.

Chapter 2

1. R. Carson, *Silent Spring* (Harmondsworth, Middlesex: Penguin Books Ltd, 1962), p. 31.
2. Ibid., pp. 193–213.
3. Ibid., pp. 240–57.
4. Ibid., p. 257.
5. B. Commoner, *The Closing Circle: Nature, Man and Technology* (New York: Alfred A. Knopf, 1972), pp. 140–44.
6. Ibid., pp. 142–3.
7. Ibid., p. 121.
8. D.H. Meadows, D.L. Meadows, J. Randers and W. Behrens, *The Limits to Growth* (New York: Universe Books and London: Earth Island Ltd, 1972), pp. 66–7 (in UK edn).
9. E. Goldsmith, R. Allen, M. Allaby, J. Davoll and S. Lawrence, 'A Blueprint for Survival' *The Ecologist* 2 (January 1972), p. 6.
10. Ibid., p. 3.
11. Ibid., p. 4.
12. J. Ellul, *The Technological Society* (trans. J. Wilkinson, New York: A.A. Knopf, 1964), p. 138.
13. T. Roszak, *The Making of a Counter Culture* (London: Faber and Faber, 1970), pp. 7–8.
14. Ibid., p. 13.
15. M. Bookchin, 'Towards a Liberatory Technology' (1971) in M. Bookchin *Post-Scarcity Anarchism* (London: Wildwood House, 1974), p. 85.
16. Ibid., p. 86.
17. Ibid.
18. D. Dickson, *Alternative Technology and*

the Politics of Technical Change (Glasgow: Fontana/Collins, 1974), p. 37.
19. Ibid., p. 39.
20. P. Harper, 'Peter Harper's Directory of Alternative Technology' Architectural Design 47 (November 1974), p. 690.
21. G. Boyle and P. Harper (eds), Radical Technology (London: Wildwood House, 1976), p. 6.
22. R. Clarke, 'Soft Technology: Blueprint for a Research Community' Undercurrents 2 (May 1972), unpaginated. (Undercurrents, the 'Journal of Radical Science and People's Technology', was formerly supplied as a series of loose-leaf items in a biodegradable cellophane bag.)
23. Dickson, Alternative Technology, p. 38.
24. Ibid., p. 38.
25. T. More, Utopia (1516; trans. P. Turner, Harmondsworth, Middlesex: Penguin Books, 1965).
26. G. Woodcock, 'Foreword' in M. Berneri Journey through Utopia (New York: Schocken Books, 1950), p. ix.
27. S. Butler, Erewhon (1872; repr. London: Everyman's Library, Dent, 1959).
28. G. Orwell, Nineteen Eighty-Four (1949; repr. Harmondsworth, Middlesex: Penguin Books, 1959).
29. A. Huxley, Brave New World (1932; repr. Harmondsworth, Middlesex: Penguin Books, 1955).
30. R. Ellman, Yeats: the Man and the Masks (London: Faber, 1961), p. 116.
31. Plato, The Republic (trans. D. Lee, Harmondsworth, Middlesex: Penguin Books, 1974), p. 124.
32. Berneri, Journey Through Utopia, p. 11.
33. Aristophanes, The Birds in Aristophanes (trans. J.H. Frere, London: George Routledge and Sons, 1886), pp. 175–281.
34. J. Andrea, Christianopolis (1619; trans. F.E. Held, New York: Oxford University Press, 1916).
35. R. Burton, The Anatomy of Melancholy (1621; repr. London: J.M. Dent and Sons Ltd, 1961).
36. T. Campanella, The City of the Sun (1623; trans. W. Gilstrap in G. Negley and J. Patrick [eds], The Quest for Utopia [College Park, Maryland: McGrath Publishing Co., 1952]).
37. S. Gott, Nova Solyma (1648; trans. W. Begley, London: 1902).
38. L. Mumford, The Story of Utopias (London: George G. Harrap and Co. Ltd, 1923), p. 85.
39. Andrea, Christianopolis, pp. 149–50.
40. Ibid., pp. 269–70.
41. Ibid., p. 269.
42. Ibid., p. 149.
43. Ibid., p. 170.
44. Ibid., p. 260.
45. Ibid., p. 165.
46. Ibid., p. 164.
47. F. Bacon, New Atlantis (1672; ed.

H. Osborne, London: University Tutorial Press, undated).
48. Ibid., pp. xviii–xix.
49. Ibid., p. 41.
50. J. Harrington, The Commonwealth of Oceana (London: 1656).
51. G. Winstanley, 'The Law of Freedom in a Platform' (1652; in C. Hill (ed.), Winstanley: the Law of Freedom and Other Writings (Harmondsworth, Middlesex: Penguin Books, 1973).
52. Berneri, Journey Through Utopia, p. 243.
53. E. Bellamy, Looking Backward (London: William Reeves, 1888), p. 49.
54. Ibid., p. 96.
55. Ibid., p. 146.
56. Ibid., p. 147.
57. Ibid., p. 90.
58. Ibid., p. 86.
59. E. Cabet, Voyage en Icarie (1845; trans. J. Patrick, in Negley and Patrick (eds), The Quest for Utopia)
60. Berneri, Journey Through Utopia, p. 222.
61. Mumford, The Story of Utopias, p. 147.
62. Quoted in J. Redmond (ed.), 'Introduction' to W. Morris News from Nowhere (1891; repr. London: Routledge and Kegan Paul, 1970), p. xxxvii.
63. F. MacCarthey, William Morris: a Life for Our Time (London: Faber and Faber, 1994), p. 584.
64. Morris, News from Nowhere, p. 18.
65. Berneri, Journey through Utopia, p. 255.
66. G. Hough, The Last Romantics (London: Duckworth, 1949), p. 109.
67. Morris, News from Nowhere, pp. 82–3.
68. Ibid., p. 38.
69. Ibid., p. 140.
70. Ibid., p. 146.
71. Y. Zamyatin, We (1926; trans. B.G. Guerney; Harmondsworth, Middlesex: Penguin Books, 1972).
72. Huxley, Brave New World.
73. Orwell, Nineteen Eighty-Four.
74. H.G. Wells, A Modern Utopia (London: Heron Books, 1905), p. 18.
75. H.G. Wells, The Sleeper Awakes & Men Like Gods (1923; repr. London: The Literary Press, The Lewisham Edition, undated), pp. 243–4.
76. E. Mannin, Bread and Roses: an Utopian Survey and Blueprint (London: Macdonald and Co. Ltd, 1944).
77. B. Skinner, Walden Two (1948; repr. New York: Macmillan, 1976).
78. Ibid., p. 279.
79. A. Huxley, Island (1962; repr. London: Chatto and Windus, 1972).
80. Ibid., p. 144.
81. Ibid., p. 146.
82. E. Callenbach, Ecotopia (Berkeley, California: Banyan Tree Books, 1975).
83. Ibid., p 18.
84. U. Le Guin, The Dispossessed (London:

Panther Books, 1975).
85. M. Piercy, Woman on the Edge of Time (1976; repr. London: The Women's Press Ltd, 1979).
86. Le Guin, The Dispossessed, p. 88.
87. Piercy, Woman on the Edge of Time, p. 154.
88. B. Vale, Albion: a Romance of the 21st Century (Barnstaple: Spindlewood Press, 1982), p. 58.
89. Ibid., p. 170.
90. Ibid., p. 70–71.
91. G. Robertson, 'New Paradigms for Ecobalance' in New Zealand Planning Institute Proceedings of New Zealand Planning Institute Conference 1993 (Auckland, New Zealand: Centre for Continuing Education, The University of Auckland, 1993), p. 26.
92. A. Pike, 'The Alexander Pike Autonomous House, Cambridge' Architectural Design 47 (November 1974), p. 681.
93. Le Guin, The Dispossessed, p. 88.
94. C.H. Pout, 'Relating CO_2 Emissions to End-uses of Energy in the UK' in Buildings and the Environment: Proceedings of the First International Conference (organized by CIB Task Group 8 'Environmental Assessment of Buildings' 16–20 May 1994; Garston, Watford: Building Research Establishment, 1994), p. 4.
95. L. Brown, C. Flavin, H. French, L. Starke, State of the World 1995: a Worldwatch Institute Report on Progress Toward a Sustainable Society (New York: W.W. Norton and Company, 1995), p. 6.
96. N. Schoon, 'Bills Doubled for Low-income Families after Switch to Meters' The Independent (21 February 1994), p. 7.
97. 'Symposium Discussion: Prospect. Limits of the Earth: Materials and Ideas' in W. Thomas (ed.), Man's Role in Changing the Face of the Earth (Chicago: University of Chicago Press, 1956), Volume 2, p. 1080.
98. Poem by Professor Kenneth Boulding quoted by Dr Sol Tax (Professor of Anthropology at the University of Chicago, and editor of American Anthropologist) in 'Symposium discussion ...', p. 1087.
99. G. Rattray Taylor, The Doomsday Book (London: Thames and Hudson, 1970), p. 284.
100. C. Moorcroft, 'Designing for Survival' Architectural Design 44 (July 1972), p. 415.
101. Ibid.

Chapter 3
1. Data taken from Department of the Environment, Climate Change: Our National Programme for CO_2 Emissions (London: Department of the Environment, 1992), p. 6.
2. Data taken from Department of the Environment, The UK Environment

(London: Government Statistical Service, HMSO, 1992), p. 214.
3. Data taken from C.H. Pout, 'Relating CO_2 Emissions to End-uses of Energy in the UK' in *Buildings and the Environment: Proceedings of the First International Conference* (organized by CIB Task Group 8 'Environmental Assessment of Buildings' 16–20 May 1994; Garston, Watford: Building Research Establishment, 1994), p. 5.
4. G. Henderson, 'Housing, Energy and the Environment' in *Proceedings of the Innovative Housing '93 Conference* (21–25 June 1993; Vancouver: Minister of Supply and Services, Canada, 1993), Volume 1, p. 5.
5. Data taken from Centre for Advanced Engineering, 'Energy Efficiency Project Workshop' in *Task Group Discussion Papers, Volume 1. Residential Buildings/Commercial and Institutional Buildings/Transport* (Christchurch, New Zealand: Centre for Advanced Engineering, University of Canterbury, February 1994), p. 3.
6. Centre for Advanced Engineering, 'Energy Efficiency Project Workshop', p. 3.
7. N. Summers, *A Prospect of Southwell* (rev. edn, Southwell, Notts.: Kelham House Publications, 1988), p. 1.
8. P.L. O'Malley, 'Southwell – Its Trade and Industry – a Survey' in Southwell and District Local History Society, *Southwell: the Town and its People* (Southwell, Notts.: Southwell and District Local History Society, 1992), p. 38.
9. N. Pevsner, *The Leaves of Southwell* (London: King Penguin Books, 1945), p. 67.
10. Hickling Corporation, *Comparison Analysis Report on Advanced Houses* Ref. 4804 prepared for EMR/Canmet (Ottawa: Hickling Corporation, 8 June 1993), p. 47.
11. A.C.E. Alternative and Conservation Energies Inc., *Design of a Generic Sustainable House* (Alberta, Canada: Alberta Municipal Affairs, Innovative Housing Grants Program, November 1991), p. 1.
12. Ministry for the Environment, *Making Connections: an Overview of Agenda 21* (Wellington, New Zealand: Ministry for the Environment, Manatu mo te Taiao, undated), p. 3.
13. D. Walker, 'The Southwell Paddy' in Southwell and District Local History Society, *Southwell: the Town and its People*, pp. 169–70.
14. G. Baird, 'The Energy Requirements and Environmental Impacts of Building Materials' in A. Dawson (ed.), *Architectural Science: its Influence on the Built Environment* Proceedings of the 28th Conference of the Australian and New Zealand Architectural Science Association

(26–28 September 1994; Geelong: Deakin University, School of Architecture and Building, 1994), p. 10.
15. J. Willoughby, *John Willoughby's Energy Filofax: Part 1 – Thermal Properties* (Cheltenham: John Willoughby, undated). (This is an unpaginated set of loose-leaf data sheets.)
16. T. Sinclair, *Energy Management in the Brick and Ceramic Industry: End of Grant Report No. 646* (New South Wales: National Energy Research and Development and Demonstration Programme, Energy Authority of New South Wales, 1986), p. iv.
17. Ibid.
18. R. Merryweather, 'A Few Recollections of Easthorpe' in Southwell and District Local History Society, *Southwell: the Town and its People*, pp. 164–5.
19. D. Oppenheim, *Small Solar Buildings in Cool Northern Climates* (London: The Architectural Press, 1981), p. 21.
20. P. Achard and R. Gicquel (eds), *European Passive Solar Handbook* (Brussels: Commission of the European Communities, Directorate-General XII for Science, Research and Development, Solar Energy Division, 1986), p. 4.3.
21. R. Everett, *Passive Solar in Milton Keynes* Research Report ERG 031 (Milton Keynes: Energy Research Group, Open University, 1980), p. 39.
22. R. Lowe, J. Chapman and R. Everett, *The Pennyland Project* ERG 053 ETSU-S-1046 (Milton Keynes: Energy Research Group, Open University, 1985), p. 8.1.
23. Lowe et al., *The Pennyland Project*, p. 6.46.
24. J. Sprigg and D.Larkin, *Shaker Life, Work and Art* (London: Cassell, 1988), p. 54.
25. M. Comino, *Gimson and the Barnsleys* (London: Evans Brothers Ltd, 1980), pp. 138–40.
26. C. Alexander, *The Timeless Way of Building* (New York: Oxford University Press, 1979).
27. C. Alexander, S. Ishikawa and M. Silverstein, *A Pattern Language: Towns, Buildings, Construction* (New York: Oxford University Press, 1997).
28. S.F. Pullen, 'Embodied Energy and Operational Energy of Houses' in Dawson (ed.), *Architectural Science*, pp. 155–62.
29. M. Pawley, 'Building Revisits: Two. Hunstanton School' *The Architects' Journal* 179 (23 May 1984), p. 39.
30. P. Tutt and D. Adler (eds), *New Metric Handbook* (London: The Architectural Press, 1979), p. 9.
31. G.J.W. Marsh, *Byelaws Bring a Breakthrough in WC Design* Ifö Info 11186 (Bromolla, Sweden: Ifö Sanitär AB, 1986), unpaginated.
32. B. Vale and R. Vale, 'Ökologische

Architektur in England' in *Tagungsband Wiener Symposium für Solar-Architektur* (Messepalast, Vienna, 21–23 May 1992; Vienna: Architekten- und Ingenieurakademie, 1992), pp. 199–220.
33. E. Hodgins, *Mr. Blandings Builds his Dream House* (New York: Simon and Schuster, 1946), p. 79.

Chapter 4

1. M. Sizemore, H. Clark, W. Ostrander, *Energy Planning for Buildings* (Washington: The American Institute of Architects, 1979), p. 5.
2. J. Goulding, J. Owen Lewis and T. Steemers, *Energy in Architecture: the European Passive Solar Handbook* Publication No. EUR 13446 of the Commission of the European Communities, Luxembourg (London: Batsford, 1992), p. 66.
3. S. Szokolay, *Environmental Science Handbook* (London: The Construction Press, 1980), p. 332.
4. D. Breuer, *Energy and Comfort Performance Monitoring of Passive Solar, Energy Efficient New Zealand Residences* Report No. 171 (Wellington: New Zealand Energy Research and Development Committee, 1988), 2 volumes.
5. D. Olivier, *Energy Efficiency and Renewables: Recent Experience on Mainland Europe* (Hereford: Energy Advisory Associates, 1992), p. 58.
6. P. Lund, 'Optimum Solar House: Interplay Between Solar Aperture and Energy Storage' *International Solar Energy Society World Conference* (1993, Helsinki: University of Technology), unpaginated.
7. Olivier, *Energy Efficiency*, p. 12.
8. W. Shurcliff, *Superinsulated Houses and Double-Envelope Houses: a Preliminary Survey of Principles and Practice* (Cambridge, Mass.: W.A. Shurcliff, 1980), p. 5.07.
9. J. Page, *Climate in the United Kingdom* (London: HMSO, 1986), pp. 291–300.
10. W. Palz and T. Steemers, *Solar Houses in Europe: How They Have Worked* (Oxford: Commission of the European Communities/Pergamon Press, 1981), p. 18.
11. Buchan, Lawton, Parent Ltd, *Status Report on the Canadian Advanced Houses Program (Draft)* A Technical Paper for Innovative Housing '93, June 21, Vancouver, British Columbia (Ottawa: CANMET/Energy, Mines and Resources, Canada, 1993), p. 2.
12. Shurcliff, *Superinsulated Houses*, p. 5.07.
13. Ibid., p. 3.18.
14. Ibid., p. 5.07.
15. A. Tucker and G. Watt, 'Appendix C: Thermal Envelope: Thermal Mass' in Centre for Advanced Engineering, *Energy*

Efficiency Project Workshop: Task Group Discussion Papers (Christchurch: University of Canterbury, Centre for Advanced Engineering, 1994), Volume 1 (*Residential Buildings*), p. 36.
16. J. Littler and R. Thomas, *Design with Energy: the Conservation and Use of Energy in Buildings* (Cambridge: Cambridge University Press, 1984) p. 123.
17. P. Grimsdale, 'Timber Frame Construction' in J. Sunley and B. Bedding *Timber in Construction* (London: B.T. Batsford Ltd/TRADA, 1985), pp. 105–18.
18. Natwest Securities, *UK Building Statistics: Building Compendium: Sector: Building and Construction/Building Materials and Merchants* (London: Natwest Securities, May/June, 1994), p. 12.
19. S. Ashley, 'What the Doctor Ordered' *Building Services: the CIBSE Journal* 10 (April 1988), pp. 25–8.
20. B. Evans, 'Build it Green: Superinsulation' *The Architects' Journal* 191 (7 March 1990), pp. 65–8.
21. B. Vale and R. Vale, 'Low Energy Cottages' *Building Services: the CIBSE Journal* 14 (February 1992), pp. 199–202.
22. D. Olivier and J. Willoughby, *Review of Ultra-Low-Energy Homes Phase 2* A Report to the Building Research Energy Conservation Support Unit (Leominster: Energy Advisory Associates, 1995), pp. 16–20.
23. R. Lowe, M. Bell and D. Johnston, *A Directory of Energy Efficient Housing Practice Prepared for the Joseph Rowntree Foundation* (Draft, not to be quoted in any publication, used here by permission of Dr Lowe; Leeds: Leeds Metropolitan University, Centre for the Built Environment, 1995), p. 29.
24. Natwest Securities, *UK Building Statistics*, p. 12.
25. Architype, *Woodways Self Build Group; Self Build Scheme at Cat Lane, Sheffield: Feasibility Report* (London: Architype Ltd, April 1990).
26. Page, *Climate in the United Kingdom*, pp. 291–311.
27. Cost data from Gordon Hall, Grayson and Co., *Pair of Ecological Cottages 85 to 89 Industry Road, Darnall, Sheffield for North Sheffield Housing Association: Final Account* (Sheffield: Gordon Hall, Grayson and Co., Quantity Surveyors, 1993).
28. D. Stephens, 'Designing and Funding Solar Villages' *Green Buildings – the Next Steps* Conference Transactions (6 November 1992, Bristol Zoo Conference Suite; Bristol: Bristol Centre for the Advancement of Architecture/CORE, 1992), pp. 25–35.
29. Page, *Climate in the United Kingdom*, p. 298.
30. Grimsdale, 'Timber Frame Construction', pp. 105–18.
31. United States Department of Agriculture, *New Life for Old Dwellings: Appraisal and Rehabilitation* Agriculture Handbook No. 481 (Washington: Forest Service of the USDA, 1975); repr. as G. Sherwood, *How to Select and Renovate an Older House* (New York: Dover Publications, 1976) p. 81.
32. USDA, *New Life for Old Dwellings*, p. 81.
33. USDA, *New Life for Old Dwellings*, p. 81 quotes from USDA Forest Products Laboratory, 'Forest Products Laboratory Natural Finish' in *USDA Forest Serv. Res. Note FPL-046* (Madison, Wis.: US Department of Agriculture, Forest Service, Forest Products Laboratory, undated) and also from 'Stain, Oil; Semi-Transparent, Wood Exterior' Fed. Spec. TT-S-708a. Both publications are available from the Superintendent of Documents, US Government Printing Office, Washington DC, 20402.
34. CMHC, *Canadian Wood-Frame House Construction* (Ottawa: Canada Mortgage and Housing Corporation, 1979), p.162.
35. H. Liddell, *private communication*, (1995).
36. G. Hall, 'Treatments' in Sunley and Bedding, *Timber in Construction*, p. 42.
37. Ibid., p. 45.
38. D. Sulman, 'Appendix: Properties and Uses of Commonly Used Timbers' in Sunley and Bedding, *Timber in Construction*, pp. 195–202.
39. Ibid., p. 198.
40. Ibid., p. 202.
41. Ibid., p. 195.
42. B. Keyworth, 'Specifying Timber' in Sunley and Bedding, *Timber in Construction*, p. 49.
43. Department of Energy, *Fuel Efficiency Booklet 7* (London: HMSO, 1979).
44. Swedhouse, *private communication* (East Molesey: Swedhouse (UK) Ltd, 1993).
45. Ekstrands, Catalogue for Ekstrands Eko-Doors (East Molesey: Swedhouse (UK) Ltd, 1993).
46. F. Hall, *Heating, Ventilating and Air Conditioning* (London: The Construction Press, 1980), p. 8.
47. CIBS, *Building Energy Code: Part 1* (London: Chartered Institution of Building Services, 1980), p. 11.
48. B. Marshall and R. Argue, *The Super-Insulated Retrofit Book* (Toronto: Renewable Energy in Canada, 1981), p. 16.
49. Lowe, Bell and Johnston, *A Directory of Energy Efficient Housing Practice*, p. 99.
50. T. Esbensen and V. Korsgaard, 'Dimensioning of the Solar Heating System in the Zero Energy House in Denmark' in *European Solar Houses* Proceedings of the UK-ISES Conference at North East London Polytechnic (April 1976; London: UK International Solar Energy Society, 1976), pp. 39–51.
51. From the discussion session (p. 101) that followed presentation of paper by A. Lovins, 'Economically Efficient Energy Futures' in W. Bach, J. Pankrath and J. Williams (eds), *Interactions of Energy and Climate* Proceedings of an International Workshop held in Münster, Germany (3–6 March 1980; Dordrecht, Holland: D. Reidel Publishing Company), pp. 1–31.
52. J. Nieminen, 'Low-Energy Residential Housing' in *Energy and Buildings* 21 (1994) pp. 187–97.
53. 1991 data from J. Prior, G. Raw and J. Charlesworth, *BREEAM/New Homes Version 3/91: an Environmental Assessment for New Homes* (Garston, Watford: Building Research Establishment, 1991) p. 7; 1996 data from P. Evans, *private communication* (Garston, Watford: BRECSU, Building Research Establishment, 11 February 1997).
54. Esbensen and Korsgaard, 'Dimensioning of the Solar Heating System', p. 51.
55. Data from P. Soulsby, *private communication* (Bournemouth: Eco-Clear Ltd, 1994).
56. Data from J. Schaeffer (ed.), *The Real Goods Solar Living Source Book* (White River Junction, Vermont: Chelsea Green Publishing Company, 1994), p. 263.
57. Ibid., pp. 164 and 287.
58. Data from ADM Indux, *Room Ventilation with Heat Recovery* (Bradford: Advanced Design and Manufacture Ltd, 1995), p. 3.
59. CIBSE, *CIBSE Guide Volume A: Design Data* (London: Chartered Institution of Building Services Engineers, 1986), p. A1 4.
60. Data compiled from CIBSE, *CIBSE Guide Volume A: Design Data* and Goulding, Owen Lewis and Steemers, *Energy in Architecture: the European Passive Solar Handbook*, p. 60.
61. CIBSE, *CIBSE Guide Volume A*, Table A7.3, p. A7-4.
62. M. Peake, *Titus Groan* (1946; repr. Harmondsworth: Penguin Books, 1968), p. 61.
63. D. Taylor, *You and Your Cat* (London: Dorling Kindersley, 1986), p. 20.
64. A. Parks, *People Heaters: a People's Guide to Keeping Warm in Winter* (Andover, Mass.: Brick House Publishing, 1981), p. 53.
65. W. Shurcliff, *Superinsulated Houses and Double-Envelope Houses*, p. 2.03.
66. R. Dumont, *Advanced Houses Program Technical Requirements* Prepared for CANMET Buildings Group (Ottawa: Energy, Mines and Resources, June 1992), p. i.

67. Based on data from Dumont, *Advanced Houses Program*, pp. 28–9.
68. W. Shick, R. Jones, W. Harris and S. Konzo, *Circular C2.3, Illinois Lo-Cal House* (Urbana, Ill.: University of Illinois, Small Homes Council, 1976), p. 8.
69. Goulding, Owen Lewis and Steemers, *European Passive Solar Handbook*, p. 324.
70. Palz and Steemers, *Solar Houses in Europe: How They Have Worked*, p. 44.
71. Data from Bosch, *Fridges and Freezers* (Bosch Domestic Appliances Ltd, 1994) p. 11.
72. E. Abel, 'Low Energy Buildings' *Energy and Buildings* 21 (1994), p. 169.
73. Olivier and Willoughby, *Review of Ultra-Low-Energy Homes Phase 2*, pp. 49–54.
74. M. Bell, R. Lowe, P. Roberts and D. Johnston, *Energy Efficiency in Housing: a Literature Review for the Joseph Rowntree Foundation* (Leeds: Leeds Metropolitan University, Centre for the Built Environment, 1994), p. 15.
75. Olivier and Willoughby, *Review*.
76. S. Carpenter, *Learning from Experiences with Advanced Houses of the World* (CADDET/International Energy Agency, 1995), pp. 196–203.
77. G. Crouch, *The Autonomous Servicing of Dwellings – Design Proposals. Dissertation 3* (Cambridge: University of Cambridge, Department of Architecture, Technical Research Division, Autonomous Housing Study, July 1972).
78. B. Vale, *The Autonomous House: Dissertation 2* (Cambridge: University of Cambridge, Department of Architecture, Technical Research Division, Autonomous Housing Study, July 1972).
79. Palz and Steemers, *Solar Houses in Europe*.
80. D. Bainbridge, *The First Passive Solar Catalog* (Davis, Calif.: The Passive Solar Institute, 1978), p. 5.
81. Ibid., p. 5.
82. R. Everett, *Passive Solar in Milton Keynes* ERG 031 (Milton Keynes: The Open University, Energy Research Group, 1980), and R. Lowe, J. Chapman and R. Everett, *The Pennyland Project* Energy Research Group, Open University. ETSU Contract No. E5A/CON/1046/174/040 (Harwell: Energy Technology Support Unit, 1985).
83. R. Vale, *The Installation of a 5kW Aerogenerator in the Isle of Ely* Report to the Anglo German Foundation for the Study of Industrial Society (London: Anglo German Foundation, 1976).
84. D. Montgomery, 'Aesthetics of Alternatives to Passive and Low-Energy Facilities' in A. Bowen and R. Vagner (eds), *Passive and Low Energy Alternatives 1* Proceedings of the First Passive and Low Energy Architecture Conference (13–15 September 1982, Bermuda; New York:

Pergamon Press), pp. 2–10.
85. E. Petersen, N. Mortensen and L. Landberg, 'Wind Resource Estimation and Siting of Wind Turbines' in B. Cross (ed.), *European Directory of Renewable Energy Suppliers and Services 1994* (London: James and James Science Publishers, 1994), pp. 181–90.
86. J. Walker, 'A Method for Improving the Energy Utililization of Wind-Driven Generators and their Operation with Conventional Power Sets' in *United Nations Conference on New Sources of Energy* (Rome: United Nations, 1961), Volume 7 W/18, pp. 363–8.
87. P. Gipe, 'Wind Power' in Schaeffer (ed.), *The Real Goods Solar Living Source Book*, p. 139.
88. A. Akbarzadeh, *Remote Area Power Supply Systems* (Melbourne, Victoria: Renewable Energy Authority of Victoria (Energy Victoria), 1992), Appendix 1, p. 137.
89. R. Vale, *The Installation of a 5kW Aerogenerator*.
90. Schaeffer (ed.), *The Real Goods Solar Living Source Book*, p. 144.
91. BBC, *Farming Today* (broadcast from London: BBC Radio 4, 24 February 1995).
92. R.Vale, *Services for an Autonomous Research Community in Wales: Working Paper 5* (Cambridge: University of Cambridge, Department of Architecture, Technical Research Division, Autonomous Housing Study, 1974), p. 42.
93. W. Hiley, *Woodland Management* (London: Faber and Faber, 1967), quoted in R. Vale, *Services for an Autonomous Research Community in Wales*, p. 43.
94. L. Brandao, 'Short-Rotation Forestry for Energy and Industry' in H. Egneus and A. Ellegard (eds), *Bioenergy '84* (London: Elsevier Applied Science Publishers, 1985), Volume 2, pp. 77–85.
95. S. Szokolay, *Architecture and Climate Change* (Red Hill: Royal Australian Institute of Architects, Education Division, 1992), p. 29.
96. R. Sims, 'Chapter 7 – Biofuels' in Ministry of Commerce, *Renewable Energy Opportunities for New Zealand* (Wellington: Ministry of Commerce, May 1993), p. 7.6.
97. Ibid., p. 7.6.
98. Massey University, *End Use Database for the New Zealand Economy* (Palmerston North: Massey University, 1992) quoted in Centre for Advanced Engineering, *Energy Efficiency in the Domestic Sector* Energy Efficiency Project Workshop: Task Group Discussion Papers, (Christchurch: University of Canterbury, Centre for Advanced Engineering, 1994), Volume 1 (*Residential Buildings*), pp. 3–5.
99. Sims, 'Biofuels', p. 7.8.
100. D. Pickles, *private communication*

(Newark, Notts: Newark and Sherwood District Council, Chief Architect and Energy Manager, 1995).
101. HUDAC, *Builders' Guide to Energy Efficiency in New Housing* (Toronto: Housing and Urban Development Association of Canada/Ontario Ministry of Energy, 1980), p. 89.
102. J. Todd, 'Biomass – Improving Air Quality Through Better Combustion' in *Solar '94 Conference Proceedings* (30 November – 3 December 1994; Sydney, NSW: Australian and New Zealand Solar Energy Society, 1994), Volume 2, pp. 437–42.
103. Ibid., p. 441.
104. D. Nicholson-Lord, 'Water Firms "Tapped Homes for £300m"' *The Independent* (Thursday, 7 July 1994), p. 10; data quoted from *Which*.
105. S. Connor and F. Pearce, 'When the Water Runs Out … ' *The Independent on Sunday* (Sunday, 22 March 1992), p. 3.
106. P. Hadfield, 'The Revenge of the Rain Gods' *New Scientist* 143 (20 August 1994), pp. 14–15.
107. Editorial, 'The Englishman's Bath' *The Times* (Thursday, 21 September 1995), p. 19.
108. A. Wise, *Water, Sanitary and Waste Services for Buildings* (London: Mitchell's Professional Library, Mitchell, 1986), Table 2.10, p. 149.
109. R. Vale, 'Housing Design' *SCEME Conference, 1994* (London: Society of Chief Electrical and Mechanical Engineers in Local Government, 1994), unpaginated; Olivier and Willoughby, *Review of Ultra-Low-Energy Homes Phase 2*, pp. 16–20.
110. Wise, *Water, Sanitary and Waste Services for Buildings*, p. 149.
111. Nicholson-Lord, 'Water Firms "Tapped Homes for £300m"'.
112. P. Chapman, *Fuel's Paradise: Energy Options for Britain* (Harmondsworth, Middlesex: Penguin Books, 1975), p. 54.
113. Data from wrapper of Sainsbury's wholemeal sliced loaf dated 27 January 1995.
114. Data from wrapper of Co-op wholemeal sliced loaf loaf dated 28 January 1995.
115. Chapman, *Fuel's Paradise*, p. 54.
116. G. Leach, *Energy and Food Production* (Guildford: IPC Science and Technology Press, 1976).
117. Data for energy ratio and total energy input from Leach, *Energy and food Production* (1976), pp. 104–6 and 113–6.
118. G. Leach, *Energy and Food Production* (London: International Institute for Environment and Development, 1975), p. 8.
119. Leach, *Energy and Food Production* (1975), pp. 72–5.
120. Data from Stadtwerke Bielefeld,

quoted in K. Galewski et al., *Regenwassersammelanlage* (Bielefeld: Karl Severing Kollegschule/Rochdale: Hopwood Hall College, ROBI (Transnationales Austauschprojekt: Qualifizierung für den Umweltschutz), 1992), p. 22.

121. K. Valdmaa, *Function of the Müllbank Toilet* (Uppsala: Royal Agricultural College of Sweden, 1975).

122. BioLet USA, *BioLet* Sales leaflet (from Halesworth, Suffolk: Eastwood Services, 1995).

123. Ibid.

124. L. Hills, 'The Clivus Toilet – Sanitation Without Pollution' *Compost Science* (May/June 1972).

125. Data from P. Soulsby, *private communication* (Bournemouth: Eco-Clear Ltd, 1994).

126. Nova Scotia Department of Health, Division of Health Engineering, *The Use of Rainwater for Domestic Purposes in Nova Scotia* (Canada: Nova Scotia Department of Health, 1992), p. 9.

127. A. Fewkes and A. Turton, 'Recovering Rainwater for WC Flushing' *Environmental Health* (February 1994), p. 43.

128. Anon., 'Rapid Population Growth has Eased' *Gulf News* (Waiheke Island, 17 March 1995).

129. G. Williams, *Birds of New Zealand* (Wellington: A.H. & A.W. Reed, 1973), p. 64.

130. All data from A. Wilson (Waiheke Tank Shop, Oneroa, Waiheke Island, Auckland, New Zealand), interviewed 1 May 1995.

131. All data from Y. Maguire (NZRN, Oneroa Red Cross Centre, Waiheke Island, Auckland, New Zealand), interviewed 1 May 1995.

132. Telephone interview with J. Graham (Auckland Public Health Office, Auckland, New Zealand), 2 May 1995.

133. BRE, *Energy Conservation: a Study of Energy Consumption in Buildings and Possible Means of Saving Energy in Housing* CP56/75 (Garston, Watford: Building Research Establishment, 1975), p. 23.

134. Page, *Climate in the United Kingdom*, p. 130.

135. BRE, *Energy Conservation*, pp. 8–9.

136. S. Wozniak, *Solar Heating Systems for the UK: Design, Installation, and Economic Aspects* (London: Department of the Environment, Building Research Establishment, HMSO, 1979), p. 62.

137. Page, *Climate in the United Kingdom*, p. 179.

138. Halcrow Gilbert Associates Ltd, *Guidelines on the Grid Connection of Photovoltaic systems* ETSU S 1394-P2, (Harwell: Energy Technology Support Unit, 1993), p. 32.

139. Price from Wind and Sun Ltd,

Oxford (1994).

140. Page, *Climate in the United Kingdom*, p. 271.

141. EECA, *A Quantum Leap into Hot Water!* Demonstration Project Profile (Wellington: Energy Efficiency and Conservation Authority, September 1993).

142. J. Harrison, *personal communication* (Capenhurst, Cheshire: EA Technology, 1995).

143. J. Rotchie, J. Ehmke, A. Rodger, R. Sharpe and S. Tucker, *Greenhouse Implications for Building* Construction and Engineering Paper JFB201 (Melbourne: CSIRO, 1990).

144. The State Electricity Commission of Victoria and Energy Victoria, *Remote Area Power Supplies* (Melbourne: The State Electricity Commission of Victoria and Energy Victoria, 1993), p. 4.

145. Ibid., p. 42.

146. Data from Wind and Sun Ltd, Oxford (1993).

147. The State Electricity Commission of Victoria and Energy Victoria, *Remote Area Power Supplies*, p. 40.

148. V. Nguyen and M. Bolzon, 'Maldorky Solar Energy Demonstration Project' in *Solar '94 Conference Proceedings* (30 November – 3 December 1994; Sydney, NSW: Australian and New Zealand Solar Energy Society, 1994), Volume 2, p. 606.

149. Schaeffer (ed.), *The Real Goods Solar Living Source Book*, p. 182.

150. D. Kuhn, 'Telecom Australia's Experience with Solar Power Systems' in Department of Primary Industries and Energy, *The Australian Renewable Energy Industry: a Guide to Australian Manufacturers and Exporters of Renewable Energy Technologies and a Selection of Case Studies* (Canberra: Australian Government Publishing Service, 1993), pp. 24–8.

151. D. Pratt, 'Managing Energy Systems' in Schaeffer (ed.), *The Real Goods Solar Living Source Book*, p. 171.

152. L. Lave, C. Hendrickson and F. McMichael, 'Environmental Implications of Electric Cars' *Science* 268 (19 May 1995), p. 995.

153. J. Hecht, 'Fears over Lead from Electric Cars 'Unfounded'' *New Scientist* 146 (20 May 1995), p. 10.

154. R. Leuthold and C. Rossetti, 'Batterie' *MobilE: la Rivista Internazionale del Veicolo Elettrico* ('The International Journal on Electric Vehicles', 1994), p. 23.

155. The State Electricity Commission of Victoria and Energy Victoria, *Remote Area Power Supplies*, pp. 58–9.

156. Energy Victoria, *Remote Area Power Systems* (Melbourne: Energy Victoria, Energy Information Centre, 139 Flinders Street, 1994), p. 6.

157. M. Williams, 'The Supply of Power to Remote Areas' in Department of Primary

Industries and Energy, *The Australian Renewable Energy Industry*, p. 45.

158. A. Burnett, 'Winners '94: Part One' *Waterways World* (November 1994), p. 69.

159. K. Kiefer, V. Hoffman, T. Erge, E. Rössler, H. Rieß, P. Sprau, G. Heilscher, M. Feneberg, G. Blässer and H. Ossenbrink, *Measurement and Analysis Programme within the Thousand Roofs Programme* (Freiburg: Fraunhofer Institute for Solar Energy Systems, 1994).

160. Cost from Wind and Sun Ltd., Oxford (1994).

161. BRE, *Energy Conservation*, pp. 8–9.

162. Data from Ministry of Energy, 1989, quoted in G. Harris, S. Gale, R. Allan, C. Lucas and M. Marinkovich, *Promoting the Market for Energy Efficiency* Report to the Official Committee on Energy Policy (Wellington: Ministry of Commerce, Energy and Resources Division, May 1993), p. 106.

163. K. Wilson, 'An Examination of some Energy Consumption Aspects of Domestic Cooking Practices' in *Consumer Issues: Strategies, Solutions and Legislation: Conference Proceedings* 15th International Home Economics and Consumer Studies Research Conference (6–8 September 1995; Manchester: Manchester Metropolitan University), Volume 1, pp. 72–87.

164. All data from AEG, *Slot-in Cookers and Haus-Line Build-in Appliances* (Slough, Berks: AEG Domestic Appliances, 1994).

165. A 2-kW 12–230 Volt inverter costs £1241.65 incl. VAT; data from Wind and Sun, *Design Guide and Catalogue* (Oxford: Wind and Sun Ltd, 1994), p. 28.

166. I. MacGill and M. Watt, 'Field Experience with RAPS and Grid Supply for Residential Power in Remote Areas' in *Solar '94 Conference Proceedings*, Volume 2, p. 505.

167. D. Olivier and D. Taylor, 'The Energy Showcase' in *Proceedings* Innovative Housing '93 Conference (Vancouver, 21–25 June 1993; 1994), Volume 3 (*Applications and Demonstrations*), p. 109.

168. Carpenter, *Learning from Experiences with Advanced Houses of the World*, p. 201.

169. Shurcliff, *Superinsulated Houses*, p. 5.11.

170. I. Cook and S. Carpenter, *Waterloo Region Green Home: a Public Demonstration of Energy Efficiency and Environmental Responsibility in New Housing* (Canada: Union Gas/Ontario Ministry of Energy, 1994) pp. 9 and 20.

171. Glynwed Ltd, *private communication* (1994).

172. A. Burnett, *The New Narrowboat Builder's Book: Chapter Four* Supplement to *Waterways World* (January 1993), p. 55.

173. Anon., 'London International Boat Show '94 Report' *Waterways World*

(March, 1994), p. 50; illustrated in Anon., 'Hot and Cold: Cookers and Fridges' *Waterways World* (October 1994), p. 67.
174. Sims, 'Biofuels' p. 7.28.
175. Data from Sunbeam Appliances, Australia (1995).
176. Data on rings of cooker read off from controls of Husqvarna Culinar 60 cooker, purchased in 1979, with additional data on ovens and thermostatic ring from Husqvarna, *Operating Instructions for Reginett Build-under Hobs and Ovens, Reginett Build-in Hobs and Ovens, and Culinar Cookers* (Luton, Beds: Husqvarna Ltd, 1979), pp. 6–8.
177. George Wilkenfield and Associates, *Residential Appliances in Australia: an Assessment of Market and Technology Developments, with Particular Reference to Energy Efficiency* Report to the State Electricity Commission of Victoria (June 1991), in Harris et al., *Promoting the Market for Energy Efficiency*, p. 107.
178. Harris et al., *Promoting the Market for Energy Efficiency*, p. 108.
179. Ibid., p. 106.
180. Ibid., p. 107.
181. R. Isaacson, *Methane from Community Wastes* (New York: Elsevier Applied Science, 1991), p. 2.
182. A. Pike, 'The Alexander Pike Autonomous House, Cambridge' *Architectural Design* 44 (November 1974), pp. 681–9; B. Vale and R. Vale, *The Autonomous House: Design and Planning for Self-Sufficiency* (London: Thames and Hudson, 1975).
183. P. Harper 'The Autonomous Houses' *Architectural Design* 46 (January 1976), p. 35.
184. R. Spargo, *Methane: the Anaerobic Flame* (Tomerong, NSW: Australian Methane Gas Research, 1981).
185. G. Smith, *Economics of Water Collection and Waste Recycling: Working Paper 6* (Cambridge: University of Cambridge, Department of Architecture, Technical Research Division, Autonomous Housing Study, July 1973), p. 23.
186. O. Skadborg and A. Vikkelsø, 'Biogas' in Associated Energy and Environment Offices, *The Sustainable Energy Handbook* (Denmark: The Danish Organization for Renewable Energy, September 1993), p. 103.
187. G. Rosenburg, 'Methane Production from Farm Wastes as a Source of Tractor Fuel' paper read to the Institute of British Agricultural Engineers, 13 November 1951, published in *Agriculture* 58 (1952), pp. 487–94.

Chapter 5
1. Department of the Environment and the Welsh Office, *The Building Regulations 1991: Part L* (London: HMSO, 1991).

2. S.Carpenter, *Learning from Experiences with Advanced Houses of the World* (Sittard, The Netherlands: CADDET/International Energy Agency, 1995), pp. 196–203.
3. British Standards Institution, *BS 5628: British Standard Code of Practice for Use of Masonry. Part 3: Materials and Components, Design and Workmanship* (London: BSI, 1985).
4. J. Page, *Climate in the United Kingdom* (London: HMSO, 1986), p. 295.
5. D. Olivier, *Energy Efficiency and Renewables: Recent Experience on Mainland Europe* (Hereford: Energy Advisory Associates, 1992), p. 11.
6. Redland Plasterboard, *Redland Drywall Manual 1990* (Reigate, Surrey: Redland Plasterboard Ltd, 1990), pp. 21–5.
7. R. Lowe, M. Bell and D. Johnston, *A Directory of Energy Efficient Housing Practice Prepared for the Joseph Rowntree Foundation* (Leeds: Leeds School of the Environment, Leeds Metropolitan University, 1995), p. 26. (Draft, not for publication, quoted here with the permission of Dr R. Lowe).
8. Redland Plasterboard, *Redland Drywall Manual*, p. 26.
9. D. Olivier, 'Beyond the Building Regs', *Building Services: the CIBSE Journal* 11 (May 1989) pp. 27–9.
10. Information from Yorkshire Brick Co., *personal communication* (Barnsley: 1992).
11. Marley Building Products, *personal communication* (1993).
12. Page, *Climate in the United Kingdom*, p. 255.
13. Data derived from ibid. p. 305.
14. Data from Excel Industries Ltd, *U.Save Fibretherm Spray Cellulose Fibre Insulation* (Ebbw Vale, Gwent: Excel Industries Ltd, 1992).
15. Lowe et al., *A Directory of Energy Efficient Housing Practice*, p. 62.
16. Swedhouse UK, *personal communications* (East Horsley, Surrey: 11 and 17 February 1993).
17. Swedhouse UK, *personal communication* (1993).
18. Velux Group, *The Optimum Use of Roof Space* (Glenrothes, Scotland: The Velux Company Ltd, 1994), p. 24.
19. D. Olivier and J. Willoughby, *Review of Ultra-Low-Energy Homes: Phase 2* A Report to the Building Research Energy Conservation Support Unit (Leominster, Herefordshire: Energy Advisory Associates, 1995), p. 23; also D. Olivier, *personal communication* (1995).
20. British Standards Institution, *BS 4471: Part 1: Dimensions for Softwood: Sizes of Sawn and Planed Timber* (London: BSI, 1978).
21. B. Vale and R. Vale, 'Low Energy Cottages', *Building Services: the CIBSE*

Journal 14 (February 1992), pp. 19–22.
22. British Standards Institution, *BS 1202: Part 1: Nails* (London: BSI, 1974).
23. S. Curwell, R. Fox and C. March, *Use of CFCs in Buildings* (London: Fernsheer Ltd, 1988), p. 12.
24. Olivier and Willoughby, *Review of Ultra-Low-Energy Homes*, p. 18.
25. Ibid., p. 20.
26. Eurisol UK, *Reducing the Greenhouse Effect by Domestic Insulation* (St Albans, Herts: Eurisol UK, 1991), p. 5.
27. Data from Excel Industries Ltd, *Warmcel: the Green Way to Insulate* (Ebbw Vale, Gwent: Excel Industries Ltd, undated; received 1995) p. 2, quoting 'Report EC Ecolabelling Board, Denmark, January, 1993'.
28. Page, *Climate in the United Kingdom*, p. 295.
29. B. Vale and R. Vale, 'A Patient Approach', *Building Services: the CIBSE Journal* 16 (January 1994), pp. 28–30.
30. M. Greenberg, 'Other Natural Materials' Chapter B7 in S. Curwell, C. March and R. Venables (eds), *Buildings and Health: the Rosehaugh Guide* (London: RIBA Publications, 1990), p. 152.
31. Lowe et al., *A Directory of Energy Efficient Housing Practice*, pp. 22–3.
32. D. Olivier, *Energy Efficiency and Renewables: Recent Experience on Mainland Europe* (Credenhill, Herefordshire: Energy Advisory Associates, 1992), p. 11.
33. Lowe et al., *A Directory of Energy Efficient Housing Practice*, p. 23.
34. Ibid., p. 23.
35. S. Ashley, 'What the Doctor Ordered' *Building Services: the CIBSE Journal* 10 (April 1988), pp. 25–8.
36. B. Vale and R. Vale, 'Low Energy Cottages', pp. 19–22.
37. B. Vale and R. Vale, 'A Patient Approach', pp. 28–30.
38. Wimpey Environmental Ltd, *Thermal Performance Assessment of Conventional Timber Frame Versus Breathing Wall Constructions* File Reference Number EPE2822M/2 (Hayes, Middlesex: Wimpey Environmental Ltd, August, 1994), pp. 1–2.
39. Building Research Establishment, *Exploiting Sunshine in House Design* prepared by Eclipse Research Consultants on behalf of the Building Research Establishment for the Department of Energy's Energy Technology Support Unit, (Garston, Watford: Building Research Establishment, 1988), p. 6.
40. ADM Indux, *Room Ventilation with Heat Recovery* (Low Moor, Bradford: Advanced Design and Manufacture Ltd, undated), pp. 2–3.
41. Page, *Climate in the United Kingdom*, p. 282.
42. Anon., 'The Secret Life of a Septic

Tank Cleaner – Hugh Richards Tells All' *Gulf News* (14 April 1995), pp. 25–7.

43. Interview with Allan Wilson (The Tank Shop, Oneroa, Waiheke Island, Auckland, New Zealand) 1 May 1995.

44. Swedal (UK) Ltd, *The Clean Alternative* (Camberley, Surrey: Swedal UK Ltd, undated), p. 4.

45. To provide an annual output of 1,095 kWh, sufficient to operate the electrically assisted composter, would need about 15 m² of photovoltaic panels at a cost of £560 per m² (excluding supports and installation; price from Wind and Sun, Oxford, 1994). The use of a smaller composter would have meant that the cellar might not have been needed to accommodate it, but a cellar was deemed necessary for the water storage, and it was easier to build a cellar under the whole house than under only part of it. In fact, the cost of building the cellar (over the cost of the foundations that would have been required if the cellar had not been built) was approximately £100/m², and the composter occupies, including space for access, about 10 m², at a total cost of £1,000. (This made the cellar option cheaper than the photovoltaic option, which would have cost about £8,400 plus the cost of the supporting structure and the additional inverter capacity – a further £2,500 at least.) As a result, the total cost for the accommodation and solar operation of the electric composter was £10,900. The cost of the Clivus Multrum unit was £4,255, plus £1,000 for the cellar in which to place it, amounting to half the cost of the electrical option.

46. L. Hills, *Grow Your Own Fruit and Vegetables* (London: Faber and Faber, 1971), p. 29.

47. C. Stoner, *Goodbye to the Flush Toilet* (Emmaus, Penn.: Rodale Press, 1977), p. 97.

48. J.T. Cartwright (Chief Building Control Officer, Newark and Sherwood District Council), *personal communication* (1 October 1993).

49. Clivus Multrum, *Multrum 1 Composter* (Cambridge, Mass.: Clivus Multrum, 1993), p. 1.

50. P. Soulsby, *personal communication* (Bournemouth, Eco-Clear Ltd, 1994).

51. A. Rockefeller, *Beyond Sewers and Septic Tanks: Separated Treatment* Paper given at Northwest On-site Wastewater Disposal Short Course (University of Washington, 1–2 March 1978), p. 4.

52. Data from Eco-Clear Ltd, *personal communication* (Bournemouth, Eco-Clear Ltd, 1994).

53. Eco-Clear Ltd, *Clivus Dry Toilet System* (Bournemouth, Eco-Clear Ltd, undated), p. 2.

54. Stoner, *Goodbye to the Flush Toilet*, p. 117.

55. Data taken from I. Lyall, *The Climate of the N.E. Midlands, Measured at Newark* (privately published, undated); obtained from Southwell Public Library, Nottinghamshire County Council. The measurements were made between 1950 and 1979.

56. G. Smith, *Economics of Water Collection and Waste Recycling: Working Paper 6* (Cambridge: University of Cambridge Department of Architecture, Technical Research Division, 1973), p. 1.

57. Ibid.

58. Data for Miele Model G 685 SC from Miele, *Dishwashing* (Abingdon, Oxon: Miele Company Ltd, 1994), p. 17.

59. B. Vallely, F. Aldridge and L. Davies, *Green Living: Practical Ways to Make Your Home Environment Friendly* (London: Thorsons, 1991), p. 80.

60. Ballofix (Valves) Limited, *Flowfix* (Oldbury, West Midlands: Ballofix (Valves) Limited, undated). Catalogue of restrictor valves for shower heads

61. Gum Leaf Shower Timer, designed by Gum Leaf Energy Savings Systems in Anon. 'Products' *Soft Technology: Technology for a Sustainable Future* Journal of the Alternative Technology Association Inc., 51 (April–June 1995), p. 9.

62. Lyall, *The Climate of the N.E. Midlands.*

63. V. Shorrocks, *Copper and Human Health – a Review: TN 34* (Potters Bar, Herts: Copper Development Association, undated).

64. Data from Shurflo, *Shurflo Highflo Pump* (Reigate, Surrey: Shurflo Ltd, undated), p. 2.

65. Doulton, *World Class Ceramic Elements from Doulton* (undated, received 1994). Domestic water filter leaflet

66. IMI, *IMI Range Hot Water Storage Cylinders* (Stalybridge, Cheshire: IMI Waterheating Ltd, 1991).

67. Morsø, *The Great Morsø Heating Programme* (Mors, Denmark: N.A. Christensen and Co., undated), p. 2.

68. D. Pratt, 'Photovoltaics' in J. Schaeffer (ed.), *The Real Goods Solar Living Sourcebook* (Ukiah, Calif.: Real Goods Trading Corporation, 1994), p. 76.

Chapter 6

1. D. Olivier, *Energy Efficiency and Renewables: Recent Experience on Mainland Europe* (Credenhill, Herefordshire: Energy Advisory Associates, 1992), p. 9.

2. Data for all calculations here from J. Page, *Climate in the United Kingdom* (London: HMSO, 1986), pp. 255 (soil temperature), 291 (aerated concrete), and 305 (slab U value).

3. H. Fullard and H. Darby, *The University Atlas* (London: George Philip, 1983), p. 25.

4. Page, *Climate in the United Kingdom*, p. 224.

5. Ibid., p. 179.

6. Ibid., p. 166.

7. S. Carpenter, *Learning from Experiences with Advanced Houses of the World* (Sittard, the Netherlands: CADDET/International Energy Agency, 1995), p. 41.

8. R. Lowe, M. Bell and D. Johnston, *A Directory of Energy Efficient Housing Practice Prepared for the Joseph Rowntree Foundation* (Leeds: Leeds Metropolitan University, Leeds School of the Environment, 1995), p. 100.

9. BSI, *BS 5925: Code of Practice for Ventilation Principles and Designing for Natural Ventilation: Draft for Public Comment* (London: BSI Standards, November 1989), p. 26.

10. Carpenter, *Learning from Experiences*, pp. 44–5.

11. P. Semenenko, *Passive Stack Ventilation: Experimental Modelling* Dissertation for BSc Hons in Building Engineering and Management (Bristol: Bristol Polytechnic, Department of Construction and Environmental Health, June 1990), p. 66.

12. Data from P. Achard and R. Gicquel (eds), *European Passive Solar Handbook: preliminary edition* (Brussels: Commission of the European Communities, Directorate-General XII for Science, Research and Development, 1986), p. 3.18.

13. Ibid., p. 2.26.

14. G. Brundrett, 'Some Effects of Thermal Insulation on Design' *Applied Energy* 1.7.1975.

15. P. Höppe 'Improving Indoor Thermal Comfort by Changing Outdoor Conditions' *Energy and Buildings* 16 (1991), pp. 743–7.

16. N. Billington and B. Roberts, 'Building Services Engineering: a Review of its Development' *International Series on Building Environmental Engineering* (Oxford: Pergamon Press, 1982), Volume 1, pp. 31–2.

17. W. Keatinge, S. Coleshaw and J. Holmes, 'Changes in Seasonal Mortalities with Improvement in Home Heating in England and Wales from 1964 to 1984' *International Journal of Biometeorology* 33 (1989), pp. 71–6.

18. R. Lowe, J. Chapman and R. Everett, *The Pennyland project* ETSU Report Contract No. E5A/CON/1046/174/040 (Harwell, Oxfordshire: Energy Technology Support Unit, 1985), p. 5.24.

19. Ibid., p. 5.19.

20. D. Olivier and J. Willoughby, *Review of Ultra-Low-Energy Homes: Phase 2* A Report to the Building Research Energy Conservation Support Unit (Leominster,

Herefordshire: Energy Advisory Associates, April 1995), p. 18.
21. C. Ponting, *A Green History of the World* (London: Sinclair-Stevenson Ltd, 1991), p. 29.
22. Data from J. Griffiths, *Thermal Comfort in Buildings with Passive Solar Features – Field Study* Final Report to the Commission of the European Communities (Guildford: University of Surrey, 1990); reported in J. Goulding, J. Owen Lewis and T. Steemers, *Energy in Architecture: the European Passive Solar Handbook* Publication No. EUR 13446 of the Commission of the European Communities, Luxembourg (London: Batsford, 1992), p. 64.
23. M. Humphreys, *Field Studies of Thermal Comfort Compared and Applied* BRE Current Paper 76/75 (Garston, Watford: Building Research Establishment, 1975).
24. D. Bainbridge, *The First Passive Solar Catalog* (Davis, Calif.: The Passive Solar Institute, 1978), p. 11.
25. Ibid., p. 13.
26. M. Evans, *Housing, Climate and Comfort* (London: The Architectural Press, 1980), p. 24.
27. Ibid., p. 24.
28. Ibid., pp. 19 and 21.
29. A. Gagge, A. Burton and H. Gazatt, 'A Practical System of Units for the Description of the Heat Exchange of Man and his Environment' *Science* 94 (1941), p. 428.
30. Achard and Gicquel, *European Passive Solar Handbook*, p. 2.22.
31. N. Ruck, *Building Design and Human Performance* (New York: Van Nostrand Reinhold, 1989), pp. 7–8.
32. A. Auliciems, 'Psycho-Physiological Criteria for Global Thermal Zones of Building Design' *International Journal of Biometeorology* 26 (1982), supplement.
33. S. Szokolay, *Architecture and Climate Change* (Red Hill: Royal Australian Institute of Architects, 1992), p. 43.
34. A. Parks, *People Heaters: a People's Guide to Keeping Warm in Winter* (Andover, Mass.: Brick House Publishing, 1981), p. 64.
35. L. Schipper, A. Ketoff and A. Kahane, 'Explaining Residential Energy Use by International Bottom-up Comparisons' *Annual Review of Energy* 10 (1985), pp. 341–405.
36. D. Barker, *personal communication* (14 June 1998).

37. D. Barker, *personal communication* (23 April 1998).
38. B. Keyworth, 'Specifying timber' in J. Sunley and B. Bedding (eds), *Timber in Construction* (London: TRADA/B.T. Batsford Ltd, 1985), p. 59.
39. Page, *Climate in the United Kingdom*, p. 319.
40. J. Sunley, 'Timber Today and Tomorrow' in Sunley and Bedding, *Timber in Construction*, p, 191.
41. L. Helbro, 'Bio Fuels – Wood Heating' in Associated Energy and Environment Offices, *The Sustainable Energy Handbook* (Copenhagen: Associated Energy and Environment Offices/The Danish Organisation for Renewable Energy, 1993), p. 92.
42. Ibid., p. 93.
43. P. Fisher and A. Bender, *The Value of Food* (Oxford: Oxford University Press, 1970), p. 22.
44. G. Leach, *Energy and Food Production* (London: International Institute for Environment and Development, 1975), p. 8.
45. L. Shorrock, G. Henderson and J. Brown, *Domestic Energy Fact File* (Garston, Watford: Building Research Establishment, 1992).
46. Bell, Lowe, Roberts and Johnston, *Energy Efficiency in Housing*, p. 12.
47. J. Cargill Thompson, 'Underground Movement' *Building* (6 October 1995), pp. 60–63.
48. V. Murley, *personal communication* (1995).
49. Identification checked at the Natural History Museum, London, 23 September 1995.
50. Enermodal Engineering Ltd, *Performance of the Brampton Advanced House* (Ottawa: CANMET Energy Mines and Resources, 1992), p. 41.
51. G. Smith, *Economics of Water Collection and Waste Recycling* Working Paper 6 (Cambridge: University of Cambridge, Department of Architecture, Technical Research Division, 1973).
52. BBC Radio 4 'News Briefing' 6:00 a.m. Wednesday, 20 September 1995.
53. Editorial, 'The Englishman's Bath' *The Times* (21 September 1995).
54. Olivier and Willoughby, *Review of Ultra-Low-Energy Homes*, p. 25.
55. Cargill Thompson, 'Underground Movement'.
56. Doulton, 'World Class Ceramic Elements from Doulton' (undated,

received 1994); domestic water filter leaflet.
57. IMI, *IMI Range Hot Water Storage Cylinders* (Stalybridge, Cheshire: IMI Waterheating Ltd, 1991).
58. J. Harrison, *personal communication* (Capenhurst, Cheshire: EA Technology, 1995).
59. Page, *Climate in the United Kingdom*, p. 299.
60. I. Gunn, *personal communication* (Auckland: University of Auckland, Department of Engineering, 1995).
61. B. Boardman et al. 'Executive summary' in *DECADE Second Year Report* (Oxford: University of Oxford, Environmental Change Unit, Energy and Environment Programme, 1995), p. 2.

Appendices

1. K. Kuusimaa, 'Silicate Particle Residues in Textiles' in Associated Energy and Environment Offices, *Proceedings of the XV International Home Economics and Consumer Studies Research Conference* (6–8 September, 1995; Manchester: Manchester Metropolitan University, 1995) Part 1, pp. 99–108.
2. D. Olivier and J. Willoughby, *Review of Ultra-Low-Energy Homes: Phase 2* A Report to the Building Research Energy Conservation Support Unit (Leominster: Energy Advisory Associates, April 1995), p. 18.
3. Data from L. Shorrock, G. Henderson and J. Brown, *Domestic Energy Fact File* (Garston, Watford: Building Research Establishment, 1992), p. 30.
4. M. Bell, R. Lowe, P. Roberts and D. Johnston, *Energy Efficiency in Housing: a Literature Review for the Joseph Rowntree Foundation* (Leeds: Leeds Metropolitan University, Centre for the Built Environment, 1994), p. 12.
5. Figure for the average seasonal efficiency of a condensing gas boiler in a domestic installation, including a modern domestic hot-water calorifier and room thermostat control, taken from CIBSE, *Applications Manual: Condensing Boilers AM3: 1989* (London: Chartered Institution of Building Services Engineers, 1989), p. 53.
6. Olivier and Willoughby, *Review of Ultra-Low-Energy Homes*, p. 18.
7. Solarex Corporation, *MegaTM Modules over 39 Watts* (Frederick, Maryland: Solarex Corporation, 1994), p. 4. Information sheet

Index